Jinxed

NORMAN MACDONALD is an award-winning journalist and author, having spent most of his working life in national and local newspapers as a reporter, newsdesk executive and editor. As well as writing books, he now runs a successful public relations and media consultancy as well as a book-publishing company.

Jinxed

Mary Kelly

with

Norman Macdonald

BIRLINN

This book is dedicated to three of the most special boys in my life who were so tragically taken from us – my sons Gordon and Mark and my nephew Davie.

First published in 2009 by
Birlinn Limited
West Newington House
10 Newington Road
Edinburgh
EH9 1QS

www.birlinn.co.uk

ISBN: 978 1 84158 812 4

British Library Cataloguing-in-Publication Data
A catalogue record for this book is available from the British Library

Typeset by Iolaire Typesetting, Newtonmore
Printed and bound by CPI Cox & Wyman, Reading

Contents

A Childhood of Fear

The tears roll down my cheeks as I weep uncontrollably. The rope that has been wound round and round my arms and body tying me to a kitchen chair digs into my skin, but the physical pain is nothing compared to the hurt I feel inside.

A brute of a man stands over me, his face twisted with rage. His big hand roughly grabs my face, forcing me to lift my head to look directly in front of me – at my own pitiful image in a mirror.

Only inches from my face, I can see his neck muscles tighten and his mouth twist like a madman as he spits out the words: 'You love your hair, don't you?'

'Yes, I do,' I manage to say in nothing more than a whisper, in between the heaving sobs that punctuate my breathing.

'You think you look nice? Well, I'm going to make sure you've got no f*****g pride left by the time I'm done with you.'

Then I see the black box in his other hand and I shudder. I know there are scissors and hair clippers inside that box and I close my eyes and pray desperately to God that this man isn't going to do what I dread the most.

'Oh Sweet Mary, Mother of God, please don't let him do this to me,' I say to myself as I squeeze one more plea for mercy in prayer.

But my pleas are unanswered as he opens the box and brings out a pair of scissors and starts to chop off my beautiful shoulder-length hair. The first metallic click of the blades slicing through my hair is followed by another and another, as he grabs clumps of my blonde locks and cuts through them. After every cut he throws a handful of my hair on to the floor as if in disgust. And there was worse, much worse to come.

'I'll show people what I do to my daughters when they defy me. This will be the sorriest day of your life,' is his mantra and he delivers it almost in unison with each slice of the scissors.

'How dare you take my reputation down by going begging in this street. I'll make an example of you and I'll show them what I do to my kids when they do things like that.'

The memory of my father's 'punishment' for his twelve-year-old daughter borrowing a half-cup of sugar from a neighbour to make tablet with her friends is as clear now as it was the day it happened sixty years ago. I can still feel the fear and I shiver at the thought of someone who should have been a loving dad doing this to his young daughter.

And it didn't stop with the scissors. Oh, no, Jocky Kelly was going to make sure everyone knew he was the master of retribution in his own home and that he wielded total control over his family.

Once he had taken as much hair off with the scissors as he could, my father then picked up the hair clippers and started cutting my hair even shorter. While he was doing this he watched my face in the mirror opposite.

I couldn't bear to look at what he was doing to me, so I closed my eyes tight and dug my chin into my chest. But as soon as he saw I didn't have my eyes open, watching what he was doing to me, he would punch me to make me look at my hair falling from the teeth of the clippers as he flicked the tufts onto the floor.

When he was finished with the clippers, he got his shaving brush out, lathered it up and covered my head with the white shaving soap. Then my father took his razor and completely shaved my head. I was completely bald when he had finished with me and when I saw what I looked like, I truly wanted to die. One minute I had lovely long hair I was really proud of, the next I was looking at myself in the mirror, seeing someone I could barely recognise. I had never seen anything like this before and I thought I had been turned into the ugliest person in the world.

Although he had wrapped the clothes rope round both my body and the chair, he hadn't tied my feet. But still I was so paralysed by the terror of the ordeal I couldn't kick out or struggle. My twenty-one-year-old married sister, Frances, happened to be in the house at the time and she jumped on my father's back and tried to pull him away from me. 'Oh my God,' she screamed. 'Stop – she doesn't deserve that.' But nothing was going to stop him meting out his cruel, cruel punishment, which ended by him untying me and tossing me aside like a rag doll.

Before my father had tied me to the chair, he had given me one almighty beating with his leather belt and his fists. By the time he had finished shaving my head, the blood had started to congeal on my face, the bruises had started to appear and my lips had become swollen.

For days after this beating I was drinking through straws, my mouth was in such a mess.

And it had all started so innocently, with three girls wanting to make some tablet, since in 1947 sweets were still rationed. We stayed in a council house in the Brucehill housing scheme, in Dumbarton. My mammy, Annie, wasn't at home at the time as she had gone to Fort William in the Scottish Highlands for a few weeks to help my brother Willie and his wife Sadie with the birth of their first child. I was left at home with my father, although Frances and her husband, Davie Dalrymple, had moved in so she could look after us while my mother was away.

It was a warm September, Indian summer night when the three of us – Esther O'Malley, Kathleen Hopkinson and I – decided it would be a great idea to make some tablet. We went to Esther's house, but soon discovered we were half a cup of sugar short for the recipe.

I was asked to get the missing ingredients, but I knew my father would never let me take the sugar out of the house. Instead, I hatched a plot to ask a neighbour of ours, Mrs Connolly, to lend me the half-cup of sugar and I would sneak sugar out of our house the next day and give it back to her when my father was at work (he was a school janitor).

We made the sweet and had a great time sitting on the steps of Esther's house eating our way through what could loosely be described as tablet. Nevertheless, we had made it ourselves, it tasted wonderful and I never gave the borrowed half-cup of sugar a second thought.

The following day while I was at school, Mrs Connolly went to our door and asked Frances if she could have the sugar she gave me returned, as she had run out. On my way home from school that day I was met by my younger sister, Rose, who ran towards me and blurted out: 'Frances has told my daddy you went to Mrs Connolly's to borrow some sugar last night. He's raging and he's going to kill you when he gets his hands on you. You've to stay in the house and wait for him to get home.'

I was petrified and I knew I would be in for a beating from my father. He would look upon any member of his family asking for a loan of sugar as begging and that would embarrass him. I decided I wasn't going home, so instead I went to my friend Kathleen Hopkinson's house. I told her what had happened and that if I went anywhere near my father, I would get a beating. I knew I couldn't stay at Kathleen's all night, so I came up with the idea of running away to Fort William and I asked her to come with me. She agreed.

We didn't have a penny between us to pay our train fare to Fort William, so I sent Kathleen to the lovely woman we called Granny Boyle who lived upstairs from me to ask for a loan of some money. Now, Granny Boyle wasn't related to me, but she was a great friend of my mum's and was just like a granny to me and my brothers and sisters.

I knew Granny Boyle wouldn't let me go to Fort William, so I told Kathleen to tell her we needed a shilling to go to the cinema. We were so naïve that we thought if we got the bus to Glasgow, we could then ask a porter where to get the train to Fort William and we would sneak on and hide in the toilet until we got there. We would jump off the train and run up the road to where my mum was staying, tell her about the half-cup of sugar and she would keep me safe.

Kathleen got the shilling from Granny Boyle, we got on the bus and by the time we got to Glasgow's Queen Street Station, it was just after 6 p.m. We asked at the ticket office when was the next train to Fort William only to be told that there wasn't another one until 8.30 the next morning.

What were we to do now? I couldn't go back home and I couldn't get to Fort William. In those days the railway station waiting rooms had a coal fire in them to keep passengers warm. We decided we would spend the night in the warmth of the railway station's waiting room and catch the first train to Fort William in the morning.

The one thing we hadn't counted on was the nightly rounds of the station by the police. After an hour or so the waiting-room door opened and two big policemen stood over us. 'What are you two doing in here?' one asked.

'I'm going to Fort William to visit my mammy,' I said. Well, that was the truth, I thought. I've got a mammy, she's in Fort William and I want to go and see her. I wasn't telling lies or doing anything wrong.

'What's your mammy doing up there?' asked the policeman.

'She's living up there just now, she sent me a letter yesterday and said she wants to see me because she's getting a bit lonely and I've to bring a friend with me,' I replied, thinking I was on solid ground here and the police would believe every word I was saying.

'Is that right?' the policeman went on. 'So what made you come here so early when the train's not until the morning? You say you're from Dumbarton – why didn't you just catch the train at Dumbarton Central where it stops on its way to Fort William?' He continued his line of enquiry: 'Where did you get the money to come to Glasgow?'

'My granny gave it to me.'

'So how come your granny didn't have the sense to tell you to get the train at Dumbarton tomorrow morning? That would have saved you coming all the way to Glasgow and staying in here all night.'

I started to tell the policeman about all my relatives who lived in Fort William, but he'd had enough and interrupted: 'I think we'll take the two of you to the police station to spend the night.'

'No it's OK – we're waiting for someone else to come . . .'

'I don't think so, the two of you will be safer coming with us to the police station and we'll contact your fathers.'

At that I burst into tears and wailed: 'Please mister, don't do that. My father will kill me if he finds out.'

'Look, I can't leave you here. What have you been up to anyway?'

I told him about wanting to make tablet, borrowing the half-cup of sugar from a neighbour and my father finding out and telling me not to leave the house until he got home from work.

'It won't be that bad,' said the policeman. 'I'll need to inform both your fathers where you are so they can come to collect you.'

The two policemen took us to the station, gave us a cup of

tea and a sticky bun each and said we could sleep in the cells, but they would leave the doors open. That was the worst night of my young life; my stomach was churning with fear at the thought of my father coming to collect me in the morning. I was wishing the night would last forever.

But morning did come and just after 6 a.m. so did my father, along with Mr Hopkinson. He was fine with Kathleen and gave her a cuddle. When the policeman said that my father was waiting for me I pleaded: 'Don't make me go – he'll kill me.'

'No he won't. He gave us his word he wouldn't lay a finger on you.'

I knew that was a lie. I knew something terrible was going to happen to me when I got home. My father was full of patter to the police when I was brought out to him at the front counter of the station. 'Really sorry she's been a bother to you,' he said. 'You've no idea what I've to put up with – sometimes I think she's not right in the head.'

I might have been dreading what was going to happen once I got back to Dumbarton, but my father started on me as soon as we got out of the police station and headed towards Waterloo Street Bus Station. I thought my head was going to explode as he gave me a rabbit punch on the back of my neck.

Mr Hopkinson jumped in: 'Here – hold on a minute. There's no need for that.'

'You keep your f*****g nose out of my business,' my father replied. 'You take what belongs to you and just get.'

At that, Mr Hopkinson put his arm round Kathleen and hurried on in front of us, but not before telling my father: 'You're a real bad bastard. It's a pity the wean didn't get away from you.'

On the bus, all the way back to Dumbarton, my father punched me and told me what an embarrassment I was to him. At first, other passengers tried to stop him, but he told them to mind their own business. And in those days, that's exactly what people would do. There wasn't the children's rights legislation that we have nowadays.

When we got back into the house, my father headed straight into the kitchen and grabbed hold of the two shaving belts he had hanging in there. These were what he hit us with when we were being punished. What belt he used depended on how severe the punishment was to be. The black belt was a lot older and thinner, so if it was just a wee leathering you were getting that's the one he would use. However, if he really wanted to give you a good hiding, the brown belt would come out after the black one and you would get a few lashings with that one as well. His other trick to make you even more frightened was to send you to bring the belt to him before he meted out his retribution with it.

Naturally, the morning he collected me from the police station, in Glasgow, both the black and the brown belt came out and he started in the kitchen hitting me with them. Then it was up the hallway and into the living room, turning away from him in all directions, trying in vain to escape the constant slaps of leather on my skin and the piercing pain that followed. When he wasn't using the belt, he would use his fist to hit me and I didn't know what was worse – the dull aching thud of being punched or the sharp, stinging pain of leather on my skin.

But I would have gladly put up with all of that if it had meant he never tied me to the kitchen chair and made me watch him shaving every hair from my head. The soreness and bruising of a beating disappears within a few days and so does the swelling, but it takes a year for your hair to grow back in to what is normal for a young girl.

After I was untied I lay on the living-room floor crying my heart out, while my father packed away his haircutting and shaving kit and washed the shaving soap from his hands. I thought it was over, but I was wrong.

I thought he wouldn't want anyone to see his daughter completely bald as he would be embarrassed, but his twisted mentality had him think the opposite. He grabbed me off the floor and took me to the front door and shoved me outside on to the steps.

It was just before 9 a.m. and other children were making their way to school. The first person to see me was Joseph Connolly, who burst out laughing and shouted out: 'Come and see Mary Kelly's head.' Within minutes, it was like a circus sideshow, with everybody in the street coming over to our gate to gawp at my bald head and look at me sitting crying my eyes out on the front step.

That night, when my older brothers John and Jimmy came home and saw the state I was in, there was almost a riot. Although my brothers would get a leathering from my father when they were younger, once they grew up he stopped hitting them because he knew if they retaliated he would most definitely come off worst.

My father was at evening Mass when they came home, but Jimmy was really angry and went storming about the house shouting: 'I'm going to kill that old bastard when he gets back.' Granny Boyle was in our house and tried to calm Jimmy down saying he would end up in the jail if he did anything to his father.

When my father got back from Mass, he heard the commotion and realised what was happening. He immediately went into his bedroom and locked the door before Jimmy knew he had returned.

When Jimmy found out, he tried to break the door down with his shoulder, but there wasn't enough room in the hall for Jimmy to have a run at the door and hit it with more force to try to open it.

By this time, Granny Boyle's sons were in our house pulling Jimmy away from my father's room and upstairs into their house while he calmed down. My father was a brave man when it came to giving me a hiding, but he wouldn't dare face our Jimmy when he was out to get him back for what he'd done to me.

The next day my father sent me to school and warned me not to cover my head as he wanted everyone to see what I looked like as part of his punishment. Nowadays it's not that uncommon for girls to shave their heads, but in the late 1940s, it was unheard of. At school, everyone was pointing at me and sniggering and when I got into our first class at St Patrick's High School, my teacher Sister Mary Ignatius took me outside the room and asked what had happened to me.

She was extremely sympathetic and said I could pick a friend from the class and go up to a big house in the grounds of the school called Marymount, where I could get my lessons from two other teachers away from the embarrassment of sitting in my normal classroom. So I picked my best friend, Kathleen Carr, and off we went to Marymount.

That was the only part of the day when it wasn't torture knowing all the other kids were laughing at me. It was a terrible ordeal for me coming back from school, as there were pupils from two other boys' schools walking the same road. Kathleen said we should take another route home and so we detoured along the shore road, which was never very busy at that time of day. It made our journey longer, but I never had to suffer the gauntlet of jibes and sniggers from the other kids. This went on for six months.

It wasn't for another two weeks after my father had shaved my head that my mother was due back from Fort William. My father was still unrepentant and he sent my sister Rose and me to meet her at the railway station.

He told me I was to meet my mother off the train, show her what I was like and tell her why I had been punished by having my hair shaved off. As soon as my mother stepped off the train and saw me, she burst into tears.

But like the rest of us, she was too frightened to do

anything about what had happened to me. However, Granny Boyle was angry and was intent on taking the matter further. The night after my mother came home, Granny Boyle came into our house and said: 'I'm taking this wean to see the priest. It's terrible what that man gets away with and I'll be telling the priest exactly who did this to her.'

Granny Boyle took me to the chapel house and Father Nee came to the door. He didn't react at all to me standing in front of him with a face that looked like I'd just gone ten rounds with Mike Tyson. Then Granny Boyle said: 'Look at the state of that child's face.'

'What is it?' the priest asked.

'This is Mary Kelly, John Kelly's daughter. What did she do to deserve that? All she did was to borrow a half-cup of sugar from a neighbour and he does this to her.'

Then she pulled off the pixie hat I was wearing and showed the priest my bald head. But to our horror the priest said: 'Go away from here and don't come back complaining. I'll tell you something, she deserved all she got the way she took that man's dignity down. She's not fit to be the daughter of John Kelly. Now take her away and don't expect any sympathy from me.'

When I grew older and thought back to that night, I realised that my father must have been friendly with the priests as he was the janitor at St Patrick's High School and he would be in almost daily contact with them. He would have made sure he got his side of the story in first.

My father had been in the cavalry during the First World War and Granny Boyle used to say that he just swapped one army for another when he came out and started a family. Everything in our home had to run to a strict discipline and my father's orders had to be obeyed without question. We certainly didn't have a home like the other kids had. I know this sounds ridiculous, but we weren't allowed to speak in our house in my father's presence unless, of course, he was speaking to us. We would be having a conversation with my mother, just like any other family would, but as soon as someone said 'Here's my daddy coming' the place fell silent. The minute he entered the house, there was no talking until he spoke to you.

My father wasn't a very tall man – about five feet nine or ten – but he was quite muscular and broad. He never showed any affection towards his children and I used to feel hurt when I saw other youngsters running to their daddy and getting a cuddle. I never knew that feeling of getting a kiss and a cuddle from my father.

He was a harsh man and my earliest memory is one of him shouting abuse at me for something happening which was totally out of my control. I was just four years old and the family had just arrived in the then-popular Clyde seaside resort of Dunoon for our summer holidays. Three families had come on holiday together: Granny Boyle's, the Dobbins's and ours. We stayed in a holiday camp and slept in dormitories with rows and rows of beds.

But that earliest memory begins on the second night after we had arrived and I was in a room feeling hot and being sick. I was lying on a couch looking up at a glass case with lots of bottles inside.

There was a man – a doctor – examining me with a stethoscope and every so often my mother had to carry me over to the sink so I could be sick. After he had finished his examination of me, the doctor said to my mother: 'She's got the measles. I'm sorry she can't stay here for the rest of your holiday in case she infects all the other children. She can't go back into the dormitory.'

The next thing I heard was my father's voice and it wasn't any expressions of sympathy for me. He was shouting: 'She's a f*****g jinx and she's ruined the holiday for everybody.' I remember his big angry face and being told it was my fault we had to leave. What a sad indictment of the man that my first memory of my father is of him shouting angrily at me for getting the measles.

I was wrapped in blankets and carried out of the doctor's surgery into a big black car to be driven back to Dumbarton. In the car with me were my mother, father, Granny Boyle and Sadie, one of the Dobbin girls. The women sat in the back seat and I lay on their laps, with my father and the driver in the front. At one point in the journey my father turned round and looked into the back of the car and started shouting again about me spoiling the holiday. Then Granny Boyle told him to be quiet and behave himself.

When we got back to Dumbarton I was put straight to bed, as I was still feeling terrible. The next morning my father was at it again, shouting at me and saying I had spoiled the holiday. I felt frightened, as he was shouting into my face like a sergeant major: 'What did I do to deserve you? You've been nothing but a jinx since the day you were born.' Over the years telling me I was a jinx became one of his favourite sayings.

I was born on 31 March 1935 and I had five older brothers – Bernard, William, John, James and George – and one older sister, Frances. I had another older brother and sister – Thomas and Annie – but they both died in the same week before I was born. Thomas was three and a half when he contracted scarlet fever and tragically passed it on to Annie, who was only ten weeks old, and neither of them recovered. I was the second youngest of the family, with a sister, Rose, coming along after me.

There were also three cousins living with our family – Matilda, or Tilly as she was known, Billy and Jack Price. Their mother Wilhelmina had died when they were young. Cousins they may have been, but all my life I looked on them as my sister and brothers. I didn't know Tilly, Jack and Billy weren't my real brothers and sister until I was

fourteen, when someone at school said they were really my
cousins and their dead mother was my mammy's sister.

When I was born there were twelve of us living in the two-
bedroom council house at 14 Millburn Crescent, Silverton,
in the east end of Dumbarton. When I was ten months old
the family moved to a three-bedroom council house on the
other side of Dumbarton at 46 Bontine Avenue, in the
Brucehill housing scheme, and that's where I stayed until
I left home. By the time Rose came along, thirteen of us were
living in that house and there seemed to be beds everywhere
– even in the living room. I slept in a double bed along with
my sisters, Frances, Tilly and Rose – two at the top and two
at the bottom of the bed.

Tilly was more than fifteen years older than me and I
would stay awake at night waiting for her to come home
from the dancing so I could listen to her tell all the gossip.
Going to bed at night was a relief as it meant you were safe
from my father; he never came into the girls' bedroom. I
never felt uncomfortable about the four of us sleeping in the
one bed, as it made me feel cosy, warm and good. Our
Frances was a lovely singer and I used to bribe her with
sweets and biscuits I had saved if she would sing to me when
we were supposed to be tucked up in bed sleeping.

When I was five, Tilly managed to escape all the beatings
and leatherings my father meted out to all the children by
leaving home to join the Wrens. I was then moved into
another room and shared a single bed with Frances. Apart
from the odd complaint of someone's feet getting in the way
of your face, the bedroom was a happy place to be –
especially when Frances would give us all a wee concert
party with her wonderful singing.

Even as I was growing up and going to school there was no
escaping my father's presence. Although he was the janitor
of St Patrick's, which was a joint campus for primary and

secondary classes, none of his kids got any favours from him. It was quite the contrary. When I was eleven and still in Primary Seven, I entered an essay writing competition for pupils up to the age of sixteen from all over Dumbarton. We had been taken to look round a big house which belonged to a doctor in Church Street. We were to take in all the details of what the house was like and write an essay about it when we got back to school. I was quite good at writing essays at school, but instead of giving me encouragement like the teachers did, my father warned me that if I didn't win the contest and gave him a showing up, I would be in big trouble.

I wrote my essay and waited with some trepidation to hear how I'd got on. A week or so later I was called out of my class and told that the headmaster, 'Dinky' Mulgrew, wanted to see me (for all the years I was at school, I never heard what his real first name was). Normally, when you were called to see the headmaster you had got yourself into trouble and you left his office with sore hands after getting the belt. So, it was a very nervous Mary Kelly who made her way down the stairs to the headmaster's office. On my way I passed my father, who just ignored me.

When I got to the office the red light outside the door was on, which meant he was already in with someone and I had to wait. The waiting was terrible and I was racking my brain to think what I had done wrong to merit a summons to the headmaster. When Betty Hollern, the school secretary, came out to get me she realised I was just about to burst into tears.

'Don't cry,' she said. 'Everything's all right.'

I stepped into Mr Mulgrew's office and he turned to face me with a swish of his big black gown. 'Sit down,' he ordered me. 'You know your father is the janitor of the school and I'm sure you would like to please your father.'

'Yes, Mr Mulgrew,' I replied.

'Do you remember entering the competition to write an essay about the big house you visited? How well do you think you did?'

'I don't think I did very well at all.' I was always afraid to think I had done well at something in case that was bad luck.

'Well, I've got a surprise for you. You didn't come in third, you didn't come in second . . .'

He was spinning this one out and making me suffer as I fidgeted in the chair in front of his desk. I thought he was going to say I came something like fourteenth.

He continued: 'No, Mary Kelly – you are the winner. You came first and you've won the £5 prize. You have made your father a happy man today and he's very proud of you. He was really pleased when I told him.' I couldn't believe what I was hearing. My father had known I'd won the essay competition and yet he'd just ignored me when he saw me on the stairs.

I ran all the way home at dinner-time to tell my mammy and she was delighted, giving me a big cuddle. 'I won't get leathered today,' I told her. 'Mr Mulgrew said my daddy is dead proud of me.' I also told her that the prize was £5 – which to a youngster in those days was an absolute fortune.

My mammy said that I was to give the £5 prize to my daddy as soon as I got it. 'But can I not keep a pound of it and you could get a pound as well?' I asked her.

'No. Just give all the money to your daddy,' she replied.

A week later I was presented with my prize in front of the whole school gathered in the Assembly Hall. The money was in an envelope and I didn't even open it before handing it over to my father when I got home. As I gave him the envelope he said 'thank you' and walked into his room. I thought he would come out of the room a few minutes later and give me ten shillings, or more to the point give my mammy something. But he never did, and when I asked my mammy why, she replied: 'The main thing is that you won the competition.'

It's not as if my father needed money – he had plenty stashed away in his own room. I never remember my mother or father sleeping in the same room. Obviously they must have done to have so many children, but I can only ever remember him sleeping in a separate room, which had a bed, a dressing-table with a mirror, a cupboard, bookshelf and a writing bureau. He normally kept this room locked when he wasn't in the house, and no wonder – there was money all over the place. There were notes and coins stuffed in every drawer and on top of the dresser and writing bureau. There was a wooden box that looked like a treasure chest kept in one of the deeper drawers in the dresser. And it really was a treasure chest because it was filled with notes and coins.

As far as I was led to believe from what his step-sister told me, my father had been left a lot of money when his parents died and as school janitor he had a good job. Not that he shared this wealth with my mammy or the rest of the family on a regular basis. He only ever gave my mammy £3 a week for the housekeeping, yet he spent £5 on the Littlewoods football coupon every week.

I was a terrible one for prowling when I was a wee girl and one day when I was about five, I found the key to my father's room, which he had absentmindedly left on the kitchen table. My curiosity got the better of me and when no one was looking, I sneaked into his room. I was mesmerised by the rows and rows of coins on the dresser. There were piles of half-crowns, silver sixpences and what we called in those days wooden threepenny bits. I had a look in the bottom drawer, found the 'treasure chest' box and when I opened it, I could hardly believe my eyes when I saw the amount of money inside. I carefully put it back so no one would know I had found it.

I turned round and looked at all the books on the bookshelf and decided I wanted to take a look at them – that was to be my downfall. I got a stool from the kitchen and stood on it to reach the top shelf. As I stretched to pick one, all the books fell off the shelf on to the floor and to my horror so did lots of five-pound notes, one-pound notes and ten-shilling notes that had been hidden inside the pages. I just stood there looking aghast at the books and notes scattered over the floor and then I heard a voice at the door.

'What are you doing in here?' It was my brother Willie, who was fourteen years older than me. 'The old bastard will know someone has been in here – he marks all the pages where he's hidden the notes. You go into the living room and if he says anything I'll take the blame. He'll murder you if he finds out you've been in his room.'

Of course, I didn't know that my father knew exactly where each note had been placed in the pages of the books. Willie put the notes back between the pages, but he had no idea where exactly they should go nor did he know what order the books were placed on the shelf. I sat in the living room with Willie, dreading the sound of the front door opening and my father coming home. It wasn't long before he stormed into the living room. 'Who's been in my bed-room?' he asked.

'It was me,' said Willie.

'What were you doing in there?'

'Look, I had a wee prowl, your books fell off the shelf and the money fell out. Just get on with whatever you're going to do.'

And give Willie his due, he had a go at our father for having that kind of money stashed away. 'You're a f*****g old miser. Nobody should have money like that hidden away. You should give some of it to my mother.'

My father gave Willie a real hiding with a carpet beater, and it wasn't just on the legs or the backside – he was beaten, bruised and bloodied anywhere the blows landed. After the beating Willie went upstairs to Granny Boyle's to stay with her for a few days, and the next thing I knew was that Willie had been called up to join the navy.

Although my father was never free and easy with his money, when it came to sharing it with my mammy and the rest of the family on special occasions like Christmas and Easter, he would splash out on us. But I believe that was more for show to let everyone outside the family know that the Kellys had money and his family were well kept.

At Easter, all the children in the family would get a big chocolate egg, and he liked it when we went outside to show our pals. This was also the time of year we were taken to the local Co-op department store, where we would get the best quality clothes bought for us. But again I thought that was just for show.

He also paid for all the Christmas presents we got. After all, my mammy couldn't afford to buy them on the £3 a week he gave her to run the house. And Christmas Day was like living in the olden days with the gentry handing out favours to the staff. We would be lined up in the hall waiting to be called into his room and he would be sitting at his writing bureau with a pile of money in front of him. When your turn came you had to go in, kiss him on the cheek and say, 'Thank you, Daddy', and he would push some money, which was on top of the desk, towards you. The older children were given £5, then the younger ones £4 and the very youngest, like Rose and me, were given £2.

I was a bit older when one Christmas came shortly after I'd had a real leathering off my father and I refused to kiss him on the cheek when I went in to collect my Christmas present. I went into his room and didn't even look at him. He said: 'Well?' And I just turned and ran out of the room. I just couldn't bear to kiss that man after he would regularly erupt like a volcano and cause so much hurt

in the family. When I came out of the room and my
mammy saw I hadn't got any money she started to cry,
realising I had done something to upset my father. She
knew what was coming.

'Go and get the belts,' he shouted, after he had given out
the last of the Christmas money. I was in for a beating.

My mammy pleaded with him. 'John, wait a minute, it's
Christmas Day for God's sake.'

His reply was unrelenting: 'She defied me, she's always
defying me. Any other child in the street would go down on
their knees for money like that.'

The worst thing about the way my father treated me was
that you couldn't blame it on him drinking too much. If he
had a drink problem and was only violent through drink, it
still wouldn't be justified, but you would know the reason.
If he had been an alcoholic and his vile behaviour had been
drink-related, I could understand why he acted the way he
did. But he only had a drink at weekends and never to any
real excess.

To this day I have no idea why my father treated me and the
rest of my family the way he did. By the time I had plucked
up the courage as an adult to ask him, he had literally just
died minutes before and couldn't give me an answer.
Although shortly before he died he tried to justify his
behaviour to me.

Although I never saw any outward sign of love and
affection from him towards my mammy, he must have
loved her because after she died, in September 1961 at
the age of sixty, it was the beginning of the end for him. A
year and four months later, he was dead as well. He was
staying with Frances and her husband Davie and one night
when I was in their house visiting, he took a brain haemorrhage and went into a coma. After my mammy died he had a
habit of sitting, just staring out the window. That day he

looked extremely sad and deep in thought about his life and maybe even regretting things he had done.

I was twenty-six, and even at that age I would never have spoken to my father unless he had started the conversation. But that day he looked so sad, I plucked up the courage to say something to him.

'What's the matter with you?' I asked.

He turned to me and said: 'You think I really hurt you all your life and I was really cruel to you.'

I was still scared of him and I stupidly replied: 'No, not really.'

'Well, let me tell you why I treated you the way I did. I loved you more than the rest of my children.'

'Oh, that's good,' I said, thinking that I wished he'd hated my guts so I wouldn't have felt so much pain and suffering at his hands.

But he looked so pathetic and I realised then that I was watching a man who was slowly but surely dying before my very eyes.

He continued: 'You were perfect and I wanted you to stay perfect. I just wanted you to be like a doll, but then you got a mind of your own. But I was really proud of you because you had everything a father would want to have in a daughter.

'I wanted to keep you young and keep you like that doll and I'm sorry for what I put you through. I'm truly sorry – will you forgive me?'

Although I felt like saying: 'Why are you talking to me like this after all those years of beating me up and being horrible to me?' I could only mumble 'Yes – I forgive you.'

He then asked me: 'Was I that bad to you?'

But he looked such a pathetic sight that I didn't have the guts to tell him what I really thought: 'Bad? You were a real bastard and almost ruined my whole life.'

It was later that night that my father had a massive brain

haemorrhage and lapsed into a coma. He only lived for another three months, paralysed on one side and going in and out of consciousness.

The day before he died I was in his bedroom with my brothers Billy and John. On one of the few occasions my father came to consciousness, his eyes barely open, he pulled his hand from under the covers and said: 'I want Mary.'

Billy told me to hold his hand, but I didn't want to. The memories of all the beatings came flooding back and I still hated my father for what he had done to me over the years. Just then Frances came into the room and Billy said: 'For f**k's sake, would somebody hold his hand.' Frances walked over to the bed and put her hand in my father's. His eyes still closed, he pushed her hand away and said: 'I want Mary.' This time I held his hand and he squeezed it for a few seconds before his grip slackened and he fell back into unconsciousness. After all the years of hell he put me through, his last words to me were 'I want Mary . . .'

The following day the doctor was in my father's bedroom and when he came out he told Frances, her friend Celia Coleman and me that it wouldn't be long before my father would draw his last breath. He said that any members of the family who want to say their last goodbyes should get here quick. Frances said: 'Mary, you better go in and see your daddy. There's not long to go now.'

But I was frightened to go in as I wasn't used to seeing dead people. The only other dead people I had seen before then was my mammy and a wee boy in our street when all the kids had been brought into the house to pay their last respects. I was only ten and didn't realise what was going on. I just wondered what he was doing lying in a wooden box because the last time I'd seen him he was on his bike. But this time I knew exactly what was happening and Frances saw my hesitation.

'You get into that room,' she said. 'The rest of the family has been sent for and it won't be long until they're here.'

Frances and Celia pulled me into the room to see my father alive for the last time. They had their rosary beads out and were saying a prayer. I was pretending to look at my father, but I couldn't bring myself to watch someone dying.

The doctor was also at the bedside and after a few minutes he said: 'He's gone now – he's passed over.'

Frances and Celia left the room and I was alone with my father. I was staring at the floor not wanting to look at my dead father, lying in bed only a few feet away from me. Suddenly a strange feeling came over me and it was as if I had just been given a shot of courage and my fear had disappeared. Imagine all these years I prayed for him to be dead, I thought to myself. After all the beatings, I used to say in my prayers at night: 'Please God, let the Brucehill bus kill my daddy in the morning.'

'Imagine him dead,' I thought. 'All those years when he tortured everybody with the fear and the beatings. Why did he live a life like that? Why did he treat the people he was supposed to love and care for like that? But he can't torture anybody any more . . .' And that's when I looked at him.

I stared at my father and there was no hate any more. I couldn't feel hate. It was a different Mary Kelly who started to speak to him and ask the questions I should have had the courage to ask years before.

'Why did you waste all those years? You lived a life and never loved anybody and never allowed anybody to love you – what did you do that for?' I asked him. 'You had all that money. You could have had a wonderful life and you could have given my mammy a wonderful life. We could all have been happy. What did you do that for?'

They say that your soul is still around you an hour after it leaves your body when you die, so I said to my dead father: 'If you're still in this room I want you to know I'm not frightened of you any more. You're dead and you can't come back. But I want to know why you did all those things to us.'

I heard someone coming up the hall and I stopped talking. I wasn't angry any more – I actually felt sorry for the man. He lived in this world for seventy-odd years and he didn't let anyone love him and he never gave any love. To me that's just a wasted life. If I saw my father again I know I would have the guts to ask: 'Why did you treat me like that, you rotten old bastard?'

I wouldn't be cowering or frightened of him like I used to be. I would also ask him: 'And what about all that stuff you gave me the night before you had the brain haemorrhage – you said you treated me the way you did because you loved me more than anybody. How could you do that to someone you loved?'

Life's a Beach

This is bliss. I'm watching the white, frothy waves thrashing on to the sand and making their dash up the shoreline with that hypnotic skooshing and then hissing sound as the water retreats back to the sea.

Every one of my senses is being indulged. I can smell and even taste the fresh, tangy aroma of the salty sea in my nostrils and mouth. I can hear squeals of excitement from scores of children as I watch them play rounders and one of their teammates hits the ball and runs to the next base before they're put out. Children are also busying themselves building sandcastles with brightly coloured buckets and spades or splashing around – and each other – in the water. I close my eyes as my feet touch sand warmed by the hot afternoon sun and bury my toes as deep as I can under the soft yellow grains. But maybe best of all is the feeling I get being surrounded and protected by happy, laughing, loving people who just want me to experience the joy of such simple pleasures.

This is how I spent many a summer's Sunday camping out for the day with my mammy, brothers and sisters and Granny Boyle's children on the banks of the River Clyde at Dumbarton when I was growing up. It was always a day of escape and relief for me. A day I wished would never end, because it meant a whole day away from the fear and the reality of beatings from my ill-tempered, cruel father.

He would never come to the place known as Havoc Shore and there was always a screaming match with my mother as she got everything ready to go there for our day-long picnic.

My father hated the idea of a picnic and, even more, he hated the idea of his family going on one.

'Why do you want to eat outside like animals?' he would shout.

As he got more agitated, Granny Boyle would intervene and say: 'For goodness' sake, Jocky. We're only going to the shore like everyone else does.'

And she was right. It seemed that everyone else in Dumbarton, like us, headed for Havoc on a Sunday to set up their tent, lay out blankets and build open fires to cook their dinner on. I loved those Sundays, and the good feelings about it started the night before as I snuggled up in bed thinking myself to sleep about having a great day at the shore. That's when I had a wee happy stomach and a wee happy mind. Hours on end of carefree playing and away from the misery my father brought to my life. And by the time we got home on Sunday night there would only be time for a bath, getting into your pyjamas and then to bed without having to face his wrath. Sometimes when I think back, I feel life then was like a competition – how do you avoid getting a leathering?

But Sundays during the summer were something to look forward to. I got up at 8 a.m. and got ready to go to Mass at 9. Then it was back to the house for a big breakfast of porridge followed by ham, eggs and sausage. After the breakfast things were cleared away my mammy would then start making my father's lunch and that would have to be served to him before she could get herself ready and head for the shore with the rest of us. But her duties on a Sunday looking after my father didn't end there. My mammy had to leave us at the shore at 4.30 p.m. and return home to make his tea before coming back down for a final couple of hours.

While my mammy was getting lunch ready for my father, my brothers and sisters, Granny Boyle's kids and I would start to load up the two bogeys – home-made barrows

constructed from a big, square apple or orange box with
two old pram wheels screwed to the bottom – used to
transport everything we needed for our day out at the
shore. In one bogey we piled our two tents and blankets,
which would be laid out on the ground in front of the tents,
and the other bogey contained all the pots, pans and cutlery
needed for cooking our dinner over an open fire. Another
important piece of equipment we took with us was the
calamine lotion and cotton wool to help soothe the inevitable sunburn us kids would suffer from.

Once we got to the beach each of us knew what our task
would be after pitching the two tents (one for the girls to
change into their swimming costumes and the other for the
boys; we could also escape the burning hot sun in the tents if
it was a really scorching day). The boys mainly took jobs to
do with lighting the fire, although we all took turns heading
off into the nearby woods and doing some beachcombing
for pieces of wood of all shapes, thicknesses and sizes to
keep the fire going.

We also carried big aluminium tins with a wire handle
through holes in each side to a freshwater well further along
the shoreline. Off we'd toddle along the grass pathway
above the sand, the cans swinging by our sides until we
got to the well. We'd put the can underneath the spout and
lift the handle to make the drinking water come pouring
out. There were several of these wells along the shoreline,
but they hadn't been put there as a water supply for us day
campers – they were to refresh people out walking, and each
well had a metal cup tied to it by a chain for those happy
wanderers to use.

I just loved busying myself for an hour or so, getting
everything ready for my mammy and Granny Boyle to
arrive at Havoc. Holding this rope or that rope as the tents
were put up. Making sure the blankets were spread flat out
on the sand, staggering along the beach with my arms full of

bits and pieces of wood sticking out in all directions as I tried to balance the bundle without dropping anything. The expectation of spending hours on the shore, happy and contented, was almost as good as the day itself would turn out to be. And watching the older boys set up the fire inside a circle of bricks and stones, waiting anxiously to see if the kindling really was going to burst into flames before the bigger pieces of wood were carefully placed on the fledgling campfire, was excitement itself. Oh, how easily amused we were in those days!

Just after 1 p.m. I would see two tiny figures in the distance coming down the steep steps from the Brucehill housing scheme and heading towards the shore. As the figures got closer I could recognise it was my mammy and Granny Boyle. Now we would all be together and the happiness of the day could really begin.

By this time the campfire was well and truly ablaze and some coal would be added to the wood to give some longer-lasting heat. One of the older boys would hammer an iron pole into the ground right in the middle of the fire. This pole had three hooks at the top and this was where my mammy would hang the pots to cook dinner over the fire.

It was usually soup then mince and potatoes on the menu. The pot of home-made soup – none of your tinned or packet stuff – would have been cooked the night before and would just need to be heated on the open fire. It would be the same with the mince, which had been pre-cooked the night before. The potatoes would have been washed and peeled in the house on Sunday morning, but were cooked on the fire.

My day was filled by playing games in the sand with other children or going for a walk to the woods to pick bluebells, which would be placed in an empty jam jar for a vase and presented to my mammy as a present. Not very sophisticated, but I bet my mammy enjoyed getting those flowers just as much as if they had been an expensive bouquet.

At some point during the day we would go into the water for a paddle. That was until one day I was stung by what I thought was a baby octopus that I tried to pick up out of the water. It turned out to be a jellyfish and that certainly taught me a painful lesson about not touching jellyfish. It took a good few weeks for me to pluck up the courage to go back into the water after that little episode.

Not by any manner of means were we the only family who would spend the day along Havoc Shore – it seemed half of Dumbarton was there as well. All along the shore, as far as the eye could see, people would be gathering in small groups, some with tents up like our family, others just lying on the sand and some having a picnic on the blankets they had spread out. There was lots of laughter and shouting from the friends and neighbours who would walk by and give you a quick burst of banter. It was noisy – but it was a happy noise and that was music to my ears.

In those days the River Clyde was a busy maritime thoroughfare and when big ships would sail up or down river they would create wave after wave creeping towards and onto the shore. We would wait for those big waves and run into the water and back out again, racing the ridge of water up the shore before it would splash high up our legs. There was always the smell of cooking wafting along the shore to mingle with the tang of the dulse seaweed on the rocks, which I liked. Although I'm sure the smell of dulse wouldn't be to everyone's liking.

The bathing costume I had was made from an elasticated blue material that looked like it had thousands of bubbles on it. It wasn't too bad compared to some of the other bathing outfits – especially the boys'. They normally wore bathing trunks made from wool and when they were coming out of the water the material was so wet it made the trunks sag halfway down their legs. Poor wee things, those boys.

Then there would be the dads – certainly not mine though, as, thankfully, he never came near the shore – taking their children on their shoulders or on their back into the water. Some of the men had trunks on, but most of them just rolled their trousers up their legs as far as they would go and ran into the water with their youngsters squealing in delight. I would love to see that, although there would be just a tinge of sadness in my heart that my daddy would never do that for me.

Very few of the older women would wear a bathing costume. When they wanted to cool down, they would hitch their skirts and aprons up above their knees – no further, mind – and go for a paddle. When they weren't cooking, most of the mothers and grannies would spend their day just sitting chatting and doing their knitting or crocheting.

I loved it when Tilly was up on holiday and came to the shore with us on a Sunday. She was a trendsetter in those days and wore really fancy bathing costumes. She had one that was three different colours and it had no straps – wow, that was a bit daring! I felt really proud that my big sister was so glamorous and that people would notice her when she walked back and forth to the water's edge.

At some point in the day I and many of the other youngsters would have a sleep – crawling into the tent and curling up on a blanket. It was also a time of respite from the burning sun, as the hours spent playing on the sand or in the water would ultimately lead to bare backs, fronts, arms, legs and faces turning bright red with sunburn. That's when your mammy would come to the rescue with bottles of calamine lotion, the soothing pink liquid being poured on to lumps of cotton wool and liberally dabbed onto the burnt skin before the lotion turned powdery white as it dried.

And if the family had no calamine lotion, they would turn to more natural remedies for sunburn, mixing bicarbonate of soda with water, which was then patted onto your skin – another antidote for the burning, throbbing lobster-red skin. However, if neither of those two remedies were available, a most horrible smelling – although extremely effective – medicinal product was utilised. Sour, curdled milk was a fantastic healing agent for sunburn when it was dabbed with cotton wool onto your skin. Cooling it might have been, but even the dogs running around the shoreline would steer clear of you until the horrible smell had died down.

While all this was going on the men would head off with empty cans and basins to scour the rocks for whelks and clabbie dhus, which was the local name for the large mussels that grew in great numbers along the Clyde coast. When the men came back an hour or so later with their supply of whelks and clabbies they would send the youngsters to the wells and get them to wash them in fresh water before they were boiled in pots over the open fires. When the whelks were ready, they would be shared out and everyone was given a pin to winkle the whelk out of its shell. I could hardly bear to look at, never mind eat a whelk. When you were prising the whelk out, it looked like you were pulling a tiny eye with some gunge behind it out of the shell. Oh no, that wasn't for me.

There was an overwhelming happiness on those long summer days down at Havoc Shore – an atmosphere and a joy that would never be experienced inside the four walls of my home because of the ever-present fear and dread of my father. Even when he wasn't in the house, my father seemed to leave his dreadful presence hanging in the air. Maybe because we all knew that it wouldn't be long before he'd be back in the house again and we'd all be on tenter-hooks trying not to upset him or send him into one of his violent rages.

But those times spent on the shore really were a delight, being away from that man and all he inflicted upon us. It was wonderful to hear my mammy laughing out loud as she spent a few precious hours being happy and among happy people.

The years of the Second World War brought big changes to our house, the biggest being that my older brothers were all away serving with either the Army or the Royal Navy. Even Tilly was doing her bit with the Wrens.

My father's violent rages seemed to get worse during the war years. It might have been because of the stress of waiting for the dreaded news that one of our own had been killed in action. Or maybe it was simply the fact that the older boys were no longer living in the house and acting as a brake on his more outrageous behaviour. He gave my mother some terrible beatings, and with just Frances, George, Rose and me the only youngsters left in the house, there was not much we could do to stop him. Needless to say, my mother never complained and just got on with life looking after the family that was left in the house and commanding us: 'Don't upset your father.'

I recall one terrible leathering I got from my father when I was seven years old, and it stemmed from my ignorance and naïvety about what the war really meant to families on the home front. From time to time, I used to see a boy cycling along our street dressed in a navy-blue uniform, wearing a pillbox hat with a yellow band round it and a brown canvas satchel strapped across his chest. I would watch as he carefully leaned his bike against a garden hedge or fence and walk up the path holding a buff-coloured envelope in his hand.

I could never understand why almost every time he went to someone's door there would be a commotion with shouting and screaming. At my young age I thought that something exciting must happen every time that boy went to a door and I would wish he would come to ours. What I didn't realise was that, far from delivering welcome news, the telegram boy was bringing terrible news to families that one of their loved ones had been killed in the war. What I thought were squeals of excitement were really gasps of anguish and the wailings of despair that someone close to them had died in action.

But I soon learned the hard lesson that I couldn't have been more wrong, with a beating meted out by my father. One day I was playing in our garden with a friend, Betty Keenan, who was a neighbour's daughter, when I saw the telegram boy cycling up the road.

'I hope he is coming to us,' I said to Betty. 'We've never had the telegram boy at our door; he always goes to someone else.'

The next thing I knew, my father had grabbed me by the hair, lifted me off the ground and kicked me all the way up the garden path to the door. He was shouting: 'I'll kill her. She's not right in the head.'

Granny Boyle heard the commotion and came rushing into the house to stop the beating I was getting. I was in tears and she took me into another room to explain that I shouldn't have said that I wanted the telegram boy to come to our house, as it would mean one of my brothers had been killed. 'That's why everybody screams,' she said. 'When the telegram boy comes to a house it's usually to tell the people there that someone has been killed in the war.'

Bad as my father was, I can now understand the daily dread of that knock on the door from the telegram boy with the news that one of your children had been killed and wouldn't be coming home. It must have been terrible for my mammy and father living with that fear day after day. All the same, he didn't need to give me such a severe hiding – a few stern words of explanation would have sufficed.

At such a young age I didn't really understand what the war was all about, and all it meant to me was that lots of people I liked had to go away. It did, however, sometimes feel like a big adventure, especially when the air-raid siren went off and everyone had to head for the air-raid shelter at the back of our garden.

This circular shelter was made of corrugated iron painted green, and was shared by Granny Boyle's family and ourselves. We had put three bunk beds inside the shelter – one at the top and the other two down the sides of the shelter. There were also some chairs that Granny Boyle had put there, and bits of carpet on the floor.

When the siren went off I would be covered in a blanket and carried out of the house and into the shelter. I thought it was great fun because the adults would take sandwiches, biscuits and diluting fruit juice into the shelters, as we could be in there for up to six hours at a time.

Light would come from candles placed on what I called Wee Willie Winkie candleholders or from the big torches with long, thick round handles. We would play games of snakes and ladders, listen to Granny Boyle telling stories or have a sing-song waiting for the long, drawn-out siren of the all-clear signal that meant we could head back to our house. I hadn't the foggiest that we were in any danger, so I looked on the air-raid shelter as an extra wee house out the back door, or my own special den.

Every night before it got dark we had to cover our windows with sheets of black material in case enemy bomber pilots used the house lights shining through the windows as a target for their deadly payload. This was called the blackout, and if you were lax about blacking out your windows you would get a visit from one of the local Air Raid Precaution (ARP) wardens to make sure you carried out the task. Guess who was an ARP warden as well as the school janitor – yes, none other than my father, and you can imagine our windows were among the first in the street to be blacked out. I got to help out in those blackouts, pressing hard on the drawing pins holding the black hessian in place round the window frame. Because I was so small, I could only manage to pin the bottom of the cloth to the window frame and someone like Frances or my mammy would do up the sides and along the top.

It's amazing what other wartime events stick in the memory. In my mind, I can still see the dozens of barrage balloons in the sky above Dumbarton, which were flown as a defence against dive-bombing or low-flying German bombers. If any of the Luftwaffe planes dared fly into the balloons, the cables tying them to wagons on the ground were strong enough to damage the aircraft and bring them down. I remember the barrage balloons well because of their shape and the fins they had. At the time I thought they were sharks that had jumped out of the River Clyde and were floating in the sky. I was ever so slightly afraid that these 'sharks' were going to come back down to earth and bite me!

Rationing was another major feature of life during the war. We were registered to buy our groceries from the Co-op store in the Brucehill housing scheme and our meat from McInnes, the butcher in Dumbarton's High Street. One you had registered it meant these were the only shops where you could buy your food. My mammy kept our buff-coloured Ministry of Food ration cards and our identity cards in a wee leather handbag that was always on the floor beside her chair in the living room.

While my mammy was concerning herself with how much bacon, eggs, sugar, milk, beef, tinned fruit and tea she would be allowed to buy with her ration book, the separate sweetie coupon book was uppermost in my mind. While the shopkeeper stamped the ration books to show what you had bought, the sweetie coupons were cut off in squares depending on how many ounces of sweets you bought. We were allowed to buy eight ounces of sweets a month and, of course, when you first got your sweetie coupon book it was a huge dilemma whether to splash out on lots of sweets at the one time and have nothing left for the rest of the month or spread your ration of sweets over the whole month. Believe you me, the latter demanded a fair degree of will power and self-control.

Although you didn't have to register with any particular sweet shop, they didn't always have a supply of sweets available for sale. You were always waiting to hear which shop had sweets in and when the jungle drums began to beat that one particular shop was selling sweets it was a mad dash to get there before they were sold out. I even walked two and a half miles one day to the nearby small town of Renton, which had a shop that had just got a supply of sweets in.

Although the temptation was always there to blow your sweets ration at the one time, I was always quite disciplined and kept my limit of sweets to two ounces every week for going to the cinema on a Saturday afternoon. My favourites were penny caramels and liquorice toffee. Mmmm . . . they certainly tasted a lot better when you knew you couldn't just go out and buy them any time you wanted like we do today. There were occasions when the adults would take sweet coupons from us youngsters. This would usually be because someone was having a birthday party that we were all getting invited to and the family wanted to put on a special treat for everyone. All the sweet coupons would be pooled and there would be lots of sweets on the table for the kids coming to the party. Sometimes all you would get at a birthday party would be a jam sandwich as you came in the door.

Not that I understood this at the time, but a black market in food was rife all over the country. When my brother Willie was home on leave, he used to walk six greyhounds for a man called Paddy Dougan who kept the dogs for racing. He stayed quite close to us and I was friendly with his daughter Patsy. Many a time when I was playing in her garden, Paddy would call me into the house, hand me a canvas duffle bag and ask me to take it to Willie. I would take it to my brother, who would hand the bag to my mammy and say: 'Put these in the cupboard.' And as if by magic, tins of fruit appeared on our shelves.

One really bright spot for me in the war years was going on summer holiday to Fort William. Life was so different there and everyone seemed so happy, I thought there was no war in Fort William. I would spend six weeks of my school holidays staying with either my Uncle George Murray or my Aunt Jean Cameron in the West Highland town, and they were some of the happiest times of my life.

I used to be sent up to Fort William on the train on my own and it was a wonderful feeling the night before, with a knot of excitement in my stomach and the knowledge that I would have a whole six weeks without my father shouting at me or hitting me. I would call it supreme happiness. As the train took off along the tracks, Dumbarton disappeared into the distance, as did the fear of taking another hammering from my father. My relatives – who would be at the Fort William Railway Station to meet me – and their children were glad to see me and were really good to me.

Uncle George was my mum's brother and he was married to Ellen. They didn't have any children of their own, but had taken in Tilly's sister, Helen, when their mother died and Tilly came to live with us. Aunt Jean was my mother's cousin and she was married to Alan. They had four children – young Jean, Margaret, Angus and Duncan. Wee Duncan was a poor soul as he had been crippled as a youngster just before he was due to start school. He fell out of a tree and when he landed he broke his back and a spike took one of his eyes out. He grew up really tiny and had a hump on his back – he was only about four feet tall – and with only one eye. He didn't even have a glass eye to make him look as if he had both eyes. He was probably in his early twenties when I first saw him, but I thought he looked like an old man. He was a lovely person and was spoiled rotten by everyone. He was always telling tall stories and Aunt Jean would warn me not to take any notice of what he was saying.

If we were ever going down to the shore of Loch Linnhe in Fort William we would have to walk past some big, posh houses with lots of trees and big gates in Achintore Road. A man called Colonel Lawton would sometimes be standing at the gate leaning on his hickory walking stick when we passed by and he would always wave and ask us how we were doing and where we were going. On other occasions there would be another man, who didn't have a walking stick and who spoke slightly differently. He would give us apples off the trees in the garden, and gooseberries were another thing he gave us. Once he even gave us all money to buy an ice cream. This happened several times before I realised who this second man really was, when Aunt Jean told me I had been talking to the film star Charles Lawton, who often visited his brother in Fort William.

There was one evening every summer when it appeared as if everyone from Fort William would walk up Ben Nevis and stay there throughout the night. We would leave about 6 p.m. and there was a bothy where you could get hot drinks and sandwiches on the way up the Ben. There were lots of people there that night every year and they would be lighting campfires and sitting around the flames singing Gaelic songs and telling stories. If my father had known what I was getting up to in Fort William he would have gone off his head. And when any of my brothers who had been there with me got back to Dumbarton they wouldn't dare mention that I had been up Ben Nevis with them.

As the war came to an end, street parties began to be held in our housing scheme. One of the first parties in Brucehill was for a Mr Allardyce, who had escaped from a Japanese prisoner of war camp and was returning home. The celebrations were being held along two streets, with trestle tables laid out in the middle of the road. There was a fantastic community spirit in those days and all the neighbours had pooled their food ration coupons and the tables were laden with sandwiches, cakes, biscuits and sweets.

It seemed the whole of Brucehill had turned out – except my father of course, who frowned on such joviality – for the street party, which started at 7 p.m. When all the food was eaten and the tables cleared away a couple of men – Jock Brown and John Haggerty, better-known as Big Blin Hig – would bring out their accordions and the dancing would start on the street. In between the dancing, people would get up to sing. I was allowed out late on those nights because my mother and Granny Boyle would always be at those street parties. Of course, the party of all street parties was on VE Day – 8 May 1945. This was Victory in Europe Day, when the Nazis finally surrendered to the Allies and the war thankfully came to an end.

I was still too young to really comprehend what was going on, but I knew it was something to celebrate because my mammy told me that my brothers would soon be home from the war, and that made me happy. On VE Day there was bunting stretched back and forth across the street tied to people's chimneys, and every window had a Union Jack flying from the ledge.

I thought that with my older brothers coming back, the beatings from my father would stop because they would be bigger people now and they wouldn't let him do these things. But Bernie had got married during the war and had a house of his own, and my mammy always pleaded with her older sons not to have a go at my father, fearing things would only get worse. Many a time my older brothers would be in a rage after he had given one of us a leathering and they were ready to kill him. And kill him in their anger I believe they would have, such was the viciousness of his temper and his brutality to my mother and the younger children. But in those days the punishment for murder was hanging, and my mammy would be in tears, saying that she didn't want to see one of her sons go to the gallows; she'd be hanging onto them, stopping them from going after him. So, my father got away with it.

Even Tilly had escaped for good by marrying Raymond Round – an Englishman serving in the Commandos – only after the wedding sending a telegram home to my father to say she was a new bride.

I knew something special was happening on VE Day when my mammy made sure I was wearing one of my best dresses, clean white socks and white shoes. Everyone was rushing about organising things and I was delighted to be part of it, getting sent on errands to neighbours for all sorts of things. People were bringing chairs from their homes and lining them alongside the trestle tables in the middle of the road, and the local Co-op even lent us benches for people to sit on.

Neighbours were making hats from crepe paper and the bunting and flags were being hung out. There was a great sense of excitement that grew as the sound of music came wafting up the street as a van with a big horn on top blaring out music came motoring along the road. It was pandemonium that day, with hundreds of people out on every street in the housing scheme dancing and singing. Everybody was in a joyous mood as their families were being reunited after the war, and if dads, sons, brothers, uncles, nephews and cousins were not already home from the war, it wouldn't be long before they were.

The Second World War might have been over, but for us, we still had our own war to contend with, as there was no letting up in my father's outrageous antics.

The Great Escape

I walk into my sister Frances' living room, she takes one look at me and gasps: 'Oh Jesus, Mary and Joseph. He'll go stone mad, my daddy'll kill you when he sees you dressed like that.'

The last time Frances had seen me I was dressed in a pink, double-breasted coat, wearing flat, sensible, lace-up shoes and a beanie hat with a button on top. I had poker-straight hair and absolutely no make-up – a frumpy teenager looking like someone three or even four times her age. But what stood before Frances now was a complete transformation from the day I'd left Dumbarton fourteen months earlier to live with Tilly, her husband Raymond and daughter Jennifer in Northampton. The Mary Kelly now was nothing like the Mary Kelly then. I had been to the hairdresser's and given a completely modern style for that era – a poodle cut, with my hair in tight curls. I had make-up on – something my father would never have allowed on someone my age. And the *pièce de résistance* was a figure-hugging pencil skirt with, my goodness, a split up the back that showed off my frilly underskirt, nylons with a black seam and high-heeled shoes.

I felt absolutely fantastic standing there and all the way on the bus up to Scotland from Northampton, all I could think about was the reaction from my family when they saw what I looked like. Tilly had told me I looked stunning, and if someone as glamorous as Tilly said I was stunning, well, I was stunning. There was, however, one potential big black cloud on the horizon and that was what my father's reaction was going to be. But with my new look there also came a new confidence continually bolstered by Tilly telling me I had nothing to worry about.

This dramatic change in both my appearance and the way I felt about myself, with my new-found confidence, stemmed from my stay with Tilly, after I left home at the age of sixteen. All through my early teens in the post-war years I had had to suffer more of the same domination, punishments and violent behaviour from my father in the family home. Moving out and going to Northampton to stay with Tilly was my Great Escape.

When I was between the ages of twelve and fifteen my father never allowed me to do the things that other girls of that age were getting involved in. He forbade me to join a dancing school, never let me go to the swimming baths with my friends nor allowed me to join the school choir. It was as if he never wanted anyone to be happy. He did let me join the Girls' Guild, but that was only because the organisation was run by the Catholic Church and it was perceived to be a bit holy, although all we did there was play netball and table tennis in the gym hall of Notre Dame School. Even at Hallowe'en, he never allowed me to dress up like the other children. My early teenage years were mainly about going to school, coming home, doing homework and trying my hardest to avoid a leathering from my father. Maybe once in a while my mammy, Granny Boyle and I would go to the local cinema, but I was never allowed to go there on my own or with friends.

Life in our home was like being in an army barracks, with my father the sergeant-major barking out his orders and meting out severe punishment for those who failed to obey instantly. The greatest punishments were kept for when he thought someone had defied him and, even after taking a hammering from him, my father would tell you the exact

time he would be back to give you another leathering as part
of the same punishment.

Yes, defying my father would result in a severe beating as
my brother – or in reality, my cousin – Jack found out to his
cost. And to drive home the point my father kicked Jack out
of the house and never allowed him to set foot in it again.
Jack's crime? He was caught bringing me a glass of milk and
some tea biscuits after my father had leathered me and I had
been banished to my bedroom without any food at teatime.

It all began one Sunday when I was fourteen and both my
father and my mammy were out of the house for a few
hours. In those days we had gas-powered lights and I
noticed the gas mantle in the kitchen needed to be changed.
A mantle was a very delicate piece of equipment – a small
cloth bag which surrounded different chemicals that burned
extremely brightly when lit. I stood on the kitchen table and
started to change the mantle, but it dropped out into my
hand, bursting the delicate cloth bag, and I was left holding
a tiny mound of powder. Worse still, it was the last gas
mantle we had in the house and, being a Sunday, there were
no shops open to buy a replacement.

I knew I was in trouble and without even telling my older
brothers, who were in the house, I ran out of the house in
terror – I knew what my father would do to me when he
found out what had happened. A couple of hours later
Jimmy came looking for me and said I had to go back to the
house as my father wanted to see me. I was shaking as I
walked into the kitchen, where my father was standing.

'Did you break the mantle?' he asked.

I hesitated and, fearing a beating, said: 'No.'

'There's nothing I hate more than a liar.'

As he went to get his belt for the inevitable thrashing, I
blurted out: 'It was me, but I was only trying to help my
mammy.' My delayed honesty was to no avail and I got a
real leathering with his belt. After he was finished with me I

was ordered to get my pyjamas on and go to bed without any tea that night. As I whimpered off to my bed with my legs stinging from the lashes of the belt, my father warned me that he would return later to give me another leathering to make sure I had really learned my lesson. Just as my tears had dried, I heard the bedroom door open and there was Jack sneaking in with a glass of milk and a jam sandwich. He sat at my bedside until I had drunk the milk and finished the bread and jam. 'I'll be back later on with something else for you,' he said.

In between, my father was as good as his word and he came into my room with his belt, ordered me out of my bed and gave me another leathering. Later on Jack returned with another glass of milk and some tea biscuits and as he tried to comfort me, my father came into the room and saw me with the milk and biscuits. He was raging and gave Jack a real hammering and kicked him out of the house. When my father threw you out, you stayed out. So Jack – who would have been twenty-seven at the time – had to get lodgings in a house on the other side of Dumbarton and within a year he emigrated to Australia. I have no doubt he went to the other side of the world – leaving behind the people he loved and cared for – because of the way my father treated him.

Even the simple joys of playing with your friends out in the street or in nearby woods were frowned upon by my father. I was forbidden to do either, even to go and pick bluebells to bring home for my mammy. So, if I wanted to play the usual games of peavers (hopscotch) or skipping with ropes with my friends, I would have to make the excuse of going to see them in their house, but instead playing outside in the street away from our front door where my father could see me. He would even dictate which friends I could have come to our house to visit me. The only two he would allow in the house were Patsy Dougan, whose dad Paddy Dougan was quite well off, and the local St Patrick's Chapel Passkeeper James Carr's daughter, Kathleen.

There was one girl, who had come from Ireland to live in our scheme, who once came to our door asking for me. When my father saw who it was he pushed her off the steps and up the path with a sweeping brush and told her never to darken his door again. He didn't like her because she was Irish and he thought his family were too good to be mixing with her. That attitude – as well as being racist – was quite ironic, as my father himself was descended from Irish immigrants. His words to me were: 'Keep that Irish bastard away from my door.' And as a punishment he made me sweep the steps the girl had stood on and then scrub them with bleach and water.

His reasoning for forbidding me to do all those things that girls of my age would normally do was that he thought these children were acting like idiots. One of his favourite mantras was: 'No one belonging to me will make a fool of themselves and bring my name down.'

There were glimpses of happiness during those years, but never in our home. I loved the time spent upstairs in Granny Boyle's house away from my father and I would find any excuse to visit her as much as possible. In my early teenage years, another woman who became a good friend to me was my older brother Bernie's wife, Maureen. She was one of the few people who wasn't scared of my father and would refuse to stop talking when he came into the room – much to his severe annoyance.

Maureen, bless her, obviously felt sorry for me because of how that man was treating me. She would tell my father she was taking me to the cinema so she had company on the way home, only to take me visiting all her friends and relatives. I think she would have made up any story just to get me away from my father for a few hours.

By the time I was a teenager some of my older brothers
had become grown men and I often wondered why they
never stopped my father beating up my mammy or the
other members of the family. I was recently talking to my
only surviving brother, George, and although there was
one particular occasion when Jimmy was so mad at my
father he tried to break his bedroom door down to get to
him, I asked why none of the boys had really given my
father a taste of his own medicine. He told me how our
mammy stopped them, and would tell them that God
would never forgive them if they were to hit their father.
'Mary, you were a lot younger than the rest of us and you
only remember the screaming and shouting, but I remember the look on my mother's face as she pleaded with us
not to do anything. It wasn't as if we didn't want to give
him a doing, because my father really was an evil bastard
for what he put us all through, but my mammy really
believed this "honour thy father and thy mother" stuff.
It was just the look on my mammy's face – I just couldn't
go against her, however much I wanted to give him a
hammering.'

It wasn't just in physical ways that he would hurt his
children. My sister Frances was really clever at school and
she was accepted to go to Teacher Training School, but my
father wouldn't let her go and made her take a job in a
baker's shop in Helensburgh. Granny Boyle said he did this
out of badness – he wanted to prove his children were
intelligent, but he didn't want them actually to achieve
anything in case they became better than him and started
to look down on him.

I did well at school, took French and Latin and was
always in the top three in the class. When I was fifteen, my
father decided I was to take a test to get a job as a cashier in
the Co-op in Dumbarton's High Street. There was only one
position available and in those days they chose people by

organising an accountancy test for all the brightest pupils in the area to take. I left the house on the day of the test with my father's stern warning: 'You better f*****g get that job and not give me a showing up.'

I was desperate to get a job because I thought earning a wage would give me my independence and I would be able to get away from the clutches of my father. When I was young I had an obsession about getting away from him. I even used to pray and ask God to do some really daft things like have someone from the travelling fairground steal me and take me away from home.

I was still at school when I took the test in the Co-operative offices, but as I walked through the door of the room my heart sank. Sitting there waiting to take the test as well was my educational nemesis – Rita Guthrie. I knew I would be able to beat anyone else in the test, but Rita was one of those girls who was just as clever as me and I couldn't be sure of coming top and getting the job. And, worse still, she was from a Protestant school. I thought: 'He's going to kill me. Not only did I not come top, but I let a lassie from a Protestant school beat me.'

However, as things turned out I did come top in the exam, was offered the job and even got my name in the local paper. My mammy and Granny Boyle were delighted for me, but my father never said a word. Anyway, I was just glad I didn't get a leathering from him for showing him up.

So, after the school summer holidays in 1950, I started work as a cashier in the main Co-op grocery store in Dumbarton. It was just as well I was good at arithmetic at school, because in those days there were no computers or calculators. Instead, I was working with big ledger books, fountain pens, a box of nibs and an inkwell you dipped the pen into. I worked from 8 a.m. to 5 p.m., Monday to Friday, with a half-day off on a Wednesday, although I also worked a Saturday morning. I liked the job because it was a clean environment, and because I had a good head for figures I found it quite easy.

At the age of seventeen I had never had sexual relations with anyone, but my first encounter with a boy on those terms was a terrifying ordeal – he tried to rape me. I had been asked by a boy to go to Balloch Park for a picnic and since he seemed a decent enough lad, I agreed. I made up an excuse to meet him without my father finding out and the day started well. At first, he was well mannered and I was impressed that he had turned up with a pukka picnic basket and a rug. It was a lovely spring day and Balloch Park – where the River Leven flows into Loch Lomond – was full of people. The boy suggested we walk to a nearby field, which was quieter, and when we got there he laid out the rug. I had only been sitting on the rug for a few seconds when he jumped on top of me and pushed me flat on my back. He was pulling at my pants, trying to get them down past my knees, and I was terrified, screaming for help. Luckily for me, two men passing by heard my screams and they ran over and dragged the boy off me. One of the men gave the boy a real doing while the other man put his jacket over me until I pulled my pants up and got myself decent.

The boy managed to run away and the men said they would get the police. I pleaded with them not to as I didn't want my father to find out I was out with a boy. The two men were very kind and understanding – it turned out they knew my father and what he was like – so they took me on the bus to Dumbarton and made sure I was safe walking up the road to my house. I never told a soul in my family what had happened and put the ordeal to the back of my mind.

By this time Tilly had been married for a few years and was living in Northampton, and I kept in contact by regularly writing letters to her. I would write those letters

in Granny Boyle's house in case my father found out, and
Tilly wrote to me care of Granny Boyle's address. Imagine
what it would have been like if he had found out I was
telling Tilly how bad it was in the house, with all the rows
and beatings!

In one of her letters, Tilly told me not to worry, as when
she came up on holiday next summer things would be
different. She never said what would be different, just that
they would.

And what a difference to my life when that summer
arrived and Tilly announced that she wanted me to come
and live with her family in Northampton after they had just
been given a bigger council house. I couldn't believe Tilly
was going to stand face-to-face with my father and suggest
that I would leave home at just sixteen and live three
hundred and sixty miles away in Northampton. But that's
exactly what she did, concocting some story about her
husband Raymond working nights on the railways every
alternate week and she wanted company for her and Jennifer in the house. In reality, if she had wanted company
Tilly could have gone to Raymond's parents, who lived less
than a mile away, but my father didn't know that and he
bought Tilly's 'I'm feeling lonely' story.

While Tilly was talking my father into releasing me from
his clutches I ran up to Granny Boyle's, petrified that he was
going to explode and give me a leathering for trying to get
Tilly to talk him into letting me leave the house. I sat up
there fearing the worst until Tilly came in and nonchalantly
announced: 'He's going to let you come down south with
me.'

I couldn't believe it. This was like being in heaven,
knowing I was going to get away from my father. Even
to this day, I will never understand why he let that happen,
because it was going to change my life completely – and for
the better into the bargain. My mother was pleased that I

was being given the chance of a new life, although as any mother would, she kept asking if I was sure I was doing the right thing and made me promise to write home two or three times a week. I knew I would miss my mammy, but I certainly wasn't going to miss my father.

I was lucky enough to get a job as a cashier in the Mettoy toy factory, in Northampton, which meant I would also have cash to spend on myself after I had paid Tilly my digs money.

The first thing Tilly did when we got to Northampton was begin the transformation of a dowdy wee lassie from Dumbarton into a glamorous, sophisticated and modern-looking teenager. We arrived in Northampton on a Saturday and the following day we went to Mass, as Tilly was a devout Catholic. That Sunday night after Raymond had gone to work on the nightshift and Jennifer was put to bed, Tilly sat me down and said: 'Right, my girl, you're too frumpy and old-fashioned. You look more like a middle-aged woman than a teenager. It's time you started looking like a teenager, so next Saturday we'll get you to the hairdresser's for one of those poodle cuts everyone your age is having just now.' The hairdresser's it was the following Saturday, and what an experience it was for me. I had never been to a hairdresser before as my father had always cut my hair in the house. As I sat there in the chair with the hairdresser fussing over me it was as if I was in another world. She permed my hair and put wee curls all round my head and shaped my hair down the back of my neck.

Next in the Mary Kelly makeover was the make-up. My father had never allowed me to wear make-up, but Tilly said that I should and she showed me how to put on lipstick, and make-up on my face and eyes. Tilly was an expert at things like that as she was a real stunner, dressing and carrying herself like a real glamour girl. Then there was a new outfit of a blue taffeta dress, which was all the rage then, and a pair of high-heeled shoes. I must have looked in the mirror a million times that Saturday night before I went dancing with Tilly's young sister-in-law, Pat Round.

But there were more surprises in store for me that first night out at The Salon dance hall in Northampton. A tall, handsome young American airman from the Mildenhall air base asked me to dance and immediately I was entranced by his charm, good looks and accent. I fell head over heels in love with James Hoes that night, but there was one major problem for me – he was black and I had been warned by Tilly to stay away from the Yanks – especially black Americans. Nowadays, the colour of someone's skin should mean nothing, but in the early '50s it definitely wasn't the done thing for a white girl to be going out with a black man. Looking back, it was a terribly racist attitude – although the fact that James was black made no difference to me – but it was very prevalent in this country and back in the USA at the time.

Pat was a couple of years older and wiser than me and after James had swept me off my feet and round the dance floor for the umpteenth time, she pulled me aside and said: 'Tilly will be raging if she finds out you've been talking to a black American airman.'

'You won't tell her,' I replied.

'No I won't, but there are plenty of people here who could tell her.'

However, Pat's warning didn't deter me – I was smitten. James was from New Jersey and I would hang on every last drawl of his American accent when he spoke to me. We agreed to meet again the following week and from then on every weekend was a date. He treated me really well, taking me to the cinema, out for meals and he brought me lots of presents – chocolates, jewellery and nylons – from the air force base PX Store. That was where the American airmen and women on the base were able to buy all the stuff they would normally get back in the States.

As you can imagine, the excitement of having my first boyfriend, being taken here, there and everywhere, and James opening doors for me to walk through, was a fantastic feeling – something I had never experienced before. For the next few months I saw James every weekend, but I managed to keep the fact that he was black a secret from Tilly. I told her I was seeing an American pilot I had met at the dancing, but I didn't dare mention the colour of his skin. Then one day she dropped a bombshell: 'If this boy is so nice, why don't you bring him home here for Sunday dinner so we can meet him?'

Now it was my turn to exclaim: 'Oh Jesus, Mary and Joseph!' How was I going to get round this one? As soon as I turned up on Tilly's doorstep with a black man on my arm, she'd know I'd been telling lies. Well, maybe it wasn't quite as bad as that. Let's just say I hadn't been telling her the whole truth – he was an American pilot, after all!

Where the sneakiness came from I don't know. But I hatched a plot to bring a white American pilot from Mildenhall to meet Tilly at Sunday dinner and pretend he was the guy I had been going out with for the past four months. I spoke to James about my ploy and he persuaded a pilot friend of his from the base – Larry Gilworth, from Philadelphia – to take his place and pretend he was James Hoes.

Larry thought this was a hoot and he duly turned up at Tilly's, had his Sunday lunch, conducted himself in an extremely polite manner and acted as if he had been my boyfriend for months. Tilly thought he was a really nice young man and that I had made a sensible choice in boyfriends. As Larry headed out of the door to head back to Mildenhall later that afternoon, I breathed a sigh of relief and thought I had got away with it. Of course, the following weekend I was out with James again and when we met Larry we had a great laugh about how he was my boyfriend for an afternoon. But the deception didn't last too much longer. A few weeks after the Sunday lunch charade with Larry Gilworth, Tilly had her stern face on when she asked me to come into her kitchenette for a word. She was incandescent with anger.

'You've been making a complete fool of me and don't you ever dare do that to me again. You brought that Larry Gilworth to our house and pretended that's who you were going out with when all the time you've gone behind my back and been seeing a black man. After all I've done for you, all you do is make a mockery of me.'

Well, that was just for starters. She didn't miss me and hit the kitchen cupboards. There was no point in me denying it was true because she knew far too much detail. Someone had really dropped me in it – just like Pat had predicted the first night I met James Hoes.

I hadn't meant to cause Tilly any hurt, so I promised I wouldn't see him any more. When I told James it had to end he asked me to marry him, but I had to turn him down as I just couldn't bear to think about the ramifications of doing that. Tilly was bad enough being angry, but can you imagine what my father would have said – and, worse still, done to me – because I was marrying a black man? I was only a teenager, and still terrified of my father. I thought that even if I did marry James, he had two years left of his posting to England and my father was only a train journey away if he wanted to take his anger out on me. The colour of James's skin didn't bother me, but in the Fifties it was a big deal and racism was rife in this country.

After the James Hoes Affair died down I got on with my new life in Northampton and enjoyed every minute of it. Not only did Tilly dramatically change the way I looked, she also gave my confidence a huge boost by showing me how to conduct myself in all kinds of company as she took me with her wherever she went. She was a great mentor to me and instilled in me a belief that I shouldn't be in awe of anybody. Years later Tilly used to say she had a hell of a time building up my confidence as I was far too timorous when I first came to stay with her. Tilly knew exactly what she was doing, turning a wee ugly duckling into a swan, and one in her own image.

I wrote home to my mammy every week and she would always be asking me to send her a photograph of myself. 'When you're on a picnic with Tilly, or something like that,' she would say. Little did my mammy realise what my new life was like. Tilly wasn't one for picnics, throwing a blanket on the grass or on the beach. No, Tilly took me to restaurants, and I mean real restaurants – not fish and chip places – where a waitress would come to your table to serve you.

But Tilly told me not to bother sending any photographs of myself. 'I want them to get the shock of their lives when they see you the next time we go up to Dumbarton on holiday,' she said. So for the fourteen months I was in Northampton, we never sent any photographs and no one had any idea what the Tilly Transformation of Mary Kelly had achieved. And if it was a shock Tilly wanted to give the folks back home in Dumbarton, that's exactly what they got when I appeared for the first time since leaving home. You should have seen the look on my sister Frances's face when I walked into her living room that day.

When we arrived in Dumbarton, Tilly, Raymond and Jennifer went straight to my mammy's house while I called in to see Frances first. After Frances had got used to her new-look wee sister, both of us headed for my mammy's house in Brucehill a couple of miles away. As the bus we were on passed the house, I could see my mammy, my sister Rose and Granny Boyle standing at the gate waiting for us to arrive. As soon as we walked down the road from the bus stop to the gate, my mammy was cuddling me and crying at the same time.

'Well, what do you think of your wee girl now?' asked Tilly.

'Oh, she's beautiful,' my mammy replied.

'I knew some day that wean would come into her own,' said Granny Boyle. 'You've made a great job of her, Tilly. Come on up to my house, Mary, so the rest of us can see you.'

Granny Boyle grabbed me by the hand and led me upstairs into her house. 'Wait till you see this,' she shouted down the hall. 'It's like a film star has just arrived in our street.'

'Oh, what a change in you', and 'My God you're absolutely beautiful' were the type of comments from Granny Boyle's family. I was simply basking in the glory and if my head could have got any bigger with all these compliments it would have burst the walls of Granny Boyle's living room.

It was more of the same when I got downstairs into my own house. 'The boys in this town will be going f*****g mad when they see what you've turned into. You look f*****g great, hen,' my brother John said. He was the swearer among my brothers.

But despite all those wonderful compliments I was getting, there was one hurdle still to get over – my father was due home for his lunch and the clock hands were creeping ever closer to that time of day. I felt a little nervous about seeing him, but as long as Tilly was by my side I knew I would have the power and strength to stand up to him.

My mind was jumping ahead, thinking about what he would say to me and how I would answer him back. I was expecting the usual tirade from him: 'Get that f*****g stuff off your face, get yourself into some sensible clothes and do something with that hair.'

I could hear his footsteps coming up the hall and my

stomach was tying itself in knots at the thought of his reaction. Suddenly he was there, standing in front of me in the kitchenette. He just looked at me and, for a few seconds, said nothing. There was something different in his eyes this time and he turned to my mammy and said: 'Annie, she can have dinner with me today.'

Tilly just looked at me, winked as if to say 'that's it all over, he's not going to say anything', and walked out of the kitchen.

You could have knocked me over with my newly discovered mascara brush. The make-up, the dress, the new hairdo and the high heels and all he said was: 'she can have dinner with me'. Now, that was a real honour in our house as my mother used to serve the dinner in three sittings, with usually the older boys, who were working, first to get their meal at the table with my father.

Then, to my even further surprise, he started to have a normal conversation with me.

'So, how are you doing down there anyway?'

'It's great.'

'I hear you're working as a cashier in a toy factory.'

'Yes, that's right.'

'Aye, well it's not done you any harm. I hope you're behaving yourself.'

'Of course I am.'

Just at that precise second, a flash of fear passed through my body, wondering if maybe someone had told him I had been going out with a black American pilot. But obviously not, as nothing was said.

Then it was: 'I suppose I'll see you when I come back up the road after my work at tea time, or is Tilly taking you somewhere gallivanting?'

'No, no both of us will be here for dinner.'

To be honest, all the fear and dread about facing my father disappeared within those few fleeting seconds when we looked at each other and not a word was said. I knew he was proud of me that day – not that he would have admitted it to me, not in a million years. But when I looked at him, the horrible, hateful dislike I had seen before in his eyes was not there.

When my father came home that evening, Tilly began cementing my independence from him even more. 'Mary doesn't stay in now,' she announced. 'She goes out and enjoys herself as any seventeen-year-old should.' So, announcing that I was going to a twenty-first birthday party and dance in the Hibs Hall in Dumbarton that night wasn't a problem.

If I was walking on air with all the compliments I had been getting in the few hours since I had come home, by the time the dancing started I was on cloud nine. As we were having the buffet I could see groups of boys huddled together pointing in my direction and obviously saying: 'Is that Mary Kelly?'

'No it can't be her.'

'Aye, it is. Jeezo, she's turned into a bit of a looker.'

Of course, the last time any of these lads saw me I was wearing my ever-present beanie hat and pink checked coat. I'm not surprised some of them didn't believe it was me standing there. One of the older boys, Danny Burrell, who was a friend of my brothers came over to me and said: 'Mary Kelly, hen. You are absolutely beautiful – what a change in a lassie. I never thought anyone could change like that. I'm telling you, Mary, you're turning more than a few heads in here tonight and you've got a few hearts beating faster.' I came over all coy and started to blush. 'Well, thanks very much, Mr Burrell.' I knew fine well the boys were staring at me, but I was playing it for all it was worth, pretending I hadn't noticed.

I was never short of a partner for a dance that night, but halfway through the party my eyes fell upon a boy who would play a part in another major event that would take my life on an entirely unexpected and different course. He was Gerry Munro and he was dressed in full Teddy Boy gear – the drape jacket, drainpipe trousers and the thick, rubber-soled brothel-creeper shoes. I thought he was really handsome, with dark hair and slightly dark skin.

He caught me looking at him before I could avert my eyes and even in that second or two I knew it wouldn't be long before he would be over from the other side of the hall, where all the boys were lined up, to ask me for a dance. We had quite a few dances that night, and a few kisses as well, and he walked me home.

I was home on holiday for a fortnight, but in the first week I saw Gerry another three times – the following Monday he took me to the pictures, we went to the dancing on the Wednesday and again on the Saturday. I had fallen head over heels in love with him that first night I saw him. By the time I had been out with him a half-dozen times, I decided to drop a bombshell on Tilly: 'I'm not going back to Northampton with you,' I said.

Well, you can imagine Tilly's reaction, with her powerful personality – especially when I told her it was because of a boy I had met the week before.

'You've got another two days before we leave to think about this and I suggest you think long and hard about what you're saying. You know what your life is going to be like if you come back here – it'll go back to what it was before and you know how much you hated it. If you don't come back to Northampton with us now, don't ever ask me to take you back again. I've given you a chance to make something of yourself.'

They say love is blind, but in my case it made me stupid, too. I thought Gerry was the one for me and I ignored Tilly's good advice and insisted that I was going to come back to Dumbarton. My excuse was that I missed my family too much. Of course, my mammy was delighted and my father's predictable reaction was: 'She can come back if she wants to, but she knows the rules and regulations of living in my house.'

I managed to get my old job back at the Co-operative and I was glad I had taken the decision to come home, even though Gerry wasn't as keen on our relationship as I was. We went together from time to time and I was really keen on him. However, things didn't really get serious until Christmas time, when we became an item. We were going out as a proper couple for the first few months of 1953, until the bright flame of romance began to fade.

But when you play with fire, you get your fingers burned . . .

Not the Virgin Mary Any More

The old Irish doctor has that incredulous look on his face as I tell him that I've got tuberculosis.

'Right . . . tuberculosis you say. Why do you think you've got tuberculosis?' he asks.

'Well, I've missed two periods and I feel sick all the time and everybody knows that tuberculosis makes you miss your periods.'

Dr O'Connor glances over at my Auntie Alice who has come with me to the surgery and they exchange a knowing look.

'I don't think you'll find she's got tuberculosis,' chimes in Auntie Alice. 'Go on, tell her it's not tuberculosis that's making her feel not well.'

'Have you got a boyfriend?' asks Dr O'Connor.

'Uh huh.'

'Have you been doing anything you shouldn't have been doing?'

'No, Doctor.'

'Are you quite sure about that?'

'Uh huh.'

'You've not done anything at all that you shouldn't have been doing? I don't think you're telling me the truth.'

For some reason I can't keep my eyes off the floor and there's a deafening silence from me.

'This sickness,' continues the doctor. 'Is it worse in the morning?'

'I suppose it is now you come to mention it.'

Dr O'Connor leans towards me, and looks straight in my

face and says: 'No, I don't see any tuberculosis there. You've missed two periods, you're feeling sick and it's worse in the mornings. That's what we call morning sickness, although some people can feel like that all day. I think we'd better start again – this time with the truth. Well now, Mary Kelly, I don't think we can call you the Virgin Mary any more – you're pregnant. You're having a baby.'

His words hang in the air before giving way to the silence that surrounds the three of us in the room. That is until I start bawling my eyes out as my comfort blanket of sheer ignorance and naïvety is suddenly whipped away from me.

Dr O'Connor must have thought I was a real numbskull to think that because I had missed two periods and felt sick all day meant I had tuberculosis. But he was a really kind man and gave me something to comfort me that was worth more than a chemist shop's worth of potions and pills: a big hug and a few kind words.

'I can understand why you are crying so sore. I know you're not married and you're going to have to face Jocky Kelly and tell him you're pregnant.'

Auntie Alice interrupts: 'Oh, Doctor, that can't happen. If her father finds out he's going to kill her.'

'Well, that's a big possibility there right enough,' says Dr O'Connor.

He settles me down, sits back in his chair and clasps his hands across his stomach. 'How many times have you slept with this boy?'

'Only once,' I lie.

'Are you sure you're telling me the truth?'

'Well, maybe not. It was three times, Doctor.' And even then I was still telling lies as we'd had sex about six times.

'That's more like it,' he says. 'We're going to have to get you an appointment at the maternity clinic at the hospital.'

At that, Auntie Alice interrupts: 'Doctor, please don't go near Mary's house. The only people who know Mary's expecting are us three. And I don't know how we're going to break the news to her mother, never mind her father. Oh Jesus, Mary and Joseph, it doesn't bear thinking about. When her father finds out he'll do something terrible to Mary – she'll never be able to live in this town.'

'I'll certainly not be doing that,' says Dr O'Connor. 'But Mary will have to come to see me every week to make sure everything is OK with her and the baby.'

Trust my luck. The first time I ever have sex with a boy and I fall pregnant. Thinking back, it was amazing how naïve I was. I thought I would never get pregnant because my daddy would kill me if I did. I thought God wouldn't let me get pregnant because of what my daddy would do to me if I were having a baby. Stupid? Naïve? Probably both.

Although Auntie Alice wasn't a real auntie to me – she was Granny Boyle's daughter and eighteen years older than me – she was the first person I had told about not feeling well. Even when she was telling me that missing periods and feeling sick usually meant you were pregnant I was still adamant that I had tuberculosis. She insisted that I meet her after work the following day and we would go to the doctor's surgery.

So that's how I came to be sitting in front of old Dr O'Connor, tears streaming down my cheeks after finally accepting the inevitable fact that I was eighteen, unmarried and almost three months pregnant. And to make things worse, I had fallen out of love with the baby's father, Gerry Munro, and we had split up before I discovered I was going to have his baby.

Back at the surgery, Dr O'Connor offered to make arrangements for me to go to a home where I could stay until I had the baby. In the 1950s, a young girl having a baby out of wedlock wasn't as readily accepted as it is today and many families would see it as something to be ashamed of. There were these homes where the young pregnant girl could go to stay and where you worked for your keep by doing laundry or cleaning. The girls could stay there until the baby was adopted or the mother was fit enough to look after the baby herself.

I didn't realise it at the time, but mums-to-be had a harsh life in those homes and Auntie Alice must have known what they were like. While I was nodding my head agreeing with whatever Dr O'Connor was suggesting, Auntie Alice butted in and said adamantly: 'Mary's not going to any of those bloody places. You don't realise what kind of place you're sending her to. We'll sort something out ourselves.'

An abortion was never spoken about. As a strict Catholic family the word was never mentioned in the house and, to be honest, I didn't even know what an abortion was when I was eighteen.

But unknown to me at the time, a plan would be hatched that would see me being sent to Fort William to stay with Uncle George Murray, until it was time for me to go to hospital and have the baby. Uncle George was my mammy's brother and was now a widower in his early seventies. When I was younger we would visit him and his wife Ellen several times a year – especially in the summer, when I spent my school holidays in Fort William, as well as our other relatives in Fort William, my mammy's cousins, the Camerons. They had a young family of their own. I suppose Uncle George was chosen because he had room in his house for me and we knew him just as well as the Camerons from our holidays up there.

But first, we had to tell my mammy what had happened. I was still working at the Co-op and wasn't showing any signs of a bump so no one in the family was any the wiser. Auntie Alice and I kept our secret for a few more weeks and I would be sneaking along to the maternity clinic praying to God every time that no one would recognise me and tell my father. Thankfully, no one did.

But I couldn't go on like this and Auntie Alice decided that the best tactic would be to tell my sister Frances before deciding how best to break the news to my mammy. And when Frances found out, she immediately said we had to tell my brother Jimmy. 'If anyone can save you from your father if he finds out about you being pregnant, it's our Jimmy,' she said.

If there were ever any problems in our family, a meeting would always be called in someone's house. So Jimmy was quietly asked to go to Frances's house one night after his work. By the time Auntie Alice and I arrived, Jimmy was there and had already been told the news about me being pregnant.

'This is some state of affairs,' he said. And he could hardly look me in the face with embarrassment. 'My mother will need to be told. She can't be left in the dark any longer. What's going to happen?'

Auntie Alice told Jimmy of the doctor's suggestion about me going to one of the homes, but immediately Jimmy said he didn't like the sound of that and I wouldn't be going there. That's when Frances said I would go to Fort William to stay with old Uncle George.

I always said Jimmy was a really kind man and he proved that beyond doubt by promising me that he would make sure each member of the family gave him 2/6d (12.5 pence) every week and he would send a postal order to me so I could pay Uncle George dig money and have some left over to spend on myself. Jimmy sat there working out how much money he could collect, saying: 'Some of our family won't be keen to part with half-a-crown every week – they'll make the excuse that it was her own mistake and she should pay for it. But don't worry, I'll get the money out of them.'

He worked out that I would be getting £2 17 shillings and sixpence (just over £2.87) every week. I was to give Uncle

George 25 shillings and keep the remaining £1 12 shillings and sixpence (just over £1.62) for myself.

The following day was a Wednesday – the only day my mammy didn't go into town in the afternoon to buy groceries as the shops were closed half-day. We didn't have a fridge in those days so my mammy bought food every day apart from a Sunday, when the shops were closed. Wednesday afternoon was the only time you could guarantee my mammy would be in the house and on her own as my father would be at his work.

So Wednesday afternoon it was. That's when we were going to break the news of my pregnancy to her. I'll never forget that afternoon and even after more than fifty years I still get slight butterflies in my tummy thinking about telling my mammy I was pregnant.

It was with no little trepidation that I pushed open the kitchen door with Auntie Alice by my side. As usual my mammy was slaving away at the kitchen sink and when we walked in she was peeling a mountain of potatoes for the family dinner. Auntie Alice always called my mammy Nan, instead of her name, Anne.

'Nan – would you sit down for a minute,' said Auntie Alice.

'You know I've not got time to sit down. I've got this dinner to cook,' she replied.

I can still see her harassed wee face, God bless her. Little did my mammy know that she might not have time to sit down, but in a minute she would be lying down, flat out on the kitchen floor and I would be thinking she was dead.

'Nan,' continued Auntie Alice. 'Listen, we've got it all arranged for Mary to go to stay in Fort William for a wee while.'

'What on earth has got into you, Mary?' she said. 'You're only a few months back from staying with Tilly in Northampton and you said you wanted to come home to

Dumbarton. What is there in Fort William that you want to go to live there?'

'Will you not sit down, Nan? There's something we need to tell you.'

I was too scared to say a word, even though I was the cause of all this trouble. I thought Auntie Alice was doing just fine so far.

'Nan, Mary's pregnant.'

In a split second, my mammy fainted and as she crumpled to the floor, Auntie Alice quickly moved forward to catch her as she fell, and laid her out on the kitchen floor.

'Take that knife out of your mother's hand,' Auntie Alice told me. 'And go and get Granny Boyle.'

I had never seen anyone faint before and I thought my mammy had dropped dead in front of my very eyes. I was in a blind panic as I ran out the house and banged on Granny Boyle's door.

'My mammy's dead, my mammy's dead,' I screamed hysterically.

Of course, Granny Boyle thought my father had gone into a rage and done something to my mammy. She started to head downstairs with me pulling at the back of her pinafore, getting dragged along.

'If that man's killed her . . .' she said. 'I knew he would go too far one of these days and he would kill that woman.'

'No, it's not my father – he's not even in the house. It's because my Auntie Alice told her I'm going to Fort William.'

That stopped Granny Boyle in her tracks. 'What do you mean you're going to Fort William? You're mammy's dead and you want to go to Fort William?' she said.

Off she went again, rushing down the stairs into my mammy's house while I was still trying to explain about me being pregnant and having to go to stay with my Uncle George in Fort William.

When Granny Boyle got to the kitchen she looked at my

mammy. Auntie Alice told her that my mammy had fainted. I was only a few paces behind Granny Boyle and for the first time in her life she grabbed me and started to shake me hard. 'Why are you telling me your mother's dead?'

'She is dead.'

'She's not dead – she's just fainted.'

By this time my mammy had started to come round and she was making funny noises as Auntie Alice lifted her into a chair.

Her first words were: 'Oh God save us. Your daddy's going to murder everyone in the house when he hears about this. What are we going to do?'

At this point, Granny Boyle took over. 'Never mind. Calm down, calm down – we'll sort something out and nobody's going to get murdered.' Then she ordered Auntie Alice to come up with the solution to all the ills of the world: a cup of hot, sweet tea.

A few minutes later my mammy calmed down. Holding a cup of steaming hot tea in her hand, she looked at me and said: 'Mary, how could you have done this? How could you have done this to us?'

'Mammy, I don't know . . .' was my insubstantial reply.

At this point Frances appeared and it was time for the pow-wow round the kitchen table with even more tea to oil the wheels of inventiveness as to how they were going to get me up to Fort William without my father finding out. And it turned out that Granny Boyle had known I was pregnant, but hadn't wanted to say anything until my mammy had been told. She thought that me running to her house screaming that my mammy was dead was the result of my father finding out he was unexpectedly going to be a granddad again.

Round that kitchen table the fine details of Mary Kelly's Fort William escape plan were finalised by four wise women and a frightened and confused wee lassie who just agreed to everything.

The trip north would be disguised as a normal Sunday excursion on the train to visit the relatives in Fort William. Only this time, while three of us – Frances, Auntie Alice and I – would leave on the train going north, only two would make the return journey. These Sunday excursions were quite common for people in Scotland's central belt who had relatives in the West Highlands. The train would leave Glasgow on a Sunday morning and you would have four hours with your family and friends in Fort William before you had to catch the train back to Glasgow later in the evening. So the plan was that the three of us would tell everyone we were going to Fort William the following Sunday for an away day. No one suspected anything different and since we had to act normally I went to the dancing on the Saturday night before I left home.

Before I was due to head off to Fort William on the Sunday I got a message to my unborn baby's dad that I needed to see him. We met up and I told him about me being pregnant. He was obviously shocked, but he asked me to go to his house and speak to his mother.

At his house, Gerry said he wanted to marry me and his mother said we could live at her house. 'The only thing is,' said Gerry, who was a Protestant, 'if we get married it will have to be in the Registrar's Office because I know you won't turn and become a Protestant and I'm definitely not getting married in the chapel.'

I said no to his offer of marrying me for the best of reasons – I didn't love the boy. And since I was in enough trouble with my father by getting pregnant, if I had married a Protestant, he would really have gone off his head. To Gerry's credit he didn't want to abandon me and he was willing to live up to his responsibilities of being a father to our child. But I was so terrified of my father finding out, I just wanted to get away from Dumbarton.

I begged Gerry: 'Please don't tell anybody until after

Sunday and I'm in Fort William. If my father finds out before I get out of here, he'll murder me.'

'Can I come to the railway station and see you leave?' he asked.

'No, don't do that.'

'Give me an address and I'll write to you.'

'No, it's best if you don't. You'll never see me again because I'll never be allowed to come back to Dumbarton.' I honestly believed that I would never be back in Dumbarton because of the fear of what my father would do to me.

The first problem we had to face before I could get on the train to Fort William was how to get all my clothes and belongings into two big suitcases and out of the house without my father noticing. I would never have been able to justify lugging two suitcases to the station for a day trip to Fort William. So while my father was in the pub on Saturday night, Auntie Alice's two children, Billy and Mary, called in at our house, loaded the suitcases into a baby's pram, wheeled it down the road to Dumbarton Central railway station and left the cases in the left luggage office overnight for me to pick up the following day.

Saying goodbye to my mammy on the Sunday was a terrible experience, with everybody crying their eyes out and me thinking I would never see my mammy again. Everyone agreed that once my father found out I was pregnant I would be banished from the house forever and he would order my mammy not to try to see me.

Not a lot was said on the train journey north, with just the occasional sob from myself as I felt so lost, lonely and ashamed of myself. I had no idea what the future held for me except that my life would change forever, never mind the fact I was going to live in the Highlands with a widower in his early seventies after spending all my life in busy towns in a house full of brothers and sisters.

When we arrived at Fort William we went straight to

Uncle George's house and knocked on his door. Now, when you are a teenager like I was then, you think old people are daft, but little do you realise it's you that's daft and the old folk are the wise ones. Uncle George opened the door and Frances said: 'Hello, Uncle George, we just thought we would come and visit you.'

He looked at me with the two big suitcases at my feet and replied: 'That's a lie for a start, but come on in anyway. When did you start bringing suitcases on a Sunday excursion?'

We followed him into his sparsely furnished living room. Uncle George's single bed was along one wall and there was just about enough room for a dining table and four wooden chairs. On either side of the coal fire there was a wooden rocking chair and an armchair. There was also a cuckoo clock hanging on the wall above the fireplace. The floor was covered in linoleum with two clippy rugs placed at the side of the bed and in front of the fire. Clippy rugs were home-made hessian-backed mats made from off-cuts of clothes and curtains cut into strips, held in place by hooking them through the hessian that was stretched over a wooden frame as the rug was being made.

Auntie Alice sat on the side of the bed, Frances pulled out one of the dining-table chairs to sit on and Uncle George plonked himself on his favourite rocking chair. I stood behind the armchair, not uttering a word.

'I suppose I better make you all a cup of tea,' he said, and filled an old black kettle with water, placing it in the heart of the blazing fire to come to the boil. Uncle George didn't have a cooker in the house – everything went on the open fire. Pots were hung on a hook that hung on a bar across the base of the chimney and the kettle was plunged into the middle of the burning coals. As the kettle was heating up there was an awkward silence until Uncle George said: 'I take it only two of you will be making the journey back to

Dumbarton and the young one will be staying for a while?'

'What makes you think that?' asked Frances.

'Never you mind what makes me think that – she's with child.'

'That's a terrible thing to say,' said Frances.

'Terrible or not, I can see it in her face. I think it's time somebody told me the truth.'

The game was up.

'You know what like my daddy is,' said Frances.

'I know fine well what your daddy is like,' said Uncle George.

'My mother wants to know if you could keep Mary here for a wee while until things get sorted out at home.'

How on earth did he know I was pregnant? Even though I was almost five months gone, I was still able to wear my normal clothes.

After listening to what Frances had to say, Uncle George's attitude seemed to soften. He looked at me and said: 'There's not much here, as you can see, but what there is, you are welcome to, and you'll at least have a roof over your head. There's a spare room with a bed and a chair through there that you can have.'

I took my cases through to the spare room and he was absolutely right. All that was in the room was a bed, a chair and an old wooden chest. But having said that, the place was clean and, more to the point, it had a bed where I could sleep.

When it was time for Frances and Auntie Alice to walk back to the station for the train home that was the cue for more floods of tears. They were saying things to try to make me feel better. 'Just think what we've got to face when get back to Dumbarton, having to tell your father you're staying up here because you're pregnant,' said Frances.

I was terrified that first night in the house. There were no curtains or blinds on the windows and I lay in the bed watching the darkness fall on Loch Linnhe. The darker it got, the more afraid I became. Uncle George had gone out and my head began to fill with fanciful and ridiculous notions of ghosts and the place being haunted. When I was younger and staying at Uncle George's on holiday, I got the impression my Aunt Ellen didn't really like me. My imagination was running wild, thinking this might have been the room where she died and she was going to come back to tell me to get out of her house.

I was also being tormented by the nonsensical, but to me at the time very real, thought that I would never be going back to Dumbarton and I might not see my family and friends again. I eventually managed to doze off until a noise wakened me in the middle of the night and I started screaming. It was only my Uncle George coming in and within a few seconds he was knocking on the door asking if I was all right. I told him it was just a bad dream.

In the morning Uncle George brought me a cup of tea and told me he would be away for the most of the day. I knew he used to work in the aluminium smelter before he retired, but what I didn't realise was that even in his seventies he was as active as someone half his age. I eventually found out that he was a poacher and he would stalk deer up in the hills and shoot them before selling the animals as fresh venison to local hotels. Sometimes he would be away two or three nights in a row. And not only that, the old man had a girlfriend called Meshak Cameron he would visit every day for his meals and whatever other Highland hospitality was on offer.

Before he left, Uncle George gave me a house key and told me to amuse myself for the rest of the day. I decided to tidy the house up a bit and when I went into the kitchen the double sink was full of empty Eldorado bottles. Eldorado was a cheap fortified white wine favoured by Scots work-ing-class men – and more than a few under-age boys – as a cheap way to get drunk. My next chore was to put a fire on, but when I went to the coal cellar at the end of the hallway, it was empty. If I wanted some heat in the house I had no choice but to go into town and buy a bag of coal. Luckily, my brother Jimmy had slipped me an extra £7 before I left Dumbarton to keep me going before the first postal order arrived. So I headed into Fort William town centre in search of the coal merchant. I went into a butcher's shop to ask for directions to the coal merchant's that was at the other end of the main street.

When I got there the man recognised me. 'I've seen your face around here during the summer. You come here to stay with either the Camerons or the Murrays.'

'That's right,' I said. 'I'm staying with my Uncle George Murray for a while. Can I get a bag of coal, please? There's none left in the cellar.' The coal merchant said that wouldn't be a problem, but he wouldn't be able to deliver it for another two days.

'Can I pay for it just now and take it up to the house myself?' I asked, thinking that if I waited until Wednesday I would be frozen sitting up in that house. It was October and the winter chill was starting to set in.

'A young girl like you! You sure you want to do that?'

'I'm not leaving without a bag of coal,' I insisted.

Another man working in the coal merchant's saw either the determination or desperation in my face and he came over and said: 'Give her the coal and let her take it up the road herself. She looks like a hardy one.'

In the Highlands they describe someone who is willing and determined as being 'hardy', so that was a bit of a compliment he was paying me.

I told the men I was going to buy a few groceries, take them up to Uncle George's house and I would be back in an hour or so for the bag of coal.

Sure enough, when I came back, the hundredweight sack

of coal was waiting for me and I handed over the 3/6d (17.5p). I grabbed the top of the sack and began dragging it the mile along the main street and up the hill on Grange Road to Uncle George's house. I never realised for a moment that I might be harming my baby and that a five-months pregnant teenager shouldn't be dragging a sack of coal along the pavement. All I thought was that if I wanted to be warm that night, I had to get that coal into Uncle George's coal cellar.

I was dragging the sack of coal while walking sideways. A dozen or so steps and I would have to stop for a rest before continuing on this tortuous journey. The majority of the people on the street in the middle of the afternoon were women, as most of the men would have been working. Mainly, the people just looked at me, but a few asked if I was all right and I told them that I would manage just fine. The worst part of the journey was dragging the coal up the steep hill to Uncle George's house – I thought my back was going to break. The only respite for me was that there was a dyke all the way up the hill at Grange Road and every so often I would stop, sit on the dyke and have a rest.

But there was one final mountain to climb. Well, it seemed like a mountain to me. I had to bump the sack of coal up five steps to the pathway that led to Uncle George's house. As I dragged the coal along Uncle George's path his neighbour, Mrs Anderson, came out. 'What on earth are you doing?'

'Uncle George didn't have any coal in the house.'

'For goodness' sake, if you needed coal, you could have asked us for some before the lorry came with your delivery.'

I didn't like to ask – I was too shy. I felt I didn't deserve any help as I believed I was a bad person that nobody wanted anything to do with because I had got myself pregnant. My father had made me think that way. I could imagine him screaming at me: 'Nobody will want anything to do with you, now. You've brought nothing but shame on your family.' I was also trying to keep away from people as much as possible in case they started quizzing me closely about why I was staying with my Uncle George. I was nowhere near ready to tell the world that I was expecting a baby.

Mrs Anderson helped me get the bag inside the house and tip it into the coal cellar. 'Don't ever do that again,' she said. Goodness knows what her reaction would have been if she'd known I was five months pregnant.

Staying in Uncle George's house meant I was more or less on my own, as he would either be away on his poaching sorties or with Meshak. The only time Uncle George mentioned Meshak's name to me was one of the few nights he was in the house and we were sitting round the blazing fire. 'When the baby comes,' he said, 'I know a woman called Meshak Cameron who is quite capable of delivering a baby, so you'll be all right.'

I just nodded my head in agreement, as most women had home confinements in those days. Although he was an old man, set in his Highland ways, I have no doubt Uncle George was doing his best to look after me and make sure I didn't come to any harm.

My days were spent getting up about 8 a.m. and tidying the house, making sure there was enough food in the larder, feeding Uncle George's chickens out the back door, going into town to window shop or spend an hour or two in Joe Vacenda's Café meeting people I had known from coming to Fort William on holiday. Of course, I was telling them all the lies of the day when they asked what I was doing up there. First it would be just a holiday, and then it would be that Uncle George was lonely and he needed some company. No doubt behind my back they were saying to each other: 'Who's she kidding?' The word had probably got round by that time that I was pregnant and had been banished to the Highlands to have my baby.

Most nights I would sit in the house and read or write letters home to my family and friends. Word got back to me that, as expected, my father had exploded with rage when he was told by Auntie Alice and my brother Jimmy that I was pregnant and had gone to Fort William to stay. And true to form there was a 'Never let her darken my door again' dictum and 'I'll kill her for bringing such shame on to this family' threat. I cried when I read that part of a letter sent to me, although deep inside I'd known there would be no other reaction from my father and I should have been expecting it.

Of course, when I wrote to my mammy I had to address the letter care of Granny Boyle's, as my father would have burnt the letter in the fire if he'd got his hands on it first and recognised my writing.

The highlights of the week for me were the two nights I went to see a movie in Fort William's Picture House. It was an hour or two of escapism with Charlie Chaplin, Marilyn Monroe and Joseph Cotton movies.

By this time my bump was beginning to show and to hide it I would wrap a big scarf round my waist and hold it tight with three big kilt pins before I put a skirt or dress on. I had no idea that this might harm my baby – what was at the forefront of my mind was not to let anyone know I was pregnant.

Most days at some point I would be walking round the town and at the same time keeping an eye out for my other relatives in Fort William – Aunt Jean and Uncle Alan Cameron and their children. Although they were cousins, because they were a bit older than me I called them aunt and uncle. I didn't want them to find out I was pregnant, so I thought the best way was for them not to find out I was staying in Fort William. I knew Uncle George didn't get on with the Camerons and rarely spoke to them, but I was too naïve to realise that since Fort William was such a small place, word would soon get to them that their Dumbarton cousin was in town.

A few times I saw Aunt Jean walking along the street when I was in town, so I would hurry into a shop until she passed by. But this subterfuge didn't last very long and after only three weeks of dodging my cousins, I was caught. I saw Aunt Jean in town and quickly sidestepped my way into Cooper's, the big grocer's shop in town. I gave it a few minutes and, thinking she would have passed by, I left the shop and walked right into her; she had been standing waiting for me.

'Why haven't you been to visit us?' she asked.

'Oh, I've been that busy looking after Uncle George,' I lied. And I have never been more embarrassed at doing so.

'We'd like you to come up and visit us. Will you come up tonight?' asked Aunt Jean. I agreed.

Although Uncle George was doing his best to take care of me, Aunt Jean's house and a family full of happy, caring, chatty, warm and loving people was a much better place for someone in my condition to be. When I arrived at her house that evening there was a lovely tea waiting for me and as I was helping her set the table, Aunt Jean called me into the kitchen and closed the door.

'I know the reason you're here and I don't want you to be ashamed,' she said.

I burst into tears.

'There's no need for all this crying. I've already said you've nothing to be ashamed of. I'm going to tell you something about me that you didn't know. I was in the same position as you before I married Uncle Alan.'

She told me how she had fallen pregnant to a man who had deserted her and left Fort William. But worse was to come: her baby son died shortly after being born. Years later the child's father came back to Fort William, but he was a down-and-out and soon died. He was going to be buried in a pauper's grave, but when Aunt Jean heard this she paid for a proper burial and he was laid to rest beside the baby son he never knew in the cemetery at Fort William.

Naturally, I was shocked, but was given great heart at the same time. Here was someone close to me who had been through the trauma of what I was feeling just now. And it was someone I loved and respected.

'You know we keep a spare room for visitors in the summer and do bed and breakfast. Why don't you take that room until it's time to have the baby?'

The idea of sharing a home with Aunt Jean and Uncle Alan's family of Duncan, Angus, Jean and Margaret was very appealing. But I still had a loyalty to Uncle George, who had agreed to look after me in the first place.

'That would be great, but I can't do that. What would I say to Uncle George?'

'Don't concern yourself with Uncle George; I'll talk to him.'

'But Uncle George has arranged for this lady, Meshak Cameron, to take care of me when I have the baby.'

'You can't have a baby in your Uncle George's house with someone like Meshak Cameron looking after you. Your Uncle George shouldn't be getting involved with her anyway. She's got a bad name for taking too much drink and she shouldn't be seeing your Uncle George because although her husband has left her and her children, she's still a married woman.'

Eventually, I agreed to go and stay with the Camerons. Although I knew it was the best thing to do in my condition, I still felt disloyal to my Uncle George and I knew that, despite his gruff exterior, deep inside he would be hurt. That night I went back to Uncle George's house and thankfully he wasn't in before I went to bed. The next morning he was in the house when I got up, but I never said a thing about what had been discussed with my Aunt Jean the previous night.

Late that afternoon, Uncle George was still in the house and there was a knock at the door.

'It's Aunt Jean at the door,' I shouted to him.

He never answered and I walked back up the hall into the living room. 'What does she want here?' asked Uncle George.

'I don't know.'

He looked at my face and said: 'Stop telling me lies.'

It was as if that old man could read me like a book. He knew I was pregnant when Frances, Auntie Alice and I turned up on his doorstep as soon as he saw me, and now he knew there was something going on between the Camerons and me. Uncle George was all there and a bit more.

'So you're deserting me then.'

'Aunt Jean thinks it would be better if maybe I went into hospital to have the baby and she's taking me to see the doctor.'

'You don't need to see any doctor. You're young and healthy and people never saw doctors in my days and children were born in their millions. This is just the Camerons wanting to get one over on me.'

I could see he was getting angry and he stormed up the hall to the front door where my Aunt Jean was standing, uninvited into the house. 'I suppose you're happy now,' he said to her. 'The girl would have been fine here – but it's entirely up to her now where she wants to stay.'

He came charging back up the hall into the living room where I was standing crying. 'No use crying,' he said. 'I've never done you any harm here. I only ever wanted to help you. Remember this door will always be open to you any time because you might be glad to come back here. No doubt you have already made your choice to go and stay with the Camerons and you would rather have them than me.'

I tried to explain how I felt, but I just couldn't get the words out between my sobbing.

'Maybe you will say hello to me if you pass me in the street,' he said.

'Uncle George, don't say things like that. I love you and I know you have been good to me, but I'm frightened at night.'

'There's no reason on this earth for you to be frightened – nobody will touch you here.'

'But it's the loneliness as well,' I protested.

At that Uncle George gave up the argument. 'All right then, pack your bags and I'll carry them to the Camerons for you.'

Give him his due, he carried my two suitcases to the Camerons' house, but dropped them at the gate and refused to go inside.

'I won't come any further, if you don't mind,' he said. 'I'll bid you good evening.' With that, he turned and walked away.

I felt guilty about what had happened, but I knew I would be much happier living with a family. Over the next couple of months before I was taken into hospital I always made a point of talking to Uncle George if I saw him in town and even if he hadn't seen me I would shout over to him. He was great with me, always asking how I was doing.

Life was a lot easier for me during November and December of 1953 as I was relieved that my secret was out and I no longer had to hide the fact that I was pregnant. I was in good hands medically, having regular examinations from the local doctor, and I was starting to get visits from my family in Dumbarton. First, my sister Frances came up with her eight-month-old daughter Anne, then my brother Bernie's wife Maureen came to see me. In late December, I had the best visitor of all when my mammy came to stay for a few days. It was great to see her, talk to her and get a big cuddle from her. After all, as I would soon find out, that's what mammies are for.

But shortly before my mammy was due to go back to Dumbarton, I got news from the doctor that would put me back on my own again, away from my new-found family. The baby was in the breech position and because I was so young, it was my first pregnancy and the baby might come early, I was being sent to Raigmore Hospital in Inverness for the two months before the baby was born. I went into hospital the day before Christmas Eve and I made the then three-hour journey from Fort William to Inverness almost seventy miles away in an ambulance with my mammy and Aunt Jean.

Once again, I feared loneliness was going to become a frequent visitor as I lay there in my hospital bed. Since there was only one bus a week from Fort William to Inverness and you couldn't make the return journey on the same day, I wouldn't be getting many visitors of the usual kind.

Mum's the Word

It's the middle of the night and a terrible pain searing through my stomach wakens me from a deep sleep. I turn on to my other side hoping this will make the ache somehow go away. It subsides for a minute or two and just when I think I'm feeling better, back it comes with a vengeance. It seems that each time the pain returns, it comes back even fiercer than it was before.

No matter what position I lie in my hospital bed, the pain just won't go away. The two-bedded room in the maternity ward I'm sleeping in is in semi-darkness and total silence. I can't put up with this any longer; I'll have to go and see one of the nurses. I sweep the bedcovers to the side and gingerly sit up on the edge of the bed before shoving my feet into a pair of slippers and shuffling out of the room and the few yards along to the nurses' station along the corridor. A lovely staff nurse called Annabel MacKay is on nightshift and she asks what's the matter with me.

'I've got a sore stomach,' I reply. 'I might have eaten something that doesn't agree with me, or it might just be wind. Whatever it is, I'm in agony.'

Staff Nurse MacKay helps me back the way I came and into my bed and starts to examine me. It doesn't take her long to decide what's causing my pains. 'Absolutely nothing to do with food, Mary – the baby's coming,' she informs me. 'I'll get the doctor.'

Within minutes, the doctor is at my bedside and he too examines me. I'll never forget that doctor – Dr David Ledingham – and neither will the majority of nurses and women who came to Raigmore Hospital to have their babies. He was the spitting image of the popular American singer at that time, Johnny Ray – even down to the wisps of hair falling on to his forehead. He was such a lookalike, the nurses referred to him as Johnny Ray when he wasn't around.

By the time Johnny Ray – I mean, Dr Ledingham – was finished examining me I was in agony. I wasn't screaming, just crying my eyes out, but soon I was being wheeled to the labour suite. As soon as I got there, about 2.30 a.m., I was given an injection, but that didn't do much to ease the pain. Then it was the nitrous oxide – laughing gas – that I would breathe through a big rubber gas mask. That was quite frightening, as the only other time I experienced a mask like that was when I went to the dentist and I definitely didn't like that.

The labour pains were terrible and every five minutes I was asking how long it was going to be. The hours went by and as dawn broke they decided they should send for the maternity hospital's top consultant, Professor Hay. He insisted that if there were any complications, or if the mother was having her first child, he was to be called in. The only hint of some relief from the pain came from the gas and air from the big rubber mask and, dentist or no dentist, by that time I was extremely glad to be getting huge gasps of the stuff. It did make me feel a little hazy and it did dull the pain, but I was soon brought back to reality when I looked down and saw blood spurting everywhere.

I had a nurse at each side of me and Dr Ledingham and Professor Hay at my feet. The good professor's coat was splattered with my blood and despite his reassuring words that everything was going to be all right, I was terrified. Probably it was just as well I didn't know what haemorrhaging meant because that's what was happening to me and I was given several injections in my wrist and in my hip.

By the end, I was in such pain that I had nothing left to hang on to but the constant, comforting chat from Professor Hay. 'You'll be fine. Everything's going to be all right. It won't be long now,' he would repeat. If I had been at death's door and he'd said everything was hunky-dory, I would have believed him.

Then eight and a half hours after I first went into labour – at 10.35 a.m. on Saturday, 6 February 1954, I gave birth to a beautiful baby girl with a shock of black hair, called Alana, after my Uncle Alan, who had been so good to me. I had decided before the birth that if I had a boy the baby's name would be Alan and if a girl, Alana.

After a few moments the nurses handed Alana over to me and I felt a wave of relief sweep over me. After all the fear of my father, the embarrassment of being pregnant and un-married and the pain of childbirth, I looked down at this little bundle in my arms and thought: 'What a beautiful baby she is.'

But this didn't last too long, as the medical staff soon took Alana from me; they were still trying to stem the blood from the haemorrhaging. I became more and more aware that something wasn't quite right with all the activity going on from the doctors and nurses at the foot of my bed.

Eventually they stemmed the flow of blood and I was allowed back up to the ward while Alana was still in the nursery. By this time Sister Ross was on duty and she came over to my bed and put a lovely wee teddy bear in my locker for Alana. It was a wonderful feeling, considering the pain I had suffered since the early hours of the morning. Now I was propped up in bed, the pain was gone, I didn't have a big bulge in my stomach any more and I had a lovely baby daughter.

But my ordeal wasn't over yet. Later Sister Ross was sitting at my bedside chatting away, telling me how I would stay in bed for a couple of days and maybe be allowed up to walk around on the third day. Sounded fine to me. Sister Ross went off to tend to other mums and then I felt terror – the fright of my life. I turned round to get a glass of water from the top of the locker and I literally felt as if something was leaving my body. It was horrific, because I actually *heard* this thing coming out of me. I pushed the sheets and blankets down and looked between my legs. I screamed in horror.

Sister Ross rushed into the room and asked: 'What's wrong?'

'My insides have fallen out,' I managed to gasp in between my screams, which the entire hospital must have heard. I looked down again and shuddered as I saw what I thought was a big red jelly ball the size of a football lying on the sheets between my legs.

Sister Ross pulled the covers completely off the bed and shouted for help from the other nurses. 'Don't move, Mary,' she ordered. 'This is nothing to worry about – and your insides haven't fallen out.'

But that didn't calm me down one little bit. I was only eighteen and I saw this round ball of red jelly that had come out of my body. What else was I to think than that my insides had fallen out of me?

Another nurse came in with a towel, wrapped it round the ball of red jelly and took what I was still claiming was my insides away. Other nurses lifted me onto the chair beside my bed while the sheets and blankets were changed. While I was on the chair, Sister Ross managed to calm me down by explaining that it was a good thing that had happened. She told me that when I was giving birth I was losing too much blood and the doctors had given me an injection to make the blood clot. This had been successful in stopping the bleeding, she said, and the round ball was the clotted blood naturally coming out of my body. 'If we'd let you continue bleeding the way you were you wouldn't be alive just now,' she added.

I just wish someone had told me that was going to happen, as it would have avoided a lot of hysterical screaming and shouting on my part. But it wasn't the only thing I wasn't told when it came to giving birth.

When I was a teenager you didn't get anything like sex education, especially not in school and definitely not in a Catholic school like the one I attended. Even when I discovered I was pregnant no one told me exactly what childbirth would be like. At the time I asked Auntie Alice: 'How do they get this baby out of my stomach?' And she replied: 'It's nothing. You get a wee operation when they'll put you to sleep, open up your tummy and lift the baby out. You won't feel a thing.' Aye right, Auntie Alice. That might have been the case if someone is given a Caesarean section, which wasn't that common in 1954. She gave me the impression that was how everyone gave birth to their babies.

When I was in labour I heard one of the nurses say: 'If only her waters would break.' I had no idea what she meant and when the nurse explained what was going to happen I thought I might drown. 'My auntie says you are going to put me to sleep and when I wake up I'll have had the baby,' I said.

'Oh no, that's not going to happen,' replied the nurse. 'You are in a perfectly normal labour and you'll be able to have a natural birth.'

'So how's the baby going to get out of my body?' I asked.

And when she told me how a baby is born, I started crying even harder. 'How is something the size of a baby going to get out of there?' I said in complete horror, thinking my body was going to be ripped apart.

The nurse obviously realised I knew nothing about babies and giving birth, so she got Sister McKay to come and explain everything about the body expanding and then going back to normal size. They must have thought I was a complete idiot. I had managed to get myself pregnant, but I was asking all those stupid questions about the next bit – giving birth. I felt a bit better after her comforting words. In those days subjects like sex and childbirth weren't talked about as freely as they are today. Maybe people were too embarrassed to tell me, but at least I should have been given a vague idea of what was involved in childbirth.

I stayed in hospital for almost another three weeks. Because of my young age and the haemorrhaging problems I'd had, I was to be kept in for two weeks before being allowed home. But I was kept in a few days longer as the bus couldn't get to Fort William because of snowdrifts. I didn't mind it in the maternity unit because it wasn't long built and everything was modern.

The mums-to-be weren't sleeping in rows and rows of beds down a long ward – we were two to a room, with nice yellow and gold-coloured floral pattern curtains and bedspreads. My experience of hospitals up till then had been the old-fashioned kind with nothing but white bedcovers. Our rooms even had a coffee table – something I had never seen before.

Although I felt embarrassed and uncomfortable the first few days in hospital surrounded by married women getting daily visits from their husbands, I was soon put at ease because the nurses and doctors were really nice and I was treated no differently because I was a single mum. The nameplate on the door to my room even had my name written as Mrs Kelly. I appreciated that from the staff there.

Because of the public transport problems getting from Fort William to Inverness and back, in all my ten weeks in hospital, I only had three visits. The first was the day I was taken into hospital, the second was from Aunt Jean and her daughter, young Jean, after Alana was born and the third was when I was getting home. That's when my mammy came with Aunt Jean and it was the first time she saw her new granddaughter.

The day I came out of hospital, Alana was christened in St Mary's RC Church in Inverness and then it was straight on the bus heading for my Aunt Jean's in Fort William. My mammy said Alana was a beautiful baby, but I could see she was embarrassed with the stigma attached of me being a mum, but not married. I felt terrible that I had hurt her and made her feel that way. She stayed in Fort William for four days and in that time the subject of what was to happen to Alana and myself was broached. My father was still adamant that I was never to show my face in Dumbarton again.

Alana's future was more a topic for discussion than what was to happen to me, as my father's edict made it pretty obvious that my future lay elsewhere. My brother Bernie and his wife Maureen wanted to adopt Alana, as did young Jean, who was in her twenties and married. But once again my father was in control – not only of my life, but Alana's as well. He decided that no one was to adopt Alana and since I had made the mistake of getting pregnant, I was to pay for that mistake and take care of Alana myself. I know Bernie, Maureen and young Jean were very disappointed that they couldn't adopt Alana. Maureen, especially, was broken-hearted and she had bought lots of things expecting she was going to be bringing up a baby girl.

So, for the first three months I settled into life with my Aunt Jean and Uncle Alan in Fort William until one day a letter arrived from my mammy. It told how my father had changed his mind and Alana and I could come and live in the house in Dumbarton – as long as he didn't have to set eyes on the both of us.

As much as I loved and appreciated all that Aunt Jean and Uncle Alan had done for me, my mammy and all my brothers and sisters were back home in Dumbarton and I decided to move back there. Anyway, my father ruled the roost and he wasn't making a kind offer to have me back in the house – it was a command. I knew it wasn't going to be easy living at home again, being at the mercy of his temper and violent rages. But everyone was terrified of him, and if I didn't go home I was afraid he would take it out on my mother and others in the family.

My mammy came to Fort William to take Alana and me home. As the train pulled into Dumbarton Railway Station, the fear gripped me. It was the thought of being back in the same town as that man and what he might have in store for me. When we got off the train we got a taxi back home. It was planned that way so we wouldn't have to get a bus, where lots of people would have seen me with Alana. Auntie Alice had come to meet us at the station and when we got to our house she took Alana in her arms. This was the moment I dreaded, having to face my father for the first time since he'd found out I was pregnant and had been sent to the Highlands to have my baby.

Between my own family and Granny Boyle's there were about thirty people in the house crammed into rooms and the hallway. I was last to walk through the front door and immediately my mammy said: 'You've to go in and see him right away – he's in the living room.'

The people greeting me with hugs and kisses suddenly stopped and a nervous hush fell over everyone in the hallway. No one knew what was going to happen, but I could see from their faces that they feared the worst.

I walked to the living-room door and I could see the room was empty apart from my father sitting in his chair, his face like thunder. 'Get in here and shut that door,' he ordered and rose out of his armchair, standing ramrod straight as if he was on the parade ground. I closed the door and knew what was coming. I could see it in his face and I had seen that look of rage many, many times before. I was standing, shaking, only a few feet away from him, expecting the first slap or punch of a terrible beating.

Then the door opened and I turned round to see my brother Jimmy standing there.

'What the hell do you want?' my father shouted.

At first Jimmy ignored him and walked over to the window with his back to us. 'I'll just wait in here,' said Jimmy in a quiet but determined voice.

'Get yourself out of this room until I deal with her,' was my father's retort.

'No. Say what you've got to say, but I'm staying here.'

We couldn't see the look on Jimmy's face, but by the way he spoke, all three of us knew he was going to stand his ground. If anyone was going to be able to protect me that day, it was our Jimmy.

My father started screaming in a staccato voice: 'You . . . get . . . the . . . f**k . . . out . . . of . . . this . . . living . . . room.'

I was petrified, but Jimmy stayed calm. 'I'm not leaving here. Get on with what you've got to say and get it over with.'

Having lost the battle of wills against Jimmy, my father turned his attention to me. 'You're nothing but a dirty, low-down harlot – the scum of the earth,' he shouted, his face scarlet and eyes bulging. 'I've told all the neighbours what you've done to this family and there's not one of them will talk to you again. I knew from the day you were born you were nothing but trouble and now you've brought a bastard child under my roof.'

At that Jimmy interrupted: 'For Christ's sake, give it a rest – this is 1954, not the dark ages.'

That really set my father off and he moved forward as if he was going to slap me. In a split second, Jimmy was standing between my father and me.

'Lift a hand to her and I'll f*****g kill you,' Jimmy warned.

'I'll f*****g kill her,' my father screamed.

My father tried to push Jimmy out of the way to get to me, but Jimmy stood his ground and put his arm across his body like a shield, stopping my father getting anywhere near me.

'You better calm down,' said Jimmy in a loud but calm voice. 'If anybody is going to get killed it'll be you. Just leave her alone.'

I just hid behind Jimmy, trying to shut out the shouting and the violence going on only inches away from me. Suddenly the living-room door burst open and lots of people piled into the room thinking a fight had already erupted – well, it more or less had.

My mother was in tears and being comforted by Auntie Alice in the bedroom while Granny Boyle ushered me out of the room in the melee. I could still hear my father shouting about me bringing shame on the family and how I was going to pay dearly for what I'd done to his good name, and the voices of people trying to calm him down as I was led away down the hall.

I stayed in Granny Boyle's house for a couple of hours before word was sent upstairs that my father had gone to his bed and it was safe for me to come back into the house.

'Don't come out of your bedroom in the morning until he has gone to his work,' my mother told me. 'He still doesn't want to see either of you, so the baby can't come out either.'

I was put in my mother's bedroom. She and my young sister Rose shared a double bed and I had a single bed with the cot between us. It took my mother a couple of weeks to start using the name Alana; up till then she just referred to her as 'the baby'. It was a mixture of shame, fear of my father and not wanting to say Alana's name in case it set him off on one of his rages. Although when he wasn't in the house, my mother would be over at the cot touching Alana and making the daft baby noises adult make.

Any time my father was in the house, I had to stay in the

bedroom with Alana and I was constantly on edge, waiting to hear his footsteps coming up the path and making sure we were hidden away in the bedroom before the key turned in the front door. There was always someone either from my own house or Granny Boyle's who would keep a lookout when he was expected back. Once we heard the front door opening again and he was heading out of the house, we would get the all-clear to come back into the living room or kitchen.

This went on for about three months until one morning I was in the bedroom and I heard his footsteps in the hall. Suddenly they stopped outside the bedroom and there was a knock on the door. From the other side of the door my father said: 'Get yourself and that child into the living room.'

I didn't know whether to be terrified or happy that I was being allowed into the living room with Alana in his presence. Was it a trick? Was my brother Jimmy away to work and this was my father's chance to have another go at me in my protector's absence? I was soon to find out, as there was no way I could disobey his command to come out of the bedroom, and I would be able to tell his mood by the look on his face.

As soon as I got into the living room I knew a miracle had happened and from that moment he adored Alana like no other of his children or grandchildren. He took Alana in his arms, gave her a cuddle, turned to me and said: 'Don't you ever put your hands on that child. I don't want her soiled with you touching her. In fact, don't even look at her, let alone touch her.' After that, I only got to touch Alana when he wasn't there. I was definitely still *persona non grata* as far as my father was concerned.

My mammy was just as shocked as I was and I was sent upstairs to get Granny Boyle down so she could be told of this momentous event in the Kelly family household. It was an amazing transformation and I will never be able to explain it. My father went from referring to Alana as 'it' or 'it's' – my brother Jimmy used to joke that he must have thought the name on the birth certificate was spelled 'IT'S' – to her being the complete love of his life. Alana was given every single piece of love he had in him and she very definitely became the favoured grandchild – even to the detriment of all his other grandchildren. My mammy was delighted at my father's change of heart as it took away a major source of conflict in the house. From not wanting to set eyes on Alana, overnight he completely changed and he would always have her by his side.

He would usually sit at the table at the living-room window so he could watch what was happening in the street outside. Now another chair would be pulled up beside him, where he would sit Alana in her Moses basket. And when one of his cronies came in to see him the Moses basket would be up on the table for everyone to see. Then he would carry Alana out to the garden and stand at the front gate so everyone passing by would see her and they would come over for a look and to admire the baby. Out of the blue, he discovered a regular penchant for a breath of fresh air and he would be marching up and down the street pushing Alana in her pram. He started his work really early in the morning, at 6 a.m., and would come home for his breakfast once the school had started. He would tell my mammy not to bath Alana in the morning until he came home just after 9 a.m., as he wanted to bath her in front of the fire.

His whole life revolved around Alana and nothing was too good for her. He spoiled her rotten and bought nothing but the best for her. As Alana got older, he said that she was to call him daddy and she was to refer to me as simply Mary. Not mummy, or even Auntie Mary – just Mary.

If some of his other grandchildren were visiting and they heard the ice cream van he would give them money to go and get an ice cream cone. He was a bit of a show-off and liked people to see that he had money, so he made sure people saw that his grandchildren were never short of money when it came to ice cream and sweets. Only thing was, though, Alana always got more than any of the other grandkids and he always made sure she got what she wanted. If two other grandchildren were sitting on the two poofies that were always by the fireside and Alana came in and said she wanted to sit on one, he would kick the poofie away from under whoever was sitting on it and say: 'That's Alana's.'

Although Alana was most definitely the apple of his eye, I was still an outcast and someone he could barely tolerate. Often if he was passing me in the hallway, a split second after he had gone by I would get a sharp punch in the neck or on my back and I would hear him mutter his favourite insults: 'I'll never be able to hold my head up in this town again . . . nothing but a harlot . . . you're the lowest form of life.'

I couldn't even talk to my own daughter when he was around because that would lead to another punch. He had decided that Alana was his daughter and I was to have nothing to do with her. It's just as well Alana was bottle-fed as it would have been mighty difficult for me to feed her when I was banned from touching her.

I had believed my father when he had told me that no one in the street would want to talk to me after what happened, and I was terrified the first time I managed to sneak out of the house, taking Alana out in her pram. I thought people would walk by me and not look my way, but nothing could have been further from the truth.

Lots of people stopped to look at Alana in her pram. 'Oh, she's a lovely baby,' they would say. 'You've been away a long time – was that your daddy that made you go to Fort William? That's terrible. You having a baby is nothing to be ashamed of – young lassies who aren't married have been having babies since time began and they always will. You're not the first and you certainly won't be the last.'

I was beginning to wonder what my father was talking about when everybody wanted to see Alana and seemed more than happy to speak to me. I finally realised my father had been telling a pack of lies when one of his friends, a Mr Haggerty, was walking towards me. I thought, since he was friends with my father, he would definitely not talk to me so I decided to look straight ahead and ignore him. But as I passed him, he put his hand on the pram and said: 'Here, what are you doing walking past me, Mary Kelly?'

'My father said nobody in the street wants to talk to me because I've had Alana,' I answered.

'Don't you take your daddy on,' said Mr Haggerty. 'You've got a lovely wee baby there and you should be proud of her. See when you're wheeling her around in that pram of hers, you keep your head high because you've done nothing that other people haven't been doing for thousands of years.'

The change in my father towards Alana was almost of the proportions of Saul and his conversion on the road to Damascus. My father insisted Alana stayed with him and my mammy, even after I got married and set up home. Even when my mammy died and my father went to live with my sister Frances's family, Alana went too. God only knows what made him change his mind about Alana that morning. From that moment he never wanted her to leave his side and, as usual, he got his own way and she was there until the day he died.

My father's decision to take over parenting duties – at least, when he was in the house – gave me the chance to live as normal a life as possible for a girl of my age. That meant I could get to the dancing with my friends and that's where I met James Jennings – better known as James The Gent.

He was a big-time Mafia-style figure in our area at the time. He wasn't into violence in any way, but his *modus operandi* was robberies of cash and jewellery in partnership with safe-blowers.

I had gone to a dance in the Chapel Hall with my mammy of all people when James Jennings walked in and soon started to chat me up. Everyone knew who he was, and his reputation, but I liked the attention this older man – I was nineteen and he was twenty-four – was giving me. He was really handsome and, today, when I see pictures of the actor Dennis Quaid, it reminds me of what James Jennings looked like then. He had expensive clothes and a big black car, which was certainly different as in those days the only person you knew who had a car would be your doctor.

As we were gliding round the dance floor I was thinking, 'This is wonderful, imagine me having a man like this as a dance partner instead of the usual round of boys.' He asked me where else I would go dancing and I told him the Burgh Hall on a Wednesday and a Saturday. Sure enough, the next time I was at the Burgh Hall on a Saturday, he was there waiting for me.

James The Gent by name and James The Gent by nature – that's how I found James Jennings. Every Saturday he would drive down to an orphanage called Cardross Park Home, in the village of Cardross, between Dumbarton and Helensburgh. And when he arrived, he would hand out bundles of sweets and toys to the orphans there.

James later told me that his mother had died when he was young and he and his brothers and sisters were brought up in that orphan's home, where they had been well looked after. That's why he would visit the home every week with gifts for the youngsters. James was also very much the gentleman when we eventually started dating.

That Saturday, when James arrived at the Burgh Hall, he came right up to me and said hello. We spent most of the night dancing together and at the end he asked me to go to the cinema with him the following Saturday. After our date at the cinema, we met up again at the Burgh Hall the following Wednesday and it was then that he asked if I would like to spend the day with him in Glasgow on the Saturday.

I told my mammy that I had been asked out for the day and she said that she would make up some excuse to tell my father where I was. My mammy must have thought: 'God love her, she needs a break away from the house and all the grief she's getting from her father.' Of course, she gave me the usual warnings about boys, what they were after and how I was to be careful. She didn't need to because after conceiving Alana, I never had sex again until I was married. I was terrified of getting pregnant and having to face my father to tell him I was pregnant a second time.

James and I got the train to Glasgow and the first place he took me was the House of Fraser department store; he said he wanted to buy me perfume. I had really hit the big time. Normally the boys would buy you a quarter of sweets, a half-pound box of chocolates or, if you were really lucky, a sixpenny bag of chips on the way home from the dancing.

I was terrified standing at the perfume counter, not knowing which one to choose. At that time girls like me could only afford perfumes like California Poppy and Evening in Paris that only cost a shilling out of Woolworth's. James pointed to a bottle with the name Chanel written on it, but I was wondering: 'Chanel, or should it be Channel . . . that's something to do with the sea, so what if it smells like seaweed?'

James said: 'It's OK, pick one of the expensive ones off the top shelf.'

'Well, I usually wear that one,' I replied, pointing to a black bottle. It turned out to be Chanel Number 5, but I only chose it because I like the colour black and the bottle was black. We used to laugh about that day when I admitted that I had never heard of Chanel. 'I know, Mary, you hadn't a clue,' he would say.

After buying the perfume we went to a matinee performance at the cinema and I thought James would be desperate for the lights to go down so he could put his arm round me and kiss me passionately. Well, it didn't quite work out like that. The film was *The Caine Mutiny*, starring Humphrey Bogart, Van Johnson and Fred MacMurray. I sat there in the dark waiting for James to make his move, but it never came and he just sat there staring at the screen. I looked at other men in the cinema with their arms round their girlfriends having wee kisses in the dark. Every now and then, James would turn to me and ask if I was enjoying the film. I thought he had gone off me because every other boy I knew would have a kiss and a cuddle while the film was on.

At the intermission he got me a tub of ice cream and chatted away as if nothing was wrong. 'I've been waiting for ages to see this film,' said James. 'It's great, isn't it?' It was then that I suddenly realised he hadn't gone off me and he really did want to see the film. He was a mature man at twenty-four and had obviously been through the phase of kissing and cuddling in the back row of the picture house.

He also said that he would take me for dinner to a restaurant. Now, I had been to restaurants with my mammy and Tilly, but I had never been out for a meal with a boy. I wasn't looking forward to this. What if I spilled the soup? What if I was trying to cut a piece of roast beef and it slid off my plate? All these daft ideas were going through my head.

James took me to a posh restaurant called Madame Rombach's and all I ordered was macaroni cheese and chips. I thought macaroni cheese was the most disgusting food I had ever tasted, but I thought it was easy to eat, so that's what I asked for. James had a perplexed look on his face as he said: 'Are you sure that's all you want?'

He ordered a mixed grill and I was shocked when I saw him dipping his bread into the yolk of his eggs. I thought that was terrible manners, especially in a restaurant. After watching James eat, I thought that was the last date I'd go on with him. That's how much of a daft wee lassie I was. One minute, head over heels in love with this gent of a man and the next, going to dump him because he dipped his bread into the yolk of an egg.

We were supposed to finish off our date by going to the dancing in Dumbarton that night, but I made up an excuse of feeling unwell and told James I would have to go straight home when we got back to Dumbarton from Glasgow. I had no intention of not going to the dancing, but because of the bread-and-egg incident I decided I was going to go to the dancing with my pal Patsy McLaughlin instead of James.

That idea worked fine until I walked into the Burgh Hall and who was standing there but James Jennings. 'You recovered awful quick,' he said. 'Are you sure everything is OK? Did something happen today I don't know about?'

'No, today was fine. I wasn't feeling too good, but I'm OK now.'

By the end of the night I had got over my dipping-the-bread-in-an-egg phobia and agreed to go out with James again. On one of those dates, James said he was going up to Glasgow to see a friend of his, Johnny Ramensky, and he would like me to go with him. I had no idea who Johnny Ramensky was until James explained he was an expert at safe-cracking and safe-blowing. During the war he was in jail for robbery until the military offered him a pardon if he would use his safe-blowing expertise for the war effort. Johnny Ramensky agreed to this and went behind enemy lines in North Africa, Germany and Italy to blow safes in German military HQs and steal secret papers from the Nazis. Although he was pardoned, Johnny couldn't keep away from his life of crime after the war and he spent more time in and out of jails.

Once again, James said he didn't want to take his car and so we got the train to Glasgow one Sunday and then it was onto a tramcar to a stop outside the tenement where Johnny Ramensky lived. When we knocked on the door of the flat, Johnny's wife came to the door and she smiled as she asked us in. When we walked in Johnny was sitting listening to the radio. When he saw James he quickly got up out of the chair and they gave each other a hug. It was the first time I had seen two men doing that, despite having all those brothers and male cousins in my family.

Johnny and his wife stayed in a room and kitchen and although it was small, it was very clean and tidy. He was small in stature, but the most gentle of people – just like a kind old granddad. His wife was taller than Johnny.

I was introduced as James's girlfriend and I was made really welcome, with a pot of tea being made to go with the polite chat between us. I often wondered if Johnny Ramensky was ever on jobs with James stealing money and jewellery from safes. I never did find out because James was always reluctant to talk about that side of his life. It wasn't until many years later that I discovered that the wee man I had met with James was such a hero for his daredevil deeds during the war that folk songs were written about him.

Weeks turned into months and James and I saw each other regularly. I even heard his name being called out on a police radio one night. I was in a friend's house in Bellsmyre and we were using her big brother's radio to listen in to the police broadcasts. Apparently, there had been a robbery of the wages at a massive housebuilding project at Loch Sloy and the police were saying they were chasing a car being driven by James Jennings, who they believed was involved in the robbery. His name kept being repeated and they were talking about blocking him off at such and such a road. I don't know what happened after that or if the police had got the wrong man, but a few days later James was with me at the dancing.

James had told me he was single and I had no reason to doubt his word. That was until I was in what they called the make-up room at the dance hall a few months after we had started going out and a girl came over to me and said: 'Do you know James Jennings is a married man?'

'He told me he wasn't married,' I replied.

'Well, I can assure you he's married with two children and he stays in the Renton.'

As a wee Holy Catholic girl I thought this relationship had to stop, as a bolt of lightning would surely strike me down if I went out with a married man. When James took me home that night I was standing at the bottom of our road and I told him I couldn't see him again because he was a married man. At first he denied he was married, but as he was about to walk away he said: 'OK – I am married, but what difference does it make?'

'Well, it wasn't very nice you lying to me like that after I told you about me having a baby.'

At that we parted and it wasn't until three weeks later that I saw him again, when he turned up at the Burgh Hall dancing all suave and sophisticated, to ask me out. I loved the excitement of being with him. In true fatal attraction style, and thinking I could maybe dodge the lightning bolt, I said yes.

So that was us an item again – until wedding bells began to chime an escape from my father.

Married for the Wrong Reasons

They say that on your wedding day you should wear something old, something new, something borrowed and something blue. Well, I had all those things, only the blue turned out to be the bruises on my face after my father had given me a real hammering only an hour before I was due to be married.

To say he didn't want me to marry Robert Campbell would be an understatement, and he was even nice to me at one point as he tried to persuade me at the last minute not to go ahead with the nuptials. The niceness didn't last too long when he realised I was going ahead with the wedding and he reverted to type – the violent type.

I feel a mixture of excitement and fear as I am about to get ready with my younger sister, Rose – my maid of honour for my big day. We have just come back from 7.30 Mass that Saturday morning on 24 February 1955 and we have an hour before the taxi is due to take me to the chapel house where the marriage ceremony is being held.

My father is sitting in the living room and I know something is afoot as he would normally be at his work at this time. He has already made his feelings clear about being against the marriage and has told everyone he was having nothing to do with my wedding. He calls me in to the room and says: 'I know you've been to your wedding-day Mass, but let that be an end to it. I know you're not happy living here, but this is your last chance. If you call this off everything will be all right and you can even go back to England if you like.'

I can hardly believe what I'm hearing, as even in my late teens I was hardly allowed outside the front door unless someone was with me.

He goes on: 'Don't worry about Alana because your mother and I will look after her – she is our life now. Go and make a new life for yourself, but whatever you do, don't marry that bastard Campbell.'

'I can't do that,' I reply. 'I've said I would marry him and I can't change my mind now.'

'Yes, you can.'

'I can't give Robert a showing up in front of his family and everybody else who is turning up for the wedding.'

'You better, or you won't be fit to walk out that door and into the taxi that's supposed to take you to the chapel. I'll kill you before I let you get into that taxi. You've got an hour to think it over. Now get out my sight until you're ready to put an end to this nonsense.'

Rose and I head for the bedroom and I start getting ready. I would be dressed to the nines in a lovely pink suit, with black shoes and a black bag to match. After half-an-hour there is a rat-tat-tat on the bedroom door and I freeze. I recognise the knock and I know it's my father coming to try again to stop me going ahead with the wedding.

He opens the door and looks in the room. When he sees me dressed for the wedding he says: 'Don't do this. I'm giving you one last chance. I'll take you up to Glasgow Central and put you on a train to anywhere you want to go. Go back down to Tilly's, anywhere, and I'll make sure you've got money sent to you every week until you get yourself sorted and find a job. You'll want for nothing and you can come back and see your mother and Alana any time and there'll be no more said about this. I'll give you ten minutes to think about what I've just said.'

As he pulls the door I hear him mutter: 'And God help you if you haven't changed your mind.'

I sat on the double bed and wondered what to do. Rose said I should do what my father said and cancel the wedding. 'You don't have to marry Robert Campbell – it's not as if you're pregnant.' She had a point. Although many people thought I was pregnant and that was why I was marrying Robert, I most certainly was not having a baby. Not even I would make that mistake twice.

I was in a quandary. What should I do? On the one hand I could get out of Dumbarton and live off my father's money as long as I wanted and, despite the way he treated me and my brothers and sisters, I still wanted to please that man. If I did run away and leave Robert, I would be in my father's good books for once. His words 'you'll want for nothing' kept repeating in my head.

But then I would switch to the other side of the argument. How could I leave someone literally minutes before we were due to get married? Think of the embarrassment I would be causing the boy, I told myself. And how would I ever be able to face Robert, his family and friends again having jilted him like that? I couldn't do that to another human being.

I hadn't realised how long I had been sitting there arguing with myself. The door opened and there was my father standing in front of me.

'What are you doing? You made your mind up?'

'I'm going ahead and marrying Robert,' I told him.

He erupted. 'You f*****g bastard,' he screamed in my face. Grabbed my lapels and dragged me out the room into the hallway. He threw me against the wall and I slumped to the floor just as he started to kick me. He was wearing his work boots and it wasn't just the one kick, it was a frenzy of kicks. All I could do was roll up into a ball with my arms covering my head and face to protect myself as much as I could. I was screaming the place down and my mother rushed out of the living room and tried to pull my father off me, but she couldn't stop him giving me a good hiding. At that point there was no one else in the house to help me apart from my mammy and Rose.

After he finished the beating, he literally picked me up and threw me back into the bedroom. 'I'll be back and you better have changed your mind,' he shouted before storming into the living room and banging the door behind him.

My pink suit was torn at the lapels where he had grabbed me and there were dirty marks all over it where he had kicked me and from rolling about on the linoleum. There was no way I could wear that suit to anything now – never mind my wedding.

My mouth and lips were bleeding and there were marks on my face and neck where my father's boot had connected with me. I went to the bathroom and took my suit off before soaking a couple of face cloths and taking them and a towel back to the bedroom to get myself cleaned up. I sat in front of the dresser mirror and wiped the blood from my face. After that beating there was absolutely no way I wasn't going to get out of that madhouse at the first opportunity. And getting married that day was the perfect opportunity to get away from my father's violence.

I cleaned myself up as best I could and put more make-up on to hide the marks that were soon to turn to unsightly bruises. I turned to face Rose and asked how I looked. 'You look fine. It's just that the side of your mouth looks a bit puffed up,' she said.

Now I had to find a new outfit for my wedding from the clothes that were in my wardrobe. I looked out a plain, light-blue dress, navy-blue suede shoes and a navy-blue coat. I started to get dressed again, but before I was finished my father was back at the bedroom door and he came into the room. 'If you don't change your mind about this wedding, I'm going to f*****g kill you. It's not a wedding we'll be having today – it's a murder,' he said.

Just at that point, who should walk in behind him but Tilly. She wasn't scared of my father and told him: 'This is disgusting the way you're treating that girl on her wedding day.'

'Don't you start,' he replied. 'Any more from you and you won't be back in this house.'

But Tilly was fit for him. 'I'll be back any time I like,' she said. 'You don't frighten me – those days are long gone.' Now that really shut my father up and he turned on his heels and stormed from the bedroom.

Tilly helped me finish getting ready and I could hear raised voices coming from the living room as my brothers Willie and John along with Granny Boyle and her family had arrived to help prepare the wedding breakfast. My father was shouting: 'Get to f**k out of my house, the whole lot of you.'

And John replied: 'It's a pity it's not a hearse that's coming to this house to take you away, you old bastard, instead of a taxi to take that lassie to her wedding.' John had lost all respect for my father a long time before that day and he was up for a real ding-dong with my father.

I was shaking like a leaf and wondering how I was going to get through the hall and out of the house into the taxi unscathed with all this arguing and shouting going on. I'd known my father didn't want me to get married and there would be lots of screaming and shouting, but I hadn't thought for a minute he would try to spoil my wedding day by beating me up and causing mayhem in the house.

When my taxi arrived to take me to St Michael's chapel, people were so caught up in the arguments and the shouting they hardly noticed Tilly slipping Rose and me up the hall and out the door.

Of course, my father made it pretty clear from the

moment he set eyes on Robert that he was against the wedding. He had two objections to my marrying Robert – first, he didn't think he was good enough to marry one of his daughters and secondly, he was a Protestant and we were a devout Catholic family. But there was one other and far more important reason why I shouldn't really have been marrying Robert that day – I didn't honestly love him enough. I only agreed to marry him to get away from my father – Robert was my escape route.

Robert – or Boxer as he was known, as he had a reputation as a hard man with a penchant for fisticuffs of a weekend – was tall and good-looking and had continually asked me out since I'd returned to Dumbarton from Northampton. Every time he saw me at the dancing he would pester me for a date and no amount of prevarication on my part would put him off. Yes, Boxer was very persistent and I agreed to go out with him a good few times when other suitors weren't around. However, I was obviously giving him the wrong message, because several times he proposed to me, but I always said no. Even if he knew I was going out with someone else, he would wait until that fizzled out and he would quickly be back on the case asking me out again.

When I came back to Dumbarton with Alana, Robert still said he wanted to marry me, but although I felt safe with him and I knew he would look after me, I still said no to his proposals of marriage. I liked him a lot, but I knew I didn't love him enough to marry him.

However, my reluctance to marry Robert changed on Christmas Eve, 1953, when I got a terrible leathering from my father. One of my father's rules was that he didn't want to see any female underwear in the house and that meant we couldn't even put our bras or pants on the clothes horse to dry. All items of clothing like that had to go upstairs to Granny Boyle's and be hung on her pulley so he wouldn't see them.

My friend Patsy McLaughlin had got tickets for the big Christmas Eve Dance at Dumbarton Burgh Halls, which was the social event of the festive period in the town for people our age. I decided I would get myself and all-black outfit for the dance. So, I was going to be resplendent in the classic little black dress, black shoes, black nylons with a butterfly on the side and big pearl beads – Marilyn Monroe, eat your heart out!

I only had one black bra and I had been wearing it the day before the dance. On Christmas Eve I gave the bra a quick hand wash and was drying it in front of the coal fire thinking my father wasn't due home. Suddenly, I got a whack on the head and I tumbled sideways.

'What have I told you about seeing garments in this house that belong to females?' my father shouted. I hadn't heard him coming in and while I was lying on the floor he gave me such a kick in the ribs.

'Get that thing out of my sight, get your pyjamas on and get to bed,' he ordered.

My mother tried to intervene on my behalf. 'Come on, John – that's not fair and this is the big Christmas dance.'

'She'll not be seeing any dancing tonight and she'll not be having any tea either. She knows the rules of this house. In fact, just take that thing outside and put it in the bin.'

I lay in my bed crying my eyes out while Rose and George were getting ready for the festivities and I heard Patsy come to the door to get me for the Christmas dance.

'She's not getting to the dance – she's been up to her tricks again, upsetting everybody in here,' my father told her.

I then heard my brother Jimmy shouting from the kitchen: 'Mary's not upset anyone. She's in bed for no good reason.'

Patsy knew there was nothing could be said to change my father's mind, so she headed off into town by herself. That night I lay in my bed blubbing away thinking about everyone at the Christmas dance enjoying themselves and how cruel and horrible my father was to me. Then a thought suddenly came to me: 'The next time Robert Campbell asks me to marry him I'll say yes, and that way I'll get away from my father's clutches for good.'

Sure enough, a few days later I was in town with my mother for some shopping when we bumped into Robert as my mother was about to go into a fruit shop.

'What happened, you weren't at the big dance?' he asked.

'My father gave me a leathering and wouldn't let me go,' I replied.

'I was looking for you. I . . . eh . . . wanted to ask you something.'

'What was it?'

'This isn't really the right place, but I was going to ask you again . . . I was wanting to know if you'd marry me?'

'Yes,' I replied.

Well if you had seen the look on Robert's face! That answer was the last thing he expected to hear.

'Did you just say yes?'

'Yes, I will marry you.'

'You kidding me on?'

'No, I said I'll marry you and I will.'

'Will we get married this summer?'

'No. I want to get married as soon as we can and that's in six weeks' time. I think that's how long we'll have to wait.'

At that point my mammy came out of the shop and an incredulous Robert said to her: 'Mrs Kelly, Mary says she'll marry me in six weeks' time.'

'Mary can do whatever she likes,' my mammy replied.

'But what if she's only kidding me on?'

'No, no, she wouldn't kid you on about a thing like that. I wouldn't let her do that to you. Anyway if the two of you are going to get married you'll have to go and see the priest.'

'That's fine by me,' said Robert. 'You know I'm a

Protestant, but I'll even become a Catholic if it means marrying your Mary.'

'I'm not asking you to turn a Catholic,' I interrupted. 'Just get married in the chapel.'

So that was the marriage proposal, acceptance and wedding plans made in the space of a few minutes outside a fruit shop in Dumbarton town centre.

I'm sure my mammy must have been thinking I couldn't have any worse a life marrying Robert Campbell than what I had in the house at the hands of my father. Well, that's what I reckoned as well. I only agreed to marry Robert to get away from my father. In my head, I had the daft notion that even although I didn't really love Robert, escaping from my father was good enough reason to get married.

While all three of us were walking along the road, Robert said he would take Alana and offered to give her his name. But my mother was adamant that Alana would stay with her and my father, explaining that they loved her too much to let her go.

Before we went our separate ways, Robert arranged to come to our house the following Sunday – New Year's Day – to see my father and ask his permission to marry me. I thought my father would be glad to get rid of me, but when I mentioned this to my mother she warned me that it might not be that easy and that I was in for a rough time.

Over the next few days there were several whispered conversations in our house outwith my father's earshot. By the time Sunday came, all my brothers knew Robert was coming to the house and they agreed not to go out in case there was any trouble.

I didn't see Robert again until that Sunday afternoon, when I met him at the corner of our street to take him into the house to see my father. The rest of the family were fine about me marrying Robert as they appreciated that life couldn't be any worse for me out of the house and away from my father, but they all had reservations that I didn't love the man I was planning to marry.

Then my sister Frances warned: 'You know what he's going to think. My daddy's immediately going to accuse you of getting pregnant again and that's why you're getting married. I can see how his mind will work – why all of a sudden is Mary wanting to get married and so quickly? Anyway, are you telling me the truth that you're not pregnant?'

'Of course, I'm not pregnant,' I replied.

In the middle of the afternoon, I slipped out of the house and walked down the road to meet Robert. As we stood on the street corner I gave him a rundown of what my family were saying and warned him that he was unlikely to get a hug and a handshake from my father when he broke the news – it was more likely to be a rant and a right hook.

'He won't like you,' I told Robert. 'For a start you're a Protestant and he'll think you've got me pregnant so he's likely to give you a leathering and throw you out the house.'

'He might be able to throw me out his house, since it's his house, but there's no way he's going to give me a leathering – I'm not putting up with any of that nonsense.'

As we walked to the house, I told him how my sister Frances faced the same problem of wanting to marry a Protestant when she got engaged to Davie Dalrymple, whose family were well known for their connections to the Orange Lodge. When he came to see my father to ask permission to marry Frances my father's answer was to give him a punch in the mouth and tell him never to darken his doorstep again. There was such a melee that day, and my father was in such a rage, that Frances was smuggled out of a window and up to Granny Boyle's to get out of his way. My sister wanting to marry an Orangeman caused such a row that Frances never came back to our house until after she was married. She went straight from Granny Boyle's to stay with Davie's parents until they got married and had a house of their own.

I don't know how Robert felt walking up the path to the house, but my stomach was churning in anticipation of the Donnybrook that was about to ensue. The house was choc-a-bloc with people equally as anxious, as they expected my father to explode in anger. They were hanging around the kitchen, the bedroom and the hall. Everywhere except the living room, where my father was sitting.

Willie was the brave one who volunteered to venture forth and tell my father we had a visitor. 'There's a boy at the door and he wants to come in and have a word with you,' said Willie.

'A boy wants to see me? Who is he anyway and what does he want?'

'Well his name's Robert Campbell and I think he wants to see you to ask if it's OK to marry our Mary.'

'So, he's off his f*****g head then. Now she's bringing lunatics to the door.'

'I wouldn't say he was a lunatic,' said Willie. 'Just let him come in, and listen to what he's got to say.'

'For f**k's sake, bring him in then, but I'll not be taking him on, and get her in here as well.'

Willie came out of the living room and said both of us were to go in and see my father. My brother Jimmy pushed his way through the hall and came into the living room as well. When my father saw Jimmy he looked at him and said: 'What do you think you're doing? Get out of here – it's these two that want to see me.'

But Jimmy stood his ground and told my father he was staying. At that point, my brother Bernie's wife, Maureen, also came into the living room and said she was staying as well.

Robert thought he would try the polite approach and get round my father that way. Little did he know.

'Mr Kelly,' he started. 'I'm up to ask for your daughter's hand in marriage and . . .'

Before Robert could say anything else my father butted in: 'If it's only her hand you want, take it and get the f**k out of my house. Just leave the rest of her here, ya big eejit. Go on, get out of my sight before I kill the two of you.'

It never took very long for him to reach boiling point, and my father exploded out of his chair and swung a punch at Robert, but didn't connect. The boys, who were listening at the door, knew that my father had lost the place and they rushed in to pull him off Robert, who wasn't sure if he should hit my father back or not on the basis that there was a house full of his sons.

Willie and Jimmy hustled Robert out of the house and stood outside with him until he had calmed down. Meanwhile, inside the house I was getting battered around the living room.

'You bastard,' he shouted. 'All this on the first day of the year. My mother used to say that if anything bad happened on the first day of the year it was an omen that the rest of the year was going to be bad as well. And what do you do? You go and bring all this trouble to the house. And what kind of numbskull is that you've got yourself involved with? No sane person would want anything to do with you – you that's had a child out of wedlock. That shows you just what an idiot he is when he wants to marry you.'

I never went out for three or four days after that, but the beating I took made me even more determined to get married and get away from my father.

So, that's what led to me sitting in a taxi with my sister Rose, heading for St Michael's Chapel House Oratory to get married to a man I didn't really love. All I could think of in the taxi was that I was on my way to freedom from the beatings I had been getting from my father.

The priest who married us, Father Hugh O'Leary, was a friend of my father's and he refused to allow Robert and me to get married in the proper St Michael's Chapel. He had obviously been speaking to my father and was taking his side, so he told Robert that if we wanted him to marry us, it would have to be in the small oratory inside the chapel house. When Robert and I had gone to see the priest, he made it quite clear to us that he wasn't in favour of a mixed marriage between a Catholic and a Protestant and he was only carrying out the ceremony with great reluctance. I think he also made us get married in the oratory because it would have saved my father any embarrassment, as there was no room for any guests at the marriage ceremony. The only people in the oratory when I got married were Robert, me, Rose, the best man, John Towie, and the priest. Everyone else was back at our house waiting for us to arrive back so they could start the wedding breakfast.

Even when Father O'Leary pronounced us man and wife, he never offered us any congratulations and refused to take the customary envelope containing money for carrying out the service. He just gave Robert and me a withering look, turned away and headed out of a side door, muttering: 'You can find your own way out.'

As the four of us were leaving the chapel house, Robert turned to me and said: 'This is the most miserable day in your life, isn't it?'

'No, no. I'm really happy,' I lied.

'You don't really love me and you've married the wrong person. I'm not kidding myself on that you're madly in love with me – you're only doing this to get away from your father. But it doesn't matter why you decided to marry me. I love you and as far I'm concerned that's all that matters.'

It was also obvious to anyone looking at my face that day that I had taken a beating, and when he first saw me in the oratory Robert asked: 'Did you get a doing off your father?'

When I told him I had, he vowed that would never happen again in my life but although Robert never laid a finger on me, there were still times when Robert wasn't there and my father would slap me around.

When we got back to the house, the place was full of people and there were trestle tables we had borrowed from the local Co-op store down the middle of the living room, which seated about forty for a big fry-up breakfast of sausage, ham and eggs. Of course my father was nowhere to be seen. He had gone off to the school on the pretext of having to do some work to the boilers and everybody was saying how rotten it was of him not to be there.

Up until this point, I had thought that Robert's mother Jessie was a nice person, but I got a taster of what she could really be like when she started having wee digs about me having a baby before I was married. Tilly soon put a stop to that in the way only Tilly could, with a sharp riposte across the wedding breakfast table.

'You've no need to be concerned about your son taking on the responsibility of a child right away because Alana is staying here in this house,' she said. 'And anyway, Mary is not the first and won't be the last girl to have a baby and not be married.'

That certainly got Mrs Campbell off her high horse and after a few months' marriage it became clear to me that she objected to her son marrying a Catholic just as much as my father didn't want me marrying a Protestant. I soon got to know that one of her favourite sayings on the subject of religion was that the only good Catholics are the dead ones lying up the cemetery.

A big wedding reception was planned for later in the evening at the Dumbarton Co-operative Halls, and during the day Robert, Rose, John Towie and I went to Glasgow to the cinema. But the only thing I could think about was the joy of knowing I wouldn't have to go back to my father's house that night.

There were about a hundred people there and the place was filled with family and friends. Even the relatives from Fort William made the journey down for the wedding. As expected, my father refused to come to the wedding and he also made sure Alana wasn't there either. From the outset, he made it quite clear that Alana would be staying with him and my mammy. Although I wanted to take her to live with Robert and me, I knew in my heart of hearts that materially she would be better off with them, as he was still spoiling her rotten.

We couldn't afford to go away on honeymoon, so on our wedding night Robert and I stayed with my brother Bernie and his wife Maureen, in Castlehill, as they made themselves scarce for the weekend to give us some time on our own. Even when they came back on the Monday we stayed with them for another two weeks while we decorated our own rented tenement flat at 5 Overburn Terrace, on the other side of Dumbarton.

For better or for worse, for richer or for poorer, that was me now married, and gone was the fear of getting a beating from my father if the least thing I did upset him. It was a new start, the first day of the rest of my life. I might not have loved Robert Campbell, but life as a wee housewife couldn't be any worse than my previous nineteen years had been. Or could it . . .?

Now You See Him, Now You Don't

BOOF! A right hook lands square on my father's jaw and sends him reeling back into the chair. Robert Campbell stands over him and warns: 'Don't you ever lay your hands on her again.'

It's the first time my new husband has seen my father hit me and it was going to be the last. Boxer by nickname and Boxer by nature – Robert landed a belter on his chin seconds after my father had slapped the back of his hand across my face.

Changed days indeed and one of the benefits of getting married to Robert was that he soon put a stop to my father giving me a leathering, although there were a few times in the first few months of our marriage that my father had given me a slap but I had been too scared to tell Robert. This time, however, he didn't need to be told. He saw it with his own eyes and he certainly took exception to what he saw.

Although I wasn't growing into love with Robert, I certainly liked him and what he did for me in our first year of marriage. I felt safe with him; he never lifted his hand to me and I had my independence, with my own wee house to go to after visiting my mammy. My marriage might not have been heaven, but it was a haven – a place I could go without the fear of upsetting my father and the violent consequences if I did.

Robert was very protective and would never stand for anything untoward happening to me. Never more so than when I was sexually assaulted for the second time in my life. We had not long been married and moved into our own flat on the bottom floor of a tenement in Overburn Terrace. One of my friends stayed in the flat two storeys above ours and I would often visit her. To get to her house I would have to walk up the iron spiral staircase on the outside of the building, passing the window of the house on the second floor.

Round about this time a film called *The Outlaw* starring Jane Russell was all the rage – especially as it was the first time the voluptuous actress had worn an off-the-shoulder blouse on screen. Of course, wanting always to be the height of fashion and having a bit of a bust myself, I just had to go out and buy a couple of those rather daring-for-the-time tops known as a 'Jane Russell blouse'.

One Saturday afternoon, when Robert was watching Dumbarton Football Club and I was in the house by myself getting ready to go to my mammy's, the door went. It was the man who lived upstairs and he asked for the loan of an iron for his wife. I agreed to give him an iron and left him at the door saying I would only be a minute. I went into the house to find the iron and heard the door closing and the lock being turned.

Sensing something wasn't quite right I told him: 'Open that door.'

'When I get what I am after,' he replied.

'You better get out because my husband is due back any minute now.'

He ignored this and grabbed the top of my blouse down and started to ravage my breasts. I was shouting for him to stop and luckily for me a friend of ours, Jim Bonnar, heard me screaming and looked in the window. He saw me being attacked, ran to my door and kicked it in before dragging this beast off me. My attacker disappeared and by this time all the neighbours were out having heard the commotion. There was a lot of tut-tutting and sympathy for me, but they were saying that I should think of the man's poor wife and children before I called the police. Once again, I didn't get the police involved.

I would have to tell Robert what had happened because my blouse was ripped and there were marks on my breasts. Robert would always come to my mammy's for his tea on a Saturday and I told him what happened that day, but made him promise not to do anything to the man. I should have known better, because that night Robert waited for the man and gave him the hiding of his life. And instead of my attacker being in the dock, Robert ended up in court and was fined £10 for assaulting him. Robert's defence lawyer told the story of the man trying to ravish me, but the man told the court that I was trying to entice him by going past his window with the off-the-shoulder blouse on.

I firmly believe that a woman should be able to wear what she wants without being accused of instigating unwanted sexual advances from men. And that belief is as strong today as it was when I was young.

I was the victim of a third attack of a sexual nature a few years later, when I went to buy a three-piece suite from a furniture dealer in Old Kilpatrick. You would be able to order a suite from this man and get it a lot cheaper than buying it in the shops. He would show you a catalogue, you would order the suite and then go to his house to view the furniture in his spare room when it was delivered.

I had ordered a black leather suite from him, costing £60, and when I went to see it at his house his wife was walking out of the door. I handed him the money for the suite and he said: 'Sit down and try the couch.' I did and before I knew it he was lying on top of me. I remembered my previous ordeals and decided this time I was going to fight back. I hit him and ripped his shirt in trying to get him off me. I was lucky again because after a minute or so of the struggle, I heard his front door open and his wife come back in. He jumped off me and I flew out the door past the bemused woman.

Not only did I get a real fright being attacked this way, I
didn't even get the suite, and worse still, I left the £60
behind. After what had happened the last time I didn't tell
Robert about what had happened and told him the suite
wasn't worth the money.

But back to the early days of my marriage and, as my luck
would have it, it was only a matter of weeks after getting
married before I fell pregnant with my first child to Robert.
It was while I was expecting that the incident between
Robert and my father took place.

It was several weeks after the wedding my father never
wanted before I could go back into his house to see my
mammy. And when I was in the house, my father totally
ignored me. It was as if I was invisible and he had this
knack of being able to blank out my presence completely
when I was in the same room as him. And when Robert
and I were at my mammy's for a meal, we couldn't sit at
the same table as him. We had to wait until he had finished
and moved away from the table before we could sit down
to eat.

The night Robert knocked my father for six, I had gone to
the house to make everyone's dinner as my mammy had
tickets for a pantomime. I had only a few weeks to go before
Annette would be born, so it wasn't easy cooking for
everyone coming home. It was a Friday and my mother
had left me a note of how much of their wages my brothers
and sister, Rose – who was still living at home – were to put
in a bowl when they came home. She also wrote how much
money I was to pay the various insurance men from this
money when they called round that night.

As each of my brothers came home from work they took
their keep money from their wage packets and put it in a
bowl in the kitchen. But when Rose came home she told me
she hadn't got any wages that day – and I believed her. I
paid each of the insurance men and the man that came for

the Provident cheque payment before crossing them off my mother's list and tallying up how much cash should have been left.

After washing the dishes and clearing up after dinner, Robert and I were about to leave and were putting on our coats to head back to our own house.

'Come back here you,' my father called from the kitchen. 'There's £3 short from this money. You're a thieving bastard.'

'Here you, don't talk to Mary like that after all she's done for you today,' said Robert.

'I'll do more than f*****g talk to her.' And my father hit me across the face with the back of his hand. My cheek was still stinging from the slap when Robert punched him and sent him flying back into his chair. At that precise moment the door opened, and in walked my brothers John and Jimmy. As soon as Jimmy walked into the room he could see by the way my father was slumped in the chair that he had been knocked into it. I could see by the look on his face that he was thinking: 'What are you doing hitting my father?' And he was ready to have a go at Robert.

'Jimmy, my daddy's just hit me,' I said. 'That's why Robert punched him.'

Jimmy quickly realised what had happened. He looked at Robert and said: 'That's all right then, son.' He turned to my father and asked him: 'What the f**k are you on? Mary's expecting a wean and you're hitting her – listen, those days are over. You take it from me.'

'She stole £3 out of that bowl,' my father said.

'Jimmy, I never took the £3,' I replied. 'Count the money and you'll see for yourself.'

Jimmy looked at the piece of paper showing how much people had to leave from their wages and how much money was to be paid out. He tallied up what was left and said: 'There is £3 short here.'

'That's because Rose never left any money. She didn't get any wages this week.'

'Rose says she never got any wages, does she? Mary, Robert – you hold on till she gets back home. She won't be long, now.'

One of my father's tricks if he thought he was going to get a doing – particularly off Jimmy – was to head off to his bed and lock the bedroom door so no one could get in. But Jimmy told him to stay where he was until he had got to the bottom of the mystery of Rose's empty wage packet.

Ten minutes later Rose came in and Jimmy buttonholed her right away. 'What's this about you not getting any wages?'

'Neither I did. They were kept off me for tax.'

'Jesus Christ, you must be making some f*****g money if they are keeping £3 a week off you in tax. Even I'm only getting ten shillings a week taken off me in tax. I must get a job like yours with the money they're paying out,' said Jimmy sarcastically.

Then he grabbed Rose by the hair and shook her like a rag doll. 'Mary's expecting a baby and she takes a slap off that bastard for you. If her man wasn't here to knock him into his chair she would probably have got a good kicking. It's your turn now. I'm going to give you such a leathering and he's going to watch me do it.'

Well, Jimmy slapped her, kicked her backside and bounced her off the walls. As she slid to the floor, Rose was screaming that she was going to faint and Jimmy replied: 'Don't give me any of that acting.' And pulled her up off the ground to give her another slap. The best of it was that I was the one who jumped on Jimmy's back shouting on him to stop hitting Rose.

'For f**k's sake, Mary. No wonder people take a rise out of you,' shouted Jimmy. 'Get out of my way. I'm not finished with her yet.' Jimmy dragged Rose into her bedroom, lifted her off the ground and threw her onto her bed. By this time I really did think she had passed out.

Jimmy came back into the living room, stared at my father and said: 'What have you got to say about that then?'

'Nothing. I'm away to my bed,' he replied.

Jimmy wasn't very tall, but what he lacked in height and build, he made up for with a big and courageous heart. He was the smallest of my brothers, but Jimmy was the one who had the bottle to stand up to my father. If ever my father doubted that, the day Jimmy gave Rose a leathering and asked him what he thought of it proved to all of us that Jimmy was a match for him.

I don't know if that incident had any lasting affect on my father, but a few weeks later an amazing thing happened as I headed off to hospital to have Annette after I had gone into labour. Because I had haemorrhaged giving birth to Alana the doctors suggested I go to Braeholm Maternity Hospital in Helensburgh – which handled complicated births – instead of the local maternity unit at Overtoun House in Dumbarton. Where my parents stayed was much closer to Helensburgh than where I was living on the other side of Dumbarton.

When I told my mammy she said that it would be better for me if I stayed at her house a week before I was due to give birth. But first she had to persuade my father that I could stay in the house. To convince him that there was a genuine medical reason to be as close as possible to Braeholm, I went to my doctor and got him to write a letter explaining the situation. When my mammy showed him the doctor's letter to convince him it wasn't all a pack of lies, my father agreed I could stay in the house prior to the birth.

In the middle of November, I temporarily moved back into my parents' house and plans were laid that my Auntie Alice would come to the hospital with me in the ambulance. In those days the fathers didn't go in to witness the birth and my mother told Robert he should just go into his work and someone would get a message to him when the baby was born.

I woke up at four on the morning of 30 November with pains in my stomach. I got out of bed and went into the kitchen where my mother was already making the porridge for everyone's breakfast. She knew right away that I was in labour, so she sent one of the boys to get Auntie Alice and call for an ambulance from a phone box.

By this time my father was up and about, but totally ignored everything that was going on. When the ambulance arrived my brother John and Auntie Alice helped me walk down the hall and she held a coat over my shoulders as it was a freezing cold morning. I was just about to step out of the door into the darkness and the waiting ambulance when I heard my father say brusquely to Auntie Alice: 'Out of the road, you.' Not an 'excuse me'. Just an 'out of the road'. Then I felt him wrap a mohair scarf round my shoulders. 'That'll keep you warm,' he said.

I couldn't believe this was happening. Up till then I hadn't even been allowed to sit in his chair because, according to him, I was such a harlot and had brought shame to the family. Now, for the first time I could remember, he was showing genuine love and affection towards me and wrapping his favourite scarf that no one was allowed to touch around my shoulders. Even to this day, I haven't worked out this great contradiction in the way he treated me that morning. It's a right puzzle.

Annette was born later that day and within a couple of weeks I was back in my own house playing the archetypal mum and housewife.

But during the second year of our marriage the cracks were beginning to appear. One of my cousins in Fort William was due to have her baby at home and she asked me if I would come up and be with her during the birth. Robert said he didn't mind, so with Annette – now several months old – I headed for Fort William. Sadly, my cousin's baby died after only a day and I ended up staying there for four weeks.

When I got back to Dumbarton, I bumped into my father's brother, Uncle Tommy, who warned me not to be spending too much time away from home as Robert had been jumping around with other women while I was away. I refused to believe him. My vanity kicked in when I got home and looked at myself in the mirror. Why would Robert want anyone else when he has someone as good-looking as me, I thought to myself. And of course, Robert denied he had been taking girls back to our house after a night at the dancing.

Then one of my friends, Annette Stewart, also told me that Robert was getting what we call a lumber – a girlfriend or boyfriend – when he would go to the dancing in Dumbarton. When I challenged Robert with this new evidence, he admitted he had taken a girl home – but it had only happened once.

I gave him the benefit of the doubt, until I discovered that the weekend card schools Robert said he was at never took place. He had told me that he played cards with his pals in the local park and naïvely I believed they would be playing cards in the park until two and three in the morning.

Unbeknown to me, one of Robert's friends, Sandy McLean, had taken a wee fancy to me and was biding his time before making his move. If we bumped into one another in the street, he was always helping me down the steps with the pram and being extremely pleasant and complimentary. I still had suspicions in the back of my mind that Robert was up to something with other women and I decided to confide in Sandy what my Uncle Tommy and Annette Stewart had told me. That was my first mistake, as that was the cue for him to make a move on me.

'Well, if both of them are saying the same thing, it must be true,' Sandy said. 'If I had a wife like you I certainly wouldn't be doing anything like that. I would give my right arm to have what he's got.'

I found myself thinking 'What a nice, understanding guy', not realising I was just being softened up with all his compliments, and my head was getting bigger and bigger. He was thinking he'd make Robert out to be a right bad bastard and take the role of Mary's champion, giving me a shoulder to cry on. He said that if Robert got up to anything, he'd let me know.

I met Sandy a few days later and he was back chasing his prey. I told him Robert had mentioned there was a card school organised again for that night.

'You meet me under the lamppost at the bottom of the road at 11 p.m. and I'll show you there's no card school,' he said. 'Don't be frightened that it's dark, I'll be there all the time with you and I'll walk you back to your house. Then you'll see he wasn't playing cards and if Robert says he was, you can say you were there and saw for yourself there was no card school going on.'

Sure enough, that night he was standing under the light waiting for me. We walked round the corner to the park and he said: 'Where's the card school? Sure, the men come here during the day to play pitch and toss and maybe cards, but nobody plays cards here at night.'

I started to cry and told Sandy that I had believed every word Robert had said about the night-time card schools in the park. Then he made his move. It was the arms round my shoulder to comfort me and he said: 'How do you feel now?'

'I'm leaving him.'

'I can't believe this, Mary. If I had what he has, I wouldn't be telling lies or staying out at night and seeing the lassie he's been seeing.'

More tears and more comforting from the wily Sandy. He walked me back to my door and I asked him in for a cup of tea. By this time rage had taken over from the hurt and I was set on revenge. Was I not just playing right into Sandy's hands, who was saying: 'Yes, Mary a wee taste of his own medicine might do Robert some good and bring him to his senses.'

'If that's the kind of thing Robert Campbell's been up to, then I'll be doing it a lot more than he has and I won't be doing it on the fly. I can do whatever he's been doing.'

I ended up in bed with Sandy that night – getting my revenge on Robert or, as Sandy described it, being comforted through my emotional trauma. And what made me really angry was that that week I had bought him a new suit and overcoat. I'd got myself into debt to make sure Robert was smartly turned out and now he was dressed to the nines impressing other women.

I decided to stay up and wait for Robert to come home so I could confront him. It was about 6 a.m. before he eventually appeared.

'What are you doing sitting up and still dressed?' he asked when he saw me sitting in the living room.

'Never mind that – where have you been?'

'I told you. There was a card school on.'

'Well, tell me about the card school.'

I let him ramble on for a minute, then I interrupted. 'There was no card school. I went down to the park and the place was deserted.'

'You never went down to the park on your own in the pitch dark.'

'You're right. I wasn't on my own – Sandy McLean was with me.'

'What are you talking about? Sandy was at the card school.'

'That's strange because Sandy has been in bed with me

tonight and I'm going to be seeing Sandy from now on. What you did to me I'll be doing ten times more to you and I won't be sneaking around behind people's backs. I'll be walking down the High Street arm in arm with him. See how you like living with that. And by the way, you just get your stuff and get out of here or I'm off and I'm taking the baby with me.'

'I'll f*****g kill that Sandy McLean,' shouted Robert. 'I'm getting the f**k out of here.'

That's exactly what he did, although he never went near Sandy McLean. The next thing I knew was that he had headed for England where there was plenty work for welders. He'd already stormed out of the house twice before and had gone back to stay with his mother for a couple of weeks.

After Robert left the house I went out with Sandy McLean only a few times. He was never going to mean anything to me other than a way of getting back at Robert. And anyway, every time Robert was off the scene I would take up with James 'The Gent' Jennings again. I thought I was still in love with him and it was only after I was married that I first had sex with him. I think what attracted me to him was the excitement and the danger of me going out with a gangster.

Sometimes even when Robert was at home I would meet up with James if we happened to bump into one another – and he wasn't banged up in a cell somewhere – and he asked me out to Glasgow for a meal or to go to the cinema. I don't know how I justified this to myself at the time, but I did. In my mind, I must have split myself between normality and the exciting part of my life. One part of me was the doting housewife who was cooking her man's meals, looking after his children and buying him clothes and making sure he was well dressed when he went out. The other part of me was the daft wee lassie, all taken on by James The Gent because he was the gangster type and I was loving the excitement. I just couldn't stop seeing James the Gent. I wanted to, but every time we saw each other in town he would say: 'Come out with me. One more time won't make any difference – just for old times' sake.' And I always agreed.

I know some people might say this was a very self-centred way of looking at things, but I justified it by telling myself that Robert had been running around with other women and that he knew I didn't love him when he continually asked me to marry him. I kept telling myself he shouldn't have married me when he knew I didn't really love him.

It was always the same during our tempestuous marriage. We'd have a big fall-out, he'd head off to his mother's – who never really wanted him to marry me in the first place – and she would give him money to get down to England where he would find work for a few weeks or even months if the notion took him to stay away longer. With Robert, it was a case of now you see him, now you don't!

However, it always ended the same. A knock on the door and there would be Robert, hangdog look on his face. 'I'm sorry for what I've done,' he would say. 'I love you and I couldn't stay away. We'll make a fresh start and everything will be different.'

I always fell for that and we would try to patch up our marriage and make it work – until the next time we had a row and he would disappear down south.

This behaviour pattern punctuated our marriage for years and the biggest problem I had was that when Robert was away in England he never sent me any money and that meant I had to suffer the indignity of queuing up at the Social Security offices every Monday morning asking for a cash handout to see me and the children through the week.

I was mortified having to stand in the long queue in the big Nissen hut that was the social security office in Dumbarton. Once you reached the counter you gave them your name and they told you to sit down. Then they called your name out in front of everyone else and you made your way to one of the booths to be interviewed, with everyone hearing what was being said. There was no privacy and you'd be thinking everyone was sitting there saying: 'Aye, that's her man done a runner again.'

Sometimes after the interview you had to sit for hours until someone shouted your name so you could go to the counter and collect your money. There were no cheques sent out to you or money paid direct into your bank account in those days.

There was one particular member of the Social Security staff who, as you could see by his face, enjoyed shouting out loud: 'Mrs Mary Campbell, one pound seven shillings and sixpence. And for your daughter, Annette Campbell, three shillings and sixpence. Come forward and get your money.'

It was humiliating the way everyone could hear what the Social Security staff were asking you and it made you feel like a beggar.

And to make matters worse, my father went apoplectic with rage when he found out I was claiming Social Security. 'This family's never had to beg money off anyone,' he said to me the first time someone told him they had seen me at the Social Security. 'Now you're standing in a queue every Monday degrading us all with your begging and all because you married a f*****g idiot and riff-raff. You're just like Oliver Twist begging for more gruel.'

Robert or no Robert, life went on although he was around long enough for me to become pregnant again. But it wasn't long after we discovered I was expecting when he was off on his travels again. At the end of November 1956, while I was pregnant with young Robert, I had to give up the tenement flat at Overburn Terrace because I couldn't afford to pay the rent. People today should think themselves lucky, because there was no such thing as housing benefit in those days. Annette and I moved in with my brother Willie and his wife Sadie, who had a spare bedroom in their house in the Castlehill area of Dumbarton. Staying in Castlehill meant I was closer to my mammy's and I visited her most days.

I hadn't long moved in with Willie and Sadie when like a bolt from the blue I discovered there really was something called love at first sight. I was visiting a friend of our family, Liza Vallance, who stayed across the road from my mammy's, and we were sitting having a chat when her living-room door opened and in walked a teenage boy with his father.

I never even noticed the father as I was stunned by the boy's good looks and I couldn't take my eyes off him. Liza introduced the older man as Patrick Smith, her brother-in-law, and his 16-year-old son, Patsy.

I could not believe how I was feeling in those few minutes after meeting him. I wasn't one for all that romantic love at first sight nonsense, but I did fall in love with that boy, right there and then. He had the bluest eyes I had ever seen in my life, jet-black hair, slim with a handsome face and he was smartly dressed in the Teddy Boy gear that was so fashionable in that era.

He was only in the house for a few minutes, but in that time I had fallen in love with the boy. I had a wee argument with myself:

'I've fallen in love.'

'Don't be so bloody ridiculous – you have only just met him. He's just sixteen and you're twenty-two, with two children and a third on the way.'

'No, something tells me he will be in my life and the way he's looking at me says he's got the same feeling.'

'You're off your head – he's just a boy. Someone like you doesn't fall in love with a teenager you've only just met.'

'But I've got this amazing feeling in my stomach. I think he's beautiful and I must have fallen in love with him.'

My mind was in turmoil. I knew I didn't love Robert and I was really disappointed that Patsy didn't stay longer at his aunt's house. I wondered how I was ever going to see him again. I didn't want to let Liza know that I had fallen head over heels for her nephew, so I just asked a couple of questions about him and said I thought he was a nice, polite boy. I was desperate to ask a million questions about Patsy, but I didn't dare.

For days after that fateful meeting I couldn't get Patsy out of my mind, but I was careful not to mention how I felt even to my closest friends. If I had they would have said I was mad and should be locked up for cradle snatching!

Although I was only twenty-two, because of what had happened in my life, in the eyes of many people I was a lot older than my age. I was married. I had two children and was expecting a third, and I was expected to dress and act like someone a lot older in that situation. I'm sure when people looked at me and my life, they would have me down as someone in their thirties. Although I certainly didn't look that age, it was what people expected from me.

A perfect example of how you are pigeon-holed because of your circumstances was the day I went out wearing a pair of pedal-pushers – they would be called cropped trousers nowadays. I was pregnant with young Robert and went into town wearing the fashionable pedal-pushers with a red and white striped blouse when I bumped into my mother-in-law.

'That's a disgrace you going around dressed like that,' she said. 'A woman in your circumstances shouldn't be wearing clothes made for a young lassie.'

That was me put in a box and I thought that maybe I shouldn't be dressing like that at my age and that I should act like an older woman. I was easily influenced and it was after that incident that I started to dress in a very dowdy and old-fashioned way. I stayed in that frame of mind for almost two years until someone pulled me aside and said: 'What's happened to you? You've fairly let yourself go and you used to be that glamorous.'

I told them what had happened when I was wearing the pedal-pushers. 'Robert's mother said I shouldn't dress like I was a young thing,' I said.

'Don't you be taking her on. She's only saying that because she couldn't get away with wearing them,' came the reply.

For the next few weeks I was a regular visitor to Liza and every time I was in her house I would ask a surreptitious question or two about Patsy without trying to arouse any suspicion. And much to my disappointment, he was never there when I called round.

All this time I had this burning desire to kiss Patsy. It was the strangest thing. Once the thought got into my head, no matter how much I tried to ignore it, the idea of me kissing Patsy grew stronger and stronger.

At the end of January 1957 Robert returned and once again I took him back, but my brother Willie, whose house I was still staying in, was having none of it. He wasn't happy that Robert had left while I was pregnant and said Robert wasn't welcome in his home.

'That man's made you the talk of the town,' Willie said. 'He's away and all of a sudden you start to look pregnant. People think someone other than Robert is the father and that's why he's done a runner.'

Of course, nothing could be further from the truth. Robert knew I was pregnant with his child before he left, but I suppose that's how rumours start. In any case, Willie wasn't for changing his mind and if Robert and I were getting back together again we would have to find somewhere else to live. Willie was adamant that Robert's actions had blackened the family name.

A few days after Robert had come back to Dumbarton I met him in the town and he told me someone in his work had a spare room they were willing to let out to us.

The house was at 13 Cumbrae Crescent, Castlehill, and we had one room downstairs, just across the hall from the family's living room. Robert and I were trying to make a fresh start, but after only one day in our new lodgings I got the shock of my life.

I had no idea we had moved into Patsy Smith's parents' house and I was staying in the same home as the teenage boy I had been totally infatuated with during those last few months.

My One True Love

I'm sitting on the side of the bed in our rented room trying to get Annette dressed while she wriggles around trying to slide off my knee. I hear a knock on the bedroom door and I think it's Patrick Smith senior wanting to see me about something. I get up off the bed, open the door and standing there is Patsy Smith holding a pair of Annette's shoes in his hand.

Although I'd just about got over the shock of finding out we were staying in his house, this was the first time I had seen him and my heart skipped a beat as he stood there in front of me.

Patsy broke the embarrassing silence. 'Hello, stranger,' he said. 'My dad says you left these shoes in the living room last night when he was taking a splinter out your wee girl's foot and maybe you are needing them.'

'Thanks . . . err, ehm, right, thanks very much,' I stuttered like a daft wee lassie in the school playground bumping into a boy she fancies like mad, with all her pals giggling in the background. 'It's OK. I've almost finished dressing Annette and I've got another pair of shoes for her. But thanks all the same.'

Another awkward silence and I wondered what Patsy thought about me now he'd found out I was a married woman with children and another on the way. And there was no mistaking I was pregnant because I was only a couple of weeks from the birth and there was no hiding my bump. This teenage boy had such an effect on me that I was embarrassed knowing he had found all this out about me.

'Are you off out?' he asked.

'Just going to my mammy's for the day.'

'I'll help you up the steps to the main road with the pram, then.'

'That's really good of you.'

'No problem. How long are you staying at your mother's?'

'I'll be there most of the day.'

'I could meet you on the way back and help you on the stairs again.'

'My husband is going to the football and he comes up to my mother's after the match to have his dinner and he comes back up the road with me.'

'But I would like to help you on the way back here.'

I was taken aback by how bold he was. 'I don't think my husband would like that happening,' I said, trying to put on a stern voice, but failing miserably.

'I don't care what your man likes,' he replied.

I tried to appear astonished, but at the same time was lapping all this up. Here's me, married and about to have my third child, and this teenage boy is chatting me up and wanting to see me home at night. That would be a boost to anyone's ego and I liked that.

'I know all about you. My mother told me,' he said. 'And I don't care if you have a hundred weans, or a hundred husbands either.'

How brave was this boy – or was it stupidity? Didn't he know about Robert's reputation as a hard man? I suddenly became a wee bit frightened about how all this would end. If Robert found out, he would give the boy a real doing and that would lead to Patrick Smith senior – who had a bit of a reputation himself – jumping in to the resulting rammy. Whatever the outcome of that fight might have been, one thing was for sure and that was if everything did kick off between Robert and Patsy, we would end up being thrown out of the house and be on the street with nowhere to stay.

'Let me just walk you down the road,' said Patsy. 'No one can say anything about that. I want to explain something to you.'

As we walked down the road, Patsy didn't mince his words. 'Listen, remember the day I saw you in my Aunt Liza's house? Well, I fell in love with you then,' he said. 'I have even given up my girlfriend and I'll never have another girlfriend.'

'That's silly,' I said. 'Look at the age of me compared to you.'

'I don't care about your age. I'm telling you, I haven't been able to get you out of my mind and I know you're not happy with your man because he's always away for weeks on end and you've been seen with James Jennings.'

'That might be true, but you're too young to understand these things.'

I was really taken aback about how well he had done his homework. He seemed to know a lot about my personal life and what he did know was spot on.

'I would never want to cause trouble for you,' Patsy continued. 'I'm going to get you to love me.'

Patsy left me at the bottom of Brucehill and all the way up to my mammy's my head was spinning. I was in love and it was real this time. I couldn't get all the things he had just said out of my mind. Later that night Robert and I were walking home when we passed the flagpole at the bottom of Brucehill and sure enough, there was Patsy waiting there with a few of his friends. I wondered what he was going to do, but he just shouted hello to us and we went on our way.

I felt fantastic and the dents I'd taken to my self-esteem with all of Robert's shenanigans were being well and truly straightened out by young Patsy's attentions. I thought that if a good-looking sixteen-year-old wanted me that much, and me in a roly-poly state of pregnancy, I couldn't be that bad-looking. That was the vanity kicking in.

Although I could hardly take my mind off Patsy and how I felt about him, I was only two weeks from giving birth to young Robert and that certainly brought some sense of reality back to me. The room we lived in had a bed, a tallboy for our clothes and a blanket chest. There was also Annette's cot squeezed in and a Moses basket waiting for the arrival of the new baby. There were no chairs and when Robert and I were in the room, one of us sat on the blanket chest and the other on the bed. Neither was there a television set, although Robert had a radio he would sit and listen to.

Robert was also a bit of a reader and he would lie on the bed with a book. Several times Patsy's mother Mamie would knock on the door and ask if I wanted to come through to the living room for a chat. But that friendliness soon disappeared when the Social Security people discovered the Smiths were getting £2 a week from us for renting the room and hadn't declared it. Patrick Smith had been paid off at the shipyard where he worked and was now claiming Social Security, but someone had written to the Social telling them about his new lodgers and undeclared income stream and the Social Security people told him he had better stop renting out one of his rooms if he wanted to continue claiming money.

Young Robert was born on Wednesday, 15 May 1957 in that lodgings room in the Smith house with Theresa O'Neill the midwife in attendance. Everything went fine, but as was the case in those days, a new mother was kept in bed for a week after giving birth and that was what was happening to me. That was until the day after young Robert was born. Mamie Smith came into the room and announced: 'I've got something to tell you. You'll need to get out of this house by tomorrow – the Social's been at the door.'

Although Robert was at his work the midwife was visiting me at that point and she turned round incredulously and replied: 'Mrs Campbell can't go anywhere. She just had a baby twenty-four hours ago and she needs to stay in bed for a week.'

'They need to go or we'll be in big trouble with the Social Security,' replied Mamie Smith.

But the midwife dug her heels in and called the doctor to tell him what had happened. Dr Pollachi came to the house and remonstrated with Patrick Smith, but to no avail.

'I can report you for this,' said Dr Pollachi.

'Report me to whoever you like. But get them to f**k off out of here.'

Now, the doctor was a really devout Catholic and he was shocked by the violent language. 'When Judgement Day comes you will have to face God and pay for your actions,' he told Patrick Smith.

'That's fine. I'll take my chances with God, but just get them out of this house. They've got until 4 p.m. tomorrow.'

When Robert heard about this he was none too pleased as you can imagine, but thankfully, instead of wanting to take Patrick Smith outside and give him a doing, he did the sensible thing and spoke to one of his gaffers at Denny's shipyard where he was working. Denny's used to rent out houses to their workers and he gave Robert keys to an old, damp room and kitchen which hadn't been lived in for years in the Common Lawn, in Dumbarton.

And of course, when my mammy and Frances heard about this, they too, went into action – that's what families did for each other in those days. It was decided that my mammy would take Annette for the time it took to get the house cleaned and decorated and Frances would take young Robert. I was to go to the room and kitchen with Robert.

My brother Bernie's in-laws also stayed in the Common Lawn and as soon as we had the keys to the room and kitchen, they went in and kept a fire going all day and night to try to get rid of the dampness. On the Friday, two days after I had given birth, Robert carried me, wrapped in blankets, out of the Smiths' house and into a taxi. The midwife carried young Robert and we first dropped the children off at my mammy's house and then we went on to our new tenement flat at the Common Lawn.

Although the worst of the dampness had been taken away by the fire being lit for a day and night, I could still smell mustiness and the house badly needed decorating with paper and paint. It is at times like these that you really appreciate the importance of having a family around you to help out in times of need. Bernie's in-laws, as well as keeping a fire going, brought us a pot of hot soup and made sure there was bread, milk and a caddy of loose tea in the cupboard.

Every day my mammy, Francis and the midwife came to visit me to make sure I was all right. And at night Frances's husband Davie – or Div as he got called – would come round after his work and decorate the room and kitchen. I would be lying in my bed and Div would be papering and painting round about me. And when that work was finished my mammy and Frances made sure there were nice curtains and, as best as possible, make the room and kitchen a home from home.

After a couple of weeks I was up and about and Annette and young Robert were back with us in the Common Lawn. But I couldn't go out walking my new baby in his pram until he had been christened. That was the way of things in those days if you were a Catholic, so young Robert was duly christened.

On the odd occasion when I was in the town I would pass by Patrick Smith or his wife Mamie, but they just kept on walking, eyes to the ground, not wanting to make eye contact or say anything. I reckon it was embarrassment on their part. However, one time Patrick Smith did stop me and say: 'Can I have a word with you?'

I hesitated, wondering what to do. Should I just ignore him for what he had done, or should I speak to him? What was also racing through my mind was that he was the father of the boy I had all these strange feelings about and I definitely had an urge to see Patsy again. So I stopped.

'I just want to apologise. That was a terrible thing we did to you,' he said.

Patrick Smith was a real charmer and although he was as working-class poor as the rest of us, he spoke as if he was one of the gentry and walked about the town with no little aplomb. 'But I'm sure you appreciate, Mary,' he continued. 'As needs must, one must do.'

I was very fond of both Mamie and Patrick and I couldn't help laughing at his spiel that broke the frosty atmosphere between us. Although I never expected what came next.

'Mary, my dear. You wouldn't happen to have the price of ten cigarettes on you? Just a small loan for a short time – one-and-ninepence would suffice.'

That was Patrick Smith all over and, as we used to say, he would get a piece at anybody's door. When he asked you for something he made you feel he was doing you the favour and bestowing some honour on you. Of course, you never got anything back from Patrick and I knew he would never repay the money I couldn't help myself giving him.

'Here's two bob, Patrick. Get yourself a box of matches as well,' I said, ruefully handing over the silver coin.

He was certainly what you would call a character or a local worthie. He might have acted like he was a toff, but he was never slow to give someone a doing if they annoyed him, and he was handy with his fists.

There was one occasion when Patrick Smith went looking for someone who had apparently insulted him behind his back. This poor fellow was unaware of the leathering he was about to get from Patrick Smith as he sat having a fish tea in Nutini's Fish and Chip Shop in Dumbarton's High

Street. In marched the bold Patrick, dressed all in black with a white silk scarf swaying from side to side around his neck, past the take-away counter and straight through to the busy sit-in area where people were having their fish teas.

'Right, everyone, please listen carefully,' said Patrick in loud, but posh tones. 'I am giving you one chance and one chance only.'

He pointed to the man he was after and said: 'That one is for a real good doing. All neutrals under the table!' And sure enough, the chip shop cleared and Patrick gave the guy a bigger battering than the fish that was being served.

We only stayed in the Common Lawn for about six months, because after a few weeks of us moving in the building was condemned and everyone living in the tenement was to be given a council house. But you will never believe where our allocated council house was – a top flat at Cumbrae Crescent South, right across the road looking down on Patsy Smith's house.

While I still had feelings for Patsy, being kicked out of our lodgings, having a baby and Robert being back in the house shoved them further back in my mind, although they were definitely still there. I didn't see that much of Patsy when we first moved because it was just before Christmas and with the cold weather I wasn't out and about as much with Annette or young Robert. But as we got into the spring of 1958 and Patrick Smith started working in his garden with Patsy's help, there were more and more chances to see him. I would find myself looking forward to going out on to our balcony, hoping to catch a glimpse of Patsy either coming in or out of his front door or working in the garden with the father.

I had this sneaky wee trick that I used when I heard voices coming from the Smiths' front garden. As most women did, I put young Robert in his pram out on to the veranda to get some fresh air and when I saw Patsy was in his garden I would shout: 'Annette, you mustn't do that. Come away from the pram.' Annette would be nowhere near the pram, but I just wanted to catch Patsy's attention. He would look up and I would wave over to him and he would wave back. This sort of thing went on for weeks and every chance I had I would be out on the veranda hoping Patsy would be working in his garden.

The first real contact I had with Patsy again was after Robert went off on his travels again after another row between us. I would go to my mammy's every day for my dinner as I was only getting Social Security money, and one night as I was walking back to my house Patsy was at the flagpole at the bottom of Brucehill. As I walked by he came over and asked: 'Where's your man tonight?'

'He's away working,' I replied.

'Where?'

'I don't know.' There was no point pretending as Dumbarton was a small enough town that everyone knew everybody else's business.

Patsy walked me, Annette and young Robert up the road to my house and helped me carry the pram up the stairs to my door. 'Will you be OK?' he asked.

'I'll be fine.'

'Do you not get frightened at night in here on your own?'

I knew he only needed a tiny word of encouragement and he would have asked if he could come into the house, but although I was desperate for him to come in, I didn't have the courage to ask him. He'd have been seventeen by then, but still just a young boy compared to me and my life with a husband and three children. 'No, I'm OK,' I told him.

Then he asked me a strange thing. 'Have you enough coal in the house?'

'Well, actually, I don't have any coal left and I'm just going to go straight to my bed.' Usually I would be able to get some coal from my mammy's if my father wasn't in. My mammy would fill up a wee bag of coal and tie it to the bottom of the pram to get it up the road. That night my father was in and he was still of the view that I had made my bed and I should lie in it, so I couldn't sneak any coal out of the house.

I left him on the doorstep and went into the house to get the kids and myself ready for bed. The next morning there was a knock on the door and when I opened it there was the coalman standing there with a sack of coal and a bag of logs. The coalman asked me to open the cellar door, which was out on the landing with another door inside the house.

'I never ordered any coal,' I told him.

'You're all right, Mrs Campbell, young Patrick Smith ordered and paid for it.'

I couldn't believe a teenager would think of doing that, but I was glad of the sight of a cellar full of coal and logs, which meant the kids would have a fire on all the time for the next week or so.

With Robert still away, the following Saturday night I decided I would go to the dancing at Dumbarton Burgh Hall with a few pals and ironically it was Patsy's cousin, Margaret Vallance, who was babysitting for me. I was dancing all night and I never really noticed Patsy was there. But near the end of the night he came over to me and I said: 'I haven't seen you in here before.'

'I know. But I'd been told you were going out tonight and this was the place you usually went to on a Saturday night. Anyway, can I walk you up the road?'

'Maybe it would be better if I just met you at the bottom of Castlehill and you could walk me up the road to the house.'

'No, I want to walk out this door with you. I don't want people to think I'm ashamed of being seen with you. I'll walk you through the town and up to the house.'

'Robert Campbell will kill you if he finds out.'

'Don't you worry about me and Robert Campbell – he'll not be killing me or anyone else.'

On the way up the road I told Patsy that his cousin Margaret and her boyfriend Jim McCarthy were babysitting for me, but he said that didn't bother him.

'But if Margaret finds out you've walked me home, she'll tell her mother, who'll tell your mother and there'll be all sorts of trouble,' I warned him.

'I don't care who tells who anything,' he replied. 'So long as I'm with you I don't care what anybody says.'

I admired the boy's nerve and audacity and it was the chance for me to have a wee rebellion of my own. I've often thought because I had been under such strict control of my father when I was younger that when I became an adult, I would deliberately do things I shouldn't just to prove the point that I could, without anyone's interference.

Walking up the road, I knew I was going to ask Patsy into the house even although I was apprehensive. It was a bit like wanting my cake and eating it – I was desperate for Patsy to come in, but I didn't want anyone, especially my family, finding out.

When we walked into the living room you should have seen the look of horror on Margaret Vallance's face. 'He's my cousin, Mary.'

'I know.'

'Does he know you're a married woman with kids?'

'Yes.'

She looked at Patsy. 'What's your mother going to say about this?'

'I don't care,' he replied. 'If you want to tell her that's fine by me.'

'It's none of my business,' Margaret continued. 'But I don't think this is a very sensible thing you're doing. Robert Campbell will kill you when he comes back and finds out about this.'

'I've already told Mary, don't you worry about Robert Campbell.'

Margaret and her boyfriend got their coats and left, muttering about how they hoped we knew what we were doing. Patsy stayed the night and being with him was the way it should have been. It was both love and sex at the same time and it was the first time I had experienced that. It felt right and the fact I was a married woman with children and he was just a teenager simply disappeared from my thoughts.

The next morning, however, my embarrassment was excruciating. I couldn't even make the excuse that I was drunk – everybody knows I don't drink and my mind was as clear as anything the previous night. Patsy had been sleeping when I got up and I was in the kitchen facing out the window when he walked in and said he was going because he thought I was embarrassed.

'No, I'm not,' I said, none too convincingly.

'I hope what happened last night doesn't change anything, the way you feel about me, because every time I see you going down to your mammy's, I'll be out helping you with the pram up the stairs.'

All this time I kept my back to him. A combination of embarrassment and not believing a word he said. I thought this had been a one-night stand for him, a conquest and a young boy's daft notion of proving himself by being able to bed a married woman. I didn't think for a minute he would be waiting to help me up the stairs with the pram. And I couldn't get the image of Robert going crazy with rage out of my head if he found out about Patsy.

Later that day I was, as usual, going to my mammy's and as I headed out of my close, right on cue Patsy's door opened and out he came and walked me to the bottom of Brucehill. He didn't need me to tell him what my father was like, so even he realised that walking me to the door would have been a step too far.

He said he would be waiting at the flagpole for me coming home from my mammy's and sure enough there he was. Patsy left a group of his pals and came over to me straight away and said he would walk me up the road.

I decided that he wasn't getting to come into the house that night. It was like a test for him and to let him know he couldn't just hop in and out of my bed when he liked. I would soon find out what his true feelings were. As we approached my house I told him he wasn't coming up to the house that night. He said that was fine and there was no: 'Wait a minute, don't be rotten, Mary.'

When he said that, I felt a rush of disappointment. On the one hand, I was glad he didn't try to be pushy and sweet-talk me into letting him into the house, and he seemed to accept I was in control. But on the other hand, he could have put up a bit of a fight for a couple of minutes, tried to talk me round, and I still could have said no. There you go again, wanting to have my cake and eat it.

A couple of nights later Patsy was waiting for me at the flagpole as I made my way home from my mammy's and this time he did stay the night and we slept together. This happened two or three times a week for the next couple of months and he kept saying that he loved me and asking me to divorce Robert.

That was easier said than done because over the years I must have tried to divorce Robert dozens of times and it always ended the same way, with him saying he was sorry for the way he treated me and that he wanted us to make a fresh start. I don't know why, but I always fell for that and would put a stop to the divorce proceedings. Maybe it was because every time Robert came back, for the first few weeks he couldn't do enough for me and acted like the model husband. It got so bad that my solicitor told me one day to find another lawyer if I was thinking of divorcing Robert again as he was fed up starting proceedings and then me changing my mind at the last minute.

The more time Patsy was spending in my house the more people began to talk and, as you can imagine, his mother and father were none too enamoured of this state of affairs. One day Patsy was in my house and there was a knock at the door and then the shouting began. 'Open this door, you whore of hell. I know my boy's in there.'

I turned to Patsy: 'That's your mother out there. You'll have to do something, hide somewhere, because I'm going to have to let her in. Can you climb out the back bedroom window and climb down the drainpipe? Quick, before she knocks the door off its hinges.' And that's exactly what Patsy did, shimmied down the drainpipe and disappeared through the back greens.

I knew Mamie would be at her wits' end – her son running around with a married woman and wasting his life when he should have been courting girls of his own age. I also knew that she was ready to give me a doing if she found her boy in my house.

I opened the door. 'I'm going to kill you,' she said. 'You've got my boy in there.'

'In you come, Mrs Smith, but Patsy's not here. Come in, look for yourself.' She wasn't waiting for a second invitation and she pushed me aside and stormed into the house. She went into every room, opened every cupboard and even searched behind the settee.

Robert eventually came back and that was going to be the end of my nights with Patsy. A few days after Robert's return there was a knock at the door and there was Patsy standing there.

'Robert is back,' I said.

'I know. I saw him going to the shops this morning.'

'Please don't start anything.'

'I'm not here to cause you any trouble, Mary. I just want a word with Robert.'

I couldn't believe the bravado of this boy. He walked through to the living room and said to Robert: 'How are you doing? Remember you stayed with my mother and father across the road? Well, I've been helping your wife up and down the road with the weans. What gets into you that you would run away and leave someone who looks like that?'

You could see Robert's hackles rising. 'You cheeky bastard. Who are you to come into my house and talk to me like that?'

'I'm curious why you would leave someone like Mary and I've no idea why she would take you back the way you treat her. And I'll tell you another thing. I'm going to take Mary off you and you can do whatever you like about it. I'll take her off you, sooner or later.'

I stood in the middle of the living room stunned at what was unfolding and I expected Robert to explode with rage and start fighting with Patsy. But I think Robert was just as taken aback as I was at this teenager saying these things.

And Patsy wasn't finished. 'When you've disappeared from her, I've been in and out of the house. And see the next time you are away, I will never be away from this door. And if I see a mark on Mary – you're f******g dead. You're nothing but a big f*****g balloon treating Mary like that. You don't deserve her.'

At that, Patsy marched out of the house and for a minute Robert was speechless. Eventually he turned to me and said: 'What the f**k is he on about – he's been up and down here?'

'That boy's been good to me, buying coal and logs and bringing me groceries when I've been short of money, which is all the time,' I replied.

'And what was he getting in return?'

'Don't you dare talk to me like that,' I replied, hitting straight back. 'What were you getting up to with other women when you were in England?'

'I'm either working or staying in my digs reading.'

'Who are you kidding? If you are that busy working, how come I've never seen any of your wages? And don't give me any of your nonsense about sitting in at night reading books.'

I was in full flow now and I knew it was Patsy's bravado that was giving me the courage to say these things. 'And there's something else you should know. When you've been away I've been going to the dancing at the Burgh Hall. The days of me sitting in waiting months for you to come back are over. When you're here, I'll be your wife and do everything a wife should do. But the next time you go away, don't think I'll be sitting in all day and night waiting for you to make an appearance again. The next time you disappear I'll be going out with whoever I want to and I won't be sneaking up and down closes in the dark – it will be in broad daylight.'

'So you will, with the father you've got.'

'It's got nothing to do with my father. I'm warning you, the next time you're off to England and not sending any money home, back here in Dumbarton you'll be the laughing stock.'

Robert must have got the message because he didn't argue back and didn't storm off in the direction of the bus or train station heading south. In fact, he was desperate to stay and was begging me to take him back.

I was amazed with myself that I had stood up to him like that, especially since I hadn't been feeling too well that morning and was sick. I should have guessed straight away. Any time I've been pregnant I've had morning sickness before I missed a period and that's exactly what was happening now. Sure enough, I did miss my period and I was pregnant with Patsy's child.

After my heroics of standing up to Robert, I was back in a state of panic. What was I going to do? What was my mother going to say? She would know that I had fallen pregnant while Robert was away and that would lead to all kinds of questions and recriminations. Could I get away with trying to pretend the baby was Robert's, because after he came home, we were sleeping together? And when the baby was born, I could say I was a month early giving birth.

I decided that honesty was the best policy and I gambled that if Robert really did want to make a go of our marriage this time, he would look upon the child as his own. When I was sure I was pregnant, I plucked up the courage to tell Robert I was and the father was Patsy Smith. I put on a show of nonchalance even though I was terrified of what Robert might do – and worse, what my parents and family would think. 'Tell my mammy and daddy if you want,' I said. 'I don't care any more.'

But his reply stopped me in my tracks. 'That's OK. I want you back and I'm not going anywhere so long as you stop seeing Patsy Smith, because I'm not going to be made a fool of in this town.'

Give Robert his due, for the whole of that pregnancy he never put a foot wrong and to all intents and purposes Robert was the dad to baby John, who was born on 4 April 1959. For about eighteen months after John was born, Robert stayed the course and we played the dutiful husband and wife. That was the longest he had ever stayed without doing his disappearing act. We also got a bigger council house, this time at 76 Bontine Avenue, at the top of the street where my mammy lived.

I have no doubt my mammy, my father and my brothers and sisters all suspected Patsy was John's father, but since Robert was at home and he was acting as if he was the father, they all chose to say nothing, apart from Tilly, of course. She was a great one for seeing a baby for the first time and saying the boy or girl has this one's face or that one's face. The first time she saw John her words were: 'Where did that child come from?'

'That's John,' I replied.

'I know it's John, but he doesn't look like any of us and he doesn't look like any of the Campbells, so where did he come from?'

My face went red, I looked down at the floor without answering and Frances – who was there at the time – turned away muttering: 'I'm having nothing to do with this.'

My long-time friend Liza Vallance – Patsy's aunt – came to see John and never spoke to me again. For the rest of her life not a word passed between us and she would walk by me in the street. She was obviously disgusted about my relationship with Patsy. After her visit she left with the usual goodbyes and see-you-later chat. However she found out, ignoring me was her way of saying how appalled she was at what had happened.

Robert's stay-at-home period came to an abrupt end the day he bumped into Patsy Smith and they had a fight. The word on the street was that he couldn't get the better of Patsy, so Robert stormed into our house, started an argument accusing me of looking at Patsy and headed off into the sunset again. I reckon Robert was embarrassed at not being able to give Patsy a doing and wasn't going to hang around Dumbarton listening to people talk about that. So that was him in self-imposed exile for another while.

A couple of days after Robert had left, I answered the door to find Patsy standing on the step. That really threw me and I was mortified because he would have had to walk past my mammy's, Granny Boyle's, Frances's and his Aunt Liza's house to get there. He could see how taken aback I was and I told him he shouldn't walk past all these houses because if people saw him they would know exactly where he was going. But he pleaded with me to meet him in the town and I agreed.

We started going out together and we would meet up well away from the street where I stayed and go to the cinema. Eventually I agreed that he could come to the house, but only when it was dark; I still didn't want any of my family to know what was going on. I would have died of shame if my brother Jimmy had found out and said something. I think my brothers and sisters didn't say anything about it in case they upset my mammy.

After a couple of months, a stranger would have thought we were a wee family strolling about together – except in Bontine Avenue, of course – Patsy pushing John in his buggy and Annette and young Robert by my side. This all started one day when I was in a jeweller's in Dumbarton High Street looking at some earrings. When I turned round from the counter I saw Patsy with his face pressed against the shop window, his hand shading his eyes so he could see me inside.

When I saw him I had this feeling that my stomach was starting to do somersaults, but then the fear would kick in about how this was all going to end and I knew Patsy wasn't going to give up. Patsy loved John and I used to kid him on that he was stealing John because he would often take him in his buggy for a walk. He even took John to his mother's house, and to my surprise she took to John very well.

The more Patsy would take John for walks, the more people like Frances and Auntie Alice would say to me that allowing this to happen might not be a good idea as people would start to talk. As if they weren't already doing that. That bothered me, but as far as Patsy was concerned, he didn't care what people said.

I eventually made a stand one Sunday when I was due to go down to the shore to meet up with mammy and the rest of the family. I was with him that morning and when I told him where I was going he said: 'I understand. I know I can't go with you.' As he started to walk away, I decided enough was enough and I wasn't going to hide the fact that I was in love with this boy any more. I don't know if it was the strength that love gave me or if it was because he had done so much for me and my children that I thought I couldn't treat him like that.

'Just come with us, then,' I said. As soon as the words came out of my mouth, I thought 'Oh my God, I'm going to walk down the shore to meet my family with Annette, young Robert and John, and this teenage boy is going to be by my side. What are they going to say?'

As we walked towards Havoc I said to Patsy: 'If my mother says anything, we'll need to go away and probably no one else will talk to you.'

Tilly was up on holiday and she was the first to spot us as we came up behind the family sitting on the shoreline. Tilly said: 'Hello.'

I introduced them to each other: 'This is Patrick Smith – this is my sister Tilly.'

I was about to do the same to Frances, but when I saw the look on her face, I thought better of it. It wasn't as if she drew him a dirty look or said anything; she was just completely ignoring him. My brother George's face was like fizz. He was the type of person who believed that once you marry someone you should stay married whatever happens. But give my brother Willie his due. He chirped up: 'How're you doing, Patsy?'

My mammy was somewhere in between. She didn't have a conversation with Patsy, but when it came to dishing out the dinner, my mammy put out a plate for him. Although she never handed it to him directly, she gave the plate to me saying: 'Pass it over to that young boy.'

I had hoped my mammy would understand how I felt about Patsy and if I was happy with him, she should be happy for me. Sure, Robert was my husband, but he was always away and Patsy treated my children and me really well. He would always make sure there was food in the kitchen cupboards, the children had clothes and he made me happy.

When Robert wasn't around, Patsy would stay two or three nights a week but we never lived together as partners on a permanent basis. And of course, when Robert made a reappearance that would stop and I would go back to being his wife again. And when Robert was away, Patsy was back on the scene.

My family might be turning a blind eye to my relationship with Patsy, but that wasn't the case with some of Patsy's relatives. One of his aunts went to a local priest complaining about me and asked him to make me stop seeing Patsy. That resulted in the priest walking into my house and punching me. And this was one of the times when I wasn't seeing Patsy because Robert was back in the house.

I was in the kitchen at teatime with a friend, Agnes McMartin, making the dinner when the priest walked into the house. This wasn't unusual because in those days no one kept their doors locked during the day and people walked in and out of other people's houses without knocking.

I was in the process of draining the boiling water from a pot of potatoes that had been cooking when, as if from nowhere, the priest was standing by my side. Without saying a word he punched me on one shoulder and then the other. I reeled backwards, spilling the pot of potatoes.

'You're ruining the life of a young man and I've had his aunt down to see me, breaking her heart,' he said. 'You're the scum of the earth. You shouldn't be encouraging a young boy when he should be making a life for himself with a single girl.'

By this time Agnes had grabbed a ladle and was standing up. The priest went to hit me again and Agnes shouted: 'You touch her again and I'll crack this ladle right over your head.' At that the front door opened and Robert walked in and the priest made his way out of the kitchen and into the hallway.

'He's just after hitting Mary,' shouted Agnes.

There was a scuffle in the hallway between Robert and the priest.

'What the f**k do you think you're doing?' shouted Robert.

'She deserves all she got,' the priest replied.

When Patsy found out about the priest hitting me, he took the law into his own hands and waited for him one Monday night after the Girls' Guild. As the priest walked down the avenue leading from the convent, Patsy confronted him and gave him a doing. When I heard about this I thought that the priest was bound to go to the police and Patsy would end up in jail, but the police were never involved. I reckon that was because the priest realised that if he reported Patsy, it would come out – and there was a witness – that he had assaulted me.

This strange state of on–off affairs went on for several years until Patsy had a mental breakdown and ended up in a psychiatric hospital. Through his illness he became violent and ended up being sent to the State Hospital, Carstairs. Of course, Patsy's mother blamed me for her son's illness, and why not? His father also put a 'curse' on me. One day, shortly after Patsy had been sent to Carstairs, I met Patrick Smith in the street and he said: 'Do you know the sunshine of my life has gone away for ever and it's your fault. I hope some day you will see your son where I have seen mine and you'll know how we feel seeing our boy in a mental hospital.' I could only feel guilt for the way things had turned out between Patsy and me.

Years later when my son John was just fifteen, he also had a mental breakdown and I did end up having to see him in a psychiatric hospital, so the 'curse' came true. Of course, I'm not saying what Patrick Smith said caused John's breakdown, but isn't it tragically ironic that Patsy's son suffered the same way he did? I have spoken to my GP about this and she told me that there was more than a 50 per cent chance that John would have inherited the same genes that would lead to him having a breakdown. John still suffers from this illness to this day.

It's fair to say that even after all this time I still feel so much love for Patsy, even although he died a few years ago. I regularly visit his grave at Dumbarton Cemetery. I have no doubt he was the best man I have ever known and as for true love, Patsy was my first and last real true love. Although there were a few impostors in my life along the way.

My Mammy's Gone

My mammy slumps down on to the chair by the fireside, lets out the saddest sigh I have ever heard and says: 'I'm awful weary, Mary. Weary for my Anne and Thomas.'

I'm taken aback by what my mammy has just said. I knew she had lost two of her children before I was born, but it's the first time she has ever spoken to me about them.

'But they're dead,' I say without thinking how unfeeling I was sounding. 'They've been dead for years, Mammy. You shouldn't get yourself worked up about that now.'

She takes a couple of sips from the cup of tea I've just made her and continues. 'Yes, Mary – I know all that, but a mother can get awful weary when she hasn't seen her children for a long time.'

I was in my mid twenties when I had this conversation with my mammy and I wish I'd known then what I know now about the devastating effect losing one of your children has on you. If I had realised, I would have been much more sympathetic and understanding about the torment my mammy must have gone through.

'Why are you upsetting yourself about all this now?' I asked her. 'You haven't mentioned feeling like this before. Anyway you've got all of us, all your other children.'

'I know, but you could have a hundred children and still feel the same about the ones you've lost,' she replied. 'I'll never forget my Thomas – he was beautiful. He had lovely blue eyes and blond, blond hair. He followed me everywhere. And Annie was a beautiful wee baby born with red curly hair. She was like a wee cherub, a wee angel . . . and then they were taken away from me.'

Every day on her way home from her food shopping, Mammy would come to visit me laden with two bags of groceries. She always brought me a big gingerbread cake or an icing cake and a string of lollipops for the children. I would settle her down by the coal fire and make her a cup of tea. I was about five months pregnant with Gordon the day she revealed to me her sadness about the two children she'd lost.

It was quite unnerving that Thursday afternoon as I hadn't heard talk like this before. Granny Boyle had told me about Thomas, who had contracted scarlet fever when he was coming up for four and then tragically passed it on to his sister of ten weeks. Both Thomas and Annie died of that dreadful disease in the same week. Granny Boyle's eyes filled with tears and she told me about the two tiny white coffins in our house before they were laid to rest.

The following day, Friday, Frances came to see me and said the doctor had been called in to see my mammy as her 'nerves were bad'. She added that the priest was also coming in to see my mammy to give her the Last Rites.

'But you only get the Last Rites when you're about to die,' I said. 'What is my mammy getting the Last Rites for if it's her nerves that are bad?'

'No, sometimes they do that to make people feel better and it helps them get better quicker,' Frances replied.

'Aye well, maybe that's right enough.'

Frances knew I would believe anything she said if she made it sound convincing enough. And naïvely I did believe her, though the reality was a lot different. My mammy had suffered a heart attack and was in a bad way. The doctor feared the worst and had suggested that Tilly and Jimmy, who were both living in England, should come home straightaway. But because I was five months pregnant, the family didn't want to risk me having a miscarriage, so they decided they would say she had nervous exhaustion and not tell me the truth until they really had to.

In those days, when someone in a Catholic household was seriously ill the priest would come in every day and say prayers. When the priest came to the door a member of the family would meet him with a lit candle and lead him to where the sick person was so he could give them Communion. Not a word was spoken when the priest was being led to the sick bed as he was supposed to be carrying the Host in his pocket and bringing the Lord into the house.

Frances told me I was to carry out the task of meeting the priest at the door early on Saturday morning and, oblivious to what was really going on, I was there at 6 a.m. to do my duty leading the priest to my mother.

Everyone else was waiting in the kitchen as I was standing in the hallway holding the lit candle waiting for the priest to arrive. There was a knock on the door and I opened it. Standing there in front of me was the same priest who had punched me and who Patsy had given a doing.

He stared at me and said: 'Get out of my sight.' The priest just stood on the doorstep, refusing to come into the house.

I had been well warned not to utter a word when the priest came and I just thought, 'My father will kill me if the priest refuses to come into the house to see my mammy because I am here.'

I walked back up the hall and into the kitchen and my brother Willie whispered: 'What's going on?'

'The priest won't come into the house and he says I've to get out of his sight.'

Willie grabbed the candle from me and went to the door to get the priest. The others shuffled into my mammy's bedroom, but I was told to stay in the kitchen. I sat down on a chair behind the door and I noticed there was a pot of boiling water on the cooker with a syringe in it being sterilised.

After a while, I heard our family GP, Dr Pollachi's voice coming from my mammy's bedroom asking her where the pain was worst. I heard my mammy's voice – as strong as it ever was – say the pain was in her back. Because my mother's voice was so unfaltering, I thought she couldn't be that ill and the syringe in the pot would be for a painkilling injection. But then the penny began to drop. 'Why is everyone here at this time of the morning and my mother getting the Last Rites if she's just got nervous exhaustion?' I asked myself.

Just then Dr Pollachi came into the kitchen, but because I was sitting behind the door, he didn't see me. He went over to the cooker, turned the gas off, but just left the syringe in the pot. He leaned his elbow on the cooker and sobbed quietly.

I had to say something. 'Are you all right, Doctor?'

'Ah, so you're the girl having the baby. Do you know your mother's gone?'

'No, is she going to the hospital?'

Doctor Pollachi hesitated and squeezed the top of his nose with his thumb and forefinger. He must have been embarrassed when he realised that I had seen him crying. His next problem was how to break it to me that my mammy had died after I had been told she just had nervous exhaustion.

'No, Mary,' he said in a soft voice. 'Your mother's passed away. She had a very serious heart attack on Thursday night and another one today. She hasn't survived the second heart attack. I'm sorry.'

I was speechless and I marched out of the kitchen and up the hall towards the front door. Frances's husband, Davie, saw me and pulled me back. 'Where are you going?' he asked.

'I'm getting out of here because you lot told me lies about my mammy. You said her nerves were bothering her and the doctor's just told me she'd had a heart attack.'

God love him, for Davie took me aside and said: 'Listen, Mary, this is the kind of day that if you could offer five years off your own life for it not to happen you would do that. And maybe if we had all done that she would have been here for a lot longer. I'll miss your mother something terrible, so come back in and don't do anything silly like walk out of the house in the state you're in.'

'But I should have been told – everybody else must have known.'

'They were scared you would have a miscarriage and the doctor agreed.'

I still think I should have been told, because I would have spent even more time by my mammy's bedside if I had known she'd had a heart attack. But Davie managed to calm me down and I went into the living room with him to be with other members of the family who were also in there.

It was while I was in the living room that I remembered what my mammy had said about Thomas and Annie and being weary for them. I was in shock, but I also felt a wave of self-pity come over me. I'm ashamed to say in that moment of extreme grief I had some very selfish thoughts. At that very point, I resented my poor dead brother and sister and I was saying to myself: 'Those rotten swines. They'll have my mammy now forever and we're left without her. Here's me pregnant and my mammy's gone. What am I going to do without my mammy?'

By this time all the boys in the family had arrived at the house and they were screaming in anguish. They adored their mother and it was frightening to hear these grown men weep and wail so loudly. But such was their love for my mammy it was completely understandable. The next thing Frances – who was with my mammy when she died – came into the living room and told me to go into the bedroom and see her. 'I can't. I'm frightened and I don't want to see any dead person and certainly not my . . .'

Before I could finish the sentence Frances gave me a slap across the face. 'Your mother never did you any harm when she was alive, so she's certainly not going to do you any harm in death. Get into that bedroom and don't dare say you don't want to see our mother.'

I was literally dragged into the room, petrified out of my wits, and when I got into the bedroom I held my eyes shut tight. Frances was wise to this one and she ordered: 'Open your eyes and don't be so stupid.'

I looked at my mother lying on the bed with her head on the pillow just where she had died. It was as if she had just fallen asleep, but there was a difference. My mammy looked as if she was eighteen – just like a teenage lassie with her jet-black hair and although she was sixty she had the loveliest face.

As I have said before, it wasn't just my mammy who died that day, Saturday, 30 September 1961 – it was like my father had died as well. All the life seemed to drain out of him. After my mammy's funeral he changed completely. The bawling and shouting stopped, nobody got a row any more and he even stopped shaking his newspaper if someone was talking and he got annoyed because they had disturbed his reading.

My son Gordon was born soon after, on 28 February 1962, and for the first time, my father came to visit me at my own home. He hadn't put a foot inside any of my homes before my mother died and I got the shock of my life when I answered the door one day to find my father standing there. 'I've just come to see the baby,' he said.

From then on my father would visit me every day and just sit on the couch with Gordon in his Moses basket beside him, talking to the baby. My mammy's maiden name was Gordon and my father said: 'That's what she always wanted – a grandson called Gordon. Just a pity she's not here to see him and give him a cuddle.' Even when I had visitors, my father would just sit on the couch making those daft noises adults make to babies while Gordon lay gurgling in his Moses basket.

I felt very uncomfortable with my father sitting there just talking to Gordon and hardly saying a word to me. I found it difficult to strike up a conversation with him after all those years of only speaking when I was spoken to in his company and the terrible experiences I had suffered at his hands. I didn't know what to say to him – my own father.

The embarrassing silences got so bad that I even asked a friend of mine who stayed nearby, May Barnes, to watch for my father coming out of Frances's house where he – and Alana – were now living and then she would rush round to my house and sit and chat to him.

My mother's tragic loss of her two young children was sadly mirrored in my own life later that year, in November 1962 and again in July 1967, when I lost two babies after I had given birth.

The first time I lost a baby I only had about seven weeks to go and I started to feel pains in my stomach. The pain didn't last long and I put it down to a sign of going into an early labour, although I had never been early with any of my previous children. We sent for Dr Margaret McLean, who came to the house to examine me. She said there was nothing to worry about, but if the pain came back I was to call her immediately.

Sure enough, later that night the pains returned and Robert again walked down to the public phone box at the bottom of the road – we didn't have a phone in the house then – to call Dr McLean. This time she told Robert I was to get ready to go into hospital.

When I got to the hospital I was given a thorough examination and they said they could hear the baby's heartbeat using the Pinard stethoscope, which was better known as an ear trumpet. By this time I had definitely gone into labour and I eventually gave birth. I knew immediately something was wrong because I overheard the midwife, Sister McNab, saying to her colleagues: 'I think we've lost the baby.' She handed me the baby to hold and asked: 'It's a wee boy – do you have a name for the baby? We're going to christen him now because his heartbeat is very faint.'

'I'm going to call him David,' I said.

Then I heard Sister McNab saying: 'I christen you David, in the name of the Father, the Son and the Holy Ghost.'

I was panicking when I saw the sister walk away with the baby, but I was beginning to feel the effects of the injection they had given me. I remember asking if I could see the baby before everything went blank and I fell unconscious. I felt completely empty when I woke up and they told me baby David had died – he had only lived a few minutes. I still sit and wonder sometimes what it would have been like having another son and on his birthday – 30 November – I think about who he would have looked like and what he would be doing today.

The second time I lost a baby was when I next fell pregnant, almost five years later. I was seven months gone when I felt a cold sensation in my stomach, I couldn't feel the baby moving and I started losing weight rather than putting weight on. I asked a doctor several times about this, but was told it was probably a 'lazy baby' and that some women lose weight during pregnancy. After several weeks feeling like this, yet another call was made to my GP's practice and one of the doctors came to give me an internal examination. A few minutes later, the doctor literally ran out of the bedroom and bumped into Robert who was in the hall. 'I can't find the baby's head,' the doctor said frantically. 'I'll need to get Mrs Campbell to the hospital.'

I was examined in the hospital when I was given the horrific news that I had feared all along – my baby was dead. I was going to be operated on and before going into theatre, I was asked if I had chosen any names for a boy or a girl. By the time I woke up again they had delivered a baby girl and had christened her Tracy – the name I had said I wanted if it was a girl.

I felt a mixture of intense emotions – anger, hurt and grief that no one had listened to me when I had complained all those weeks ago and I had carried a dead baby in my stomach all that time. Once again, when wee Tracy's birthday comes around I can only think about what might have been.

The Sixties were a really bad time for me. As well as my mammy dying and losing babies David and Tracy, I suffered a condition that would haunt me for nine years. I had agoraphobia and at the same time lost an incredible amount of weight. At my lowest ebb I weighed only six stone. I can vividly recall the exact moment that terrible affliction came into my life.

It was June 1960 and I was in the Woolworths store in Dumbarton High Street with Annette and young Robert, buying a bag of nails, when I was suddenly and inexplicably overcome with a horrible feeling of desperation to be in my own house. I couldn't understand what was happening to me, but all I knew was this overpowering urge to get back to my house.

The shop assistant was about to hand me the nails in their brown bag, and my change. But I was so totally overcome with fear, I turned on my heels and dashed out of the shop, dragging my two children and bumping into other shoppers on my way out. I can't explain it – all I knew was that I had to get out of that shop. 'Wait a minute,' shouted the assistant. 'What about your nails and your change?' I didn't care about that, as nothing in the world mattered more than getting out of the shop. It was as if I was running for cover.

I was in a panic and I stood for a few seconds at the bus stop outside Woolworths. I looked down the High Street, but there was no bus in sight. I grabbed the children's hands and ran to the next bus stop. Same again, a look down the road and still no bus, so it was another demented dash to the next bus stop. By the time I'd done this four or five times I was more than halfway home and I decided to run the rest of the way, dragging the children and a couple of shopping bags behind me. I ran and ran and ran, heavily panting and out of breath, but too afraid to stop until I was at my front door. My hand was shaking as I struggled to get the key in the lock, but eventually I got the door open and was inside.

After an hour or so, I'd calmed down and I tried to go back outside and head for the small ironmonger's in the housing scheme's row of shops. But as soon as I got into the shop and saw I'd have to wait in a queue, I was engulfed by fear again, which only subsided when I was surrounded by my own four walls and the doors were tightly closed. I realised I was terrified to go outside, and it was like being in jail. Why was this happening to me?

When Robert came home I tried to explain what had happened, but he didn't understand and told me not to be so stupid and to get grip of myself. As the days went by, he thought I was going off my head – a common reaction among my family and friends who didn't know or understand agoraphobia.

Ironically, one of our closest friends, Peter McMartin, was particularly scathing of me until years later he suffered the same condition and apologised for not being more sympathetic. At the time when I had agoraphobia, Peter's reaction was typical: 'What have you been up to, Mary, that you don't want to be seen outside?' he would say. 'This whole thing must be an act – it's ridiculous. How can someone like you not want to go outside? You used to be Mrs Never-In – just open the door and walk outside and stop all this nonsense.'

The days trapped like a prisoner in my own home turned

into months and the months into years and still no one really understood how I felt. I was just an oddity to them all as agoraphobia wasn't as accepted a condition then as it is today. I'm sure everyone thought I was going mad and were sceptical when I tried to explain what was going on inside my head. Everyone apart from Tilly, who had some insight into the condition as she had had a similar experience for a short time after one of her children was born. She was quite supportive towards me any time she would be up on holiday.

Of course, all this time Robert would be going AWOL down south on a regular basis, leaving me with the children, coming back after a month or so until the next time we fell out and he'd be off again.

If it hadn't been for a couple of close pals, Agnes Hamill and May Barnes, I don't know how I would have coped bringing up a family and not being able to go outside. Agnes and May spent half their lives in my house and the other half in their own. They would make sure the shopping was done and the kids were taken places that I was too scared to go to, whether it was to the doctor's, a hospital appointment or the school or even on holiday. My daughter, Annette, was another great help during these dark days, always willing to help out with the household chores and going to the shops for me.

During those years I really missed the social life I used to have before I had agoraphobia. I was in my late twenties, watching the best years of life passing by, and me stuck in my house. I literally was a prisoner in my own home and I thought this terrible affliction was going to last forever.

At my worst times with the agoraphobia I couldn't even look out of the window, as I felt such a terror at the prospect of being outside. If anyone came to the door and I was in the house by myself I couldn't even go to let them in, as that would have meant I would see the dreaded outside world.

I was ashamed of myself. I had gone from being an outgoing person who just loved getting out and about to someone who couldn't even go to her own sons' First Communion. That's right, I was so terrified of being outside, I even missed what is for Catholics one of the most important days in a child's life. My sister Frances stood in for me and became their mother figure during young Robert, John and Gordon's First Communion celebrations in chapel. I was ashamed and I hated myself for being that way.

I also felt great shame – and still do to this day – of not being able to attend my beloved mammy's funeral because of the agoraphobia. Robert and my brother Willie had taken me the few yards from my own home to my mammy's house in the darkness with a shawl over my head shortly before she died. Although I stayed at my mammy's house for three days until after her funeral, I was too terrified to go outside – especially in daylight. People wondered what on earth was wrong with me that I wasn't going to the funeral, as there wasn't the same understanding about agoraphobia in those days. It is one of my biggest regrets that I never got to my mammy's funeral.

Although Gordon was a home confinement, when it came to being taken into hospital to have my babies David and Tracy, it was a case of carrying me out of the door into a waiting ambulance, and such was the panic at the time, it blunted my fear of going outside.

At one point during my years suffering from agoraphobia, a specialist, Dr Slorach, suggested it might help if I moved out of the house I was living in and where I had been when the traumas of my mother dying and the loss of baby David had happened. He said I should move to the other side of town, away from where I had a constant reminder of these tragedies. So in 1963 he organised with the council that I should get a move to 56 Whiteford Avenue, in the Bellsmyre housing scheme in Dumbarton.

But extreme measures had to be taken to make sure I would be able to leave my house without having a major panic attack. All our furniture was moved out of the house during the day and taken to our new home, and at midnight when it was pitch black I had a shawl wrapped round my head and shoulders so I couldn't see anything and I was led and half-carried out of my house into my brother Willie's car for the drive across town to Bellsmyre. We went through the same rigmarole a few years later when we moved to a bigger house in Carman View, which was not far from Whiteford Avenue.

All through my agoraphobia ordeal, Dr McLean was a tremendous help and support, coming to see me almost every day and trying to talk me into going out into the garden. But I just couldn't bring myself to do that. I was desperate to go outside like any normal mum, but when it came to the point of stepping through the door, it was like an invisible wall had been built in front of me and I couldn't get through it. Even although I was trapped in my house, I still got smartly dressed and wore make-up every day, trying to make the best of myself as if things were normal, hoping and praying that today would be the day my nightmare ended.

And one sunny day in August 1969 my ordeal did end – just as quickly and unexpectedly as it had begun.

It was the middle of the afternoon and a sudden urge came over me to go outside. I waited a few minutes to see if I was just imagining it. When the need to go outside didn't disappear, I walked along the hall, opened the front door and looked down the street. I knew the fear of going outside had gone – but would it stay gone? The apprehension I felt now was that if I went any further the terror would come back and I would have to rush back inside the house.

I wasn't going to take that chance, so I closed the door and went back into the living room. I paced up and down the room as the urge to go outside built and built. What was I going to do? What if this was only going to last a few minutes and when I was halfway down the street I panicked?

I made a plan to go down to the local shops and back again. But what if I had to stand in a queue and the fear came back and I had to run away? I was also very aware that people living in the scheme wouldn't have seen me for years and they would probably stare at me. After all, I was the strange woman who never went out. That would make me nervous. But the pride and vanity I had within me spurred me on. I would give them all the shock of their lives. I was wearing an orange mini skirt and a white top that day and I grabbed a pair of sunglasses to hide my face. My mission – to buy a stamp from the local Post Office.

So, with a couple of shillings tightly clasped in my hand I walked out of the door, shut it behind me and walked down the street to the Post Office. The shop was empty when I walked in and the owner, George Sloss, had a puzzled look on his face when saw me. 'I don't think I've seen you before – are you Mrs Campbell?' he asked.

'Yes.'

'I've had this shop for a few years now and I've heard people talk about you, but I've never actually seen you myself. How are you?'

'Fine, thanks.'

'What can I get you?'

'Can I have a first-class stamp, please?'

I felt no fear. I felt no panic. I just felt fantastic. Victory in the face of adversity! As I walked back up the road I could see people looking at me. I must have been like a freak to them. 'That's the woman who never comes out. I always wondered what she looked like,' they would be saying to each other.

As soon as I got home I phoned Agnes and told her what I

had done. She was delighted and came straight round to see me. That night we did a tour of all my pals' houses and Agnes would walk in first and say: 'Wait till you see the surprise I've got for you.' Then I'd step into the room with a huge grin on my face to congratulatory hugs and kisses from them all.

That part of my life truly was a nightmare. It was a part of my life stolen from me by that terrible condition that is agoraphobia. It is a most horrible thing to happen to anyone and when I hear about people suffering from it today, I still get a shiver down my spine.

Linda Lusardi – Eat Your Heart Out!

I'm sitting in the living room with a friend chatting about this and that in between the cups of tea and biscuits. We're coming away with all the usual moans and groans about coping with a family growing up, gossiping about who's doing what with who among the neighbours and even what's on the telly that night.

Inevitably, the topic of conversation comes round to money – or, to be more precise, the lack of it. We swap tales of bills so heavy coming through the letterbox, you can hear the thud as they hit the floor.

'My Robert's away again,' I tell her. 'And I don't know how I'm going to pay for all the children's Christmas presents.'

'I know how hard it is with a big family and they always want what they've last seen on the television,' she says. 'Why don't you put on a black dress and a sad face and tell the weans Santa's died!'

We have a good laugh at that one and I say: 'I could give our Gordon an empty box and tell him it's an Action Man deserter!' More laughter.

'If you didn't laugh you'd cry about how tight money is just now,' I tell her.

Then, from completely out of nowhere, she asks: 'Here, Mary – how's your bust?'

'What's my bust got to do with not having any money?' I reply.

'I know you're really short of cash just now – and I want you to know I don't do this myself – but there's a pal of mine who gets paid to pose topless for a photographer.'

It takes me a few seconds to realise exactly what she's suggesting to me.

'You're joking. Are you serious? No, you can't be serious – me pose topless? Oh my God, I'd die of embarrassment.'

'No, it's OK. Nothing goes on – you just take your top off, sit on a couch and he takes photographs,' she explains. 'You wouldn't believe who does that around here for the wee guy who takes the pictures. Anyway, you've probably seen him around – he just lives a few streets away. It's Eddie Cotogno, the old Polish man who stays in Vale-view Terrace.'

I was stunned that she would come out with something like that. 'God forgive you – imagine even suggesting something like that. And anyway, I've had several kids and stretch marks all over my stomach. Who would want to take a picture of me in that state?'

'But you've got great legs, Mary. And a beautiful face, but what like's your bust?' she asks again.

'I think they're all right.'

'Show me them then,' she says. 'And I'll tell you if you could be a topless model.'

'Away you and raffle yourself,' I tell her. 'There's no way I'm showing you my boobs.'

'Go on – don't be such a prude. You've got one of those see-through chiffon scarves. Take your bra off and let's see what they're like through the scarf.'

'What if somebody comes in and sees us – they'll think we're a couple of perverts.'

'We'll lock the front and back door, close the curtains and nobody will be any the wiser.'

So that's what we did and I went upstairs to find the chiffon scarf and to take my top and bra off. I wrapped the scarf around my neck and draped it over my chest. When I walked down the stairs and into the living room, my friend looked at me and said: 'Oh, Mary – they're crackers.

For someone who's had all those kids, you've got some body.'

'Do you really think so?'

'See if you had the courage, I know you could make money out of this. My pal gets £15 to get her photographs taken topless and her boobs are nowhere near as good as yours.'

If the truth be told, deep inside I was quite flattered by the suggestion that someone thought I could be a model – topless or otherwise. And, of course, it would appeal to my vanity. The extra money wouldn't go wrong either – especially as Robert was off on one of his jaunts, not sending any money home, and I had to feed and clothe the children on Social Security handouts.

Although part of me was maybe starting to warm to the idea, I still told my friend: 'I couldn't do it – I'd be too scared. What if he is a dirty wee swine and tried to have sex with me? But what if you came with me?'

'No he doesn't allow that. He doesn't want lots of women trekking up the stairs to his door – you'd have to go yourself. Anyway, my pal has been going up to his house to get photographed for a long time and there's never been a problem with him.'

It was 1970 at the time and I was thirty-five. Although the *Sun* newspaper had that year started to publish topless photographs on Page 3, there would still have been a scandal if people found out what was going on with women posing for photographs like that in a council estate in Dumbarton.

In those days I like to think I was still quite attractive and had a reasonable body, with 36C boobs. But I told my pal that I couldn't go through with it even though I was desperate for some extra income.

Over the next week my friend mentioned several times the idea of me making some extra cash posing topless and encouraged me to give it a go. Eventually, the lure of money – and perhaps the thought that someone wanted to photograph me just like those Page 3 girls – overcame my fears and I said yes. She contacted her friend who knew Eddie Cotogno and the arrangements were made for me to visit him for my first topless photographic session.

I was told I had to go round to the photographer's house at night when it was dark so there was less chance of people seeing me. It was the worst journey of my life so far and the butterflies in my stomach were doing somersaults. I kept looking all around me imagining every curtain in every house in the street was twitching with people staring out at me saying: 'There's that Mary Campbell going to take her clothes off and get her picture taken topless.' Of course this was nonsense and I was just another woman walking down the road.

My friend had come round to my house to babysit the children. Before I left I told her: 'If I'm not back in an hour get on the phone to the police.' So that was me, desperate to earn some money for the family, but always the coward and scared out of my wits about doing the photographs.

Eddie Cotogno's flat was on the top floor of the tenement and with every step I took on the stairs to the third floor, the more nervous I got. When I got to his front door, I hesitated. My finger on the doorbell, my heart pounding and my mind racing, I plucked up the courage and pressed the bell.

I held my breath as I heard footsteps coming up the hallway inside the house and the door opened. Standing in front of me was a wee, balding, fat man with what was left of his hair a grey colour. Seeing him for the first time you would never believe that he would be the type of man to take photographs of semi-naked women, and he didn't look the creepy type at all. He was originally from Poland, spoke broken English and still had his Polish accent. 'Just come in,' he said. And as I walked up the hallway he added: 'I hope you don't feel uncomfortable because I'm not going to do anything untoward. All you're here for is to get your photograph taken.'

He showed me into a room off the hallway that he had turned into a photographic studio. There was a camera on a tripod facing a couch and a few nice chairs. The one I noticed in particular was a nice wee pink basket chair.

On the wall behind the chairs there was a big red velvet curtain hanging on the wall that was used as a background to the photographs. He also had lots of lights – like you would see at the dancing on the walls – and there were lots of different pieces of material lying around.

After a few seconds he pointed to another room across the hall and said I could go in there and strip to the waist. When I came back into his studio room he asked me to sit on one of the chairs he had draped a piece of material over.

He seemed to know what he was doing in terms of taking photographs because he would ask me to turn slightly for a pose then another way for another pose, move my hand this way or my head another way. 'Hold it there for a moment – yes that's great. That's a lovely photograph,' he would say.

I was still a bag of nerves, especially when I wasn't posing the way he wanted and he would say: 'If I can just come over and move your hand to where I want it to go.' When he came over and moved my arm I thought to myself: 'This is it. This is when he's going to jump on top of me and try to have his way with me.'

But he obviously recognised my trepidation because he would say: 'Try to calm down. This is just a profession to me and I see this kind of thing all the time.'

He was actually a perfect gentleman and acted in a very professional manner. He never said or did anything that could be remotely described as dirty, suggestive or threatening. I was actually just frightening myself that first night.

After about an hour of him taking photographs, he said that was the session done and he gave me my £15 and asked if I would come back for more photographs later that week because he said I was very good and photographed very well.

Over the next few months I visited Eddie Cotogno's to have my photograph taken topless about twenty times. After the first few visits I was quite relaxed about the whole thing because he never suggested going any further by asking me to pose completely naked and, of course, the money came in very handy.

The third time I had my pictures taken, Eddie Cotogno asked me if I would like some colour proofs of my photographs to take away with me. I was desperate to accept his offer, but trying to act all businesslike I said no thanks. However, the next time I was there he offered me photographs again and this time I accepted.

I had long hair at the time and one of the weeks I went to his house for a photographic session, I told him I was thinking about getting my hair cut short.

'Please don't do that,' he said. 'Men like long hair as well as big boobs.'

At one point Eddie Cotogno asked if I would like to pose nude, but I said no as I wouldn't have gone that far. Anyway, after having so many children the bottom part was certainly not as good as the top part. He accepted that and never raised the subject again.

My topless 'modelling' career came to an abrupt end when my husband Robert came back to the house after yet another disappearing act, wheedled his way back into my affections and I took him back in.

If the truth be told, I was really chuffed that someone would think I was attractive enough to take photographs of me. But on the other hand I was still petrified that people would find out. I kept the pictures Eddie Cotogno had given me in a brown envelope and hid them at the bottom of the airing cupboard. It was years later I decided to look them out and when I went to the cupboard they were gone. I can only surmise that Robert had found them and ripped them up.

I had never met Eddie Cotogno before I went for the photography sessions, although I had seen him walking about the housing scheme from time to time. He turned out to be a widower who went to church every week, was always well dressed, wore a bunnet like all the men of his age in those days and looked every inch a pillar of the community. Who would have guessed what went on behind the closed doors of his tenement flat at night, taking photographs of semi-naked women and the ones that were willing to pose completely starkers?

The other thing that intrigued me about his photographic studio was that there were also hundreds of books piled high against the walls. I never asked him why he had so many books. But nine years later, when my topless photograph sessions came back to haunt me, I found out then what the books were used for.

It was the summer of 1979 and one day I was flicking through a newspaper when I saw a photograph of someone I recognised. It was Eddie Cotogno and the story was about how he had been murdered.

'God rest his soul,' I thought. 'That's the wee man who took those pictures of me. That's a terrible thing to happen to him.' But that wasn't the end of it – oh no, not by a long chalk. The following night I was watching the teatime news on television and Eddie Cotogno's picture flashed up on the screen. And what I heard from the newsreader made me almost die of shock. He said police had revealed that Mr Cotogno had been taking semi-nude and nude photographs of local women in the Dumbarton area, and his next few words made me feel even worse.

'Police confirmed they had visited a whisky bond in Dumbarton to interview some females about these photographs,' the newsreader said. 'And they are urging other women who had their photographs taken by the murder victim to come forward and be interviewed by officers investigating the crime. Anyone who does come forward will be treated in the strictest confidence.'

The newsreader went on to say that police had found photographs of the women who had posed for Mr Cotogno and they wanted to interview each of them. Those who didn't volunteer to come forward would be traced and police would visit them in their homes or at work.

Robert was back living with me at the time and I said to myself: 'Oh Jesus, Mary and Joseph – what am I going to do?'

When I first read about the murder I didn't think for a moment I would become embroiled in the investigation. As well as my husband finding out about my topless modelling escapade, I was terrified about my older brothers and sisters finding out. I thought I would have to leave town to avoid embarrassing all my family, but I hadn't a clue where I was going to go. I was getting hysterical.

After a few hours I began to calm down and I replayed in my mind what the newsreader had said. I got some courage from the line about the police treating everything in confidence, so I decided I would grasp the nettle and go to the police station. The next day I made the excuse I was going to visit my Auntie Alice, arranged to have a neighbour babysit the children and I walked to the police station. With every step closer to the police headquarters, the more embarrassment I felt. By this time Gordon was seventeen and had got himself into trouble with the police on more than a few occasions. So the police would know exactly who I was and no doubt have a good laugh at my expense.

I walked through the police station doors and up to the

desk. 'Can I help you?' said the police officer on duty, Sergeant Ian Carmichael.

'I wonder if I could see someone about Mr Cotogno.'

He just looked at me with a smirk on his face and I just knew he was loving every second of watching me squirm with embarrassment.

'Right, if you'd just hold on for a minute, I'll get someone to see you.'

It got worse when I saw the detective who came out to see me. It was PC David Cosh, who had been in our house several times about Gordon and was always on my case about his shenanigans.

'Now what was it you want to see us about? Mr Cotogno – what can you tell us about him?' he asked.

I knew that, as a uniform constable, he wouldn't be in charge of the murder investigation and I suspect he had deliberately come out to see me because of his dealings with Gordon. They were really going to milk it for all they could.

'I saw on the television that the police wanted to speak to anyone who knew Mr Cotogno,' I said.

'Well, do you know something?'

'I'd rather speak to someone who is involved in the investigation.'

I'd never seen policemen with such big smiles on their faces that day as I was led to an interview room. If I thought the embarrassment couldn't get any worse, I couldn't have been any more mistaken. There was a huge table in the middle of the room completely covered with neat piles of photographs of nude and semi-naked women they had found in Eddie Cotogno's flat – and mine was right at the top.

Detective Inspector Angus McLeod and another detective I didn't know were there and the DI started asking me questions. Did anyone else come to the house while I was there? Did I see anyone I didn't recognise going in or out of the tenement close while I was visiting Mr Cotogno? Did I ever hear any telephone conversations while I was in his house?

I couldn't tell them anything because I hadn't seen or heard anything they were asking about. I've no doubt that when they knew I had come in to the station they had put my photograph on the top to put a wee bit more pressure on me to co-operate with them.

I looked at the photographs and was really embarrassed. But then there was a wee chirpy part to it when I saw some of the other women in the photographs and thought I was much better-looking than them. 'Imagine her having the cheek to pose topless,' I said to myself.

I suppose that was the wee vain bit coming out in me – despite the shame I felt at being questioned by policemen about the topless photographs, for a fleeting second, I was still comparing myself to the other women and thinking: 'I can't be too bad-looking, after all.'

After they were finished asking me questions, DI McLeod lifted up the photograph of me and said: 'That's good of you coming in. If you hadn't come in we'd have been up at your door tomorrow because this is obviously you in the photograph.'

I then said the daftest thing. 'I'm sorry about that.' And the other detective had a wee smile on his face. 'Aye, because you got caught,' he was probably thinking.

I was so relieved when I was told that was the end of the interview, they didn't need to speak to me again and all I had to do was sign a piece of paper confirming I had been interviewed by the detectives. Unfortunately, they kept my topless photographs.

Over the following days and weeks more information about Eddie Cotogno's murder and lifestyle began to come out in the news and that's when I discovered what he did with the nude photographs he took and why he had such a huge collection of books.

When I was doing the photo sessions I thought they were just for him and maybe a few of his pals to get a cheap thrill from looking at them. But what he was really doing was placing pictures in between pages of the books and selling the books from a stall at the famous Barras Market in Glasgow at the weekend. He had been running a second-hand book-stall, but his customers wouldn't be buying the books for the literary content – they would be buying them for the nude photographs of women hidden inside the pages!

Apparently, Eddie Cotogno had been bludgeoned to death, put on top of his bed and his killer or killers had tried to set fire to the body. The only lead the police had was that a taxi driver said he had dropped two strangers off near to Eddie Cotogno's flat. To this day, his killers haven't been caught and when Angus McLeod retired years later, he told the newspapers that his only regret was not catching Eddie Cotogno's killers.

By today's standards, posing topless is nothing and people hardly bat an eyelid when they see topless pictures in the tabloid newspapers. But in the late Sixties and early Seventies there was still an element of disgust and tut-tutting at these type of photographs. As a mother, you want to give your children the best. But if you don't have the money to do that, you'll do anything you can to get that money to give your kids a better life.

My only surviving brother George and his wife Jean don't know about my topless photographic career. I love my brother and sister-in-law very much and although George is a bit strait-laced, I hope he understands why I did it and we will remain as close as ever. Jean is very quiet and unassuming, but I am sure she will be understanding. She knows my life was hard and has been shocked to learn some of the things I had to endure in my life. So, here's hoping my little haven that is George and Jean's home will still hold a welcome for me when they read this book.

By doing the topless photographs I was earning some extra cash for my family and at the same time I wasn't doing any harm to myself or anyone else for that matter. If someone wants to pay money to look at a photograph of the top half of my body – then, so what? For hundreds of years, some of the world's most famous artists painted nude women. And today in art schools up and down the country, models are posing nude for artists to paint. Anyway, if Linda Lusardi, Sam Fox and all the other Page 3 girls can get away with it, so can I. The only worry I have is that somewhere in a police evidence vault there are pictures of me topless. Oh my God – what if somebody sees them!

My Gangster Lover

We've been sitting in the hotel restaurant for a couple of hours, having dinner and chatting away quite the thing. It's the first time he has asked me out and my date is the perfect gentleman, politeness personified, making sure everything is to my liking. The meal at the former Silver Thread Hotel in Paisley is lovely, he makes sure I always have a drink – although it's just soda water and lime – and for the first time in ages I'm relaxed and having a good time.

Completely out of the blue the subject of conversation changes and he announces: 'I've booked a room for us to go upstairs for the night.'

I'm completely taken aback. I'm thinking this is only a date for dinner, a few drinks and some pleasant conversation – an escape from the drudgery and dreariness of my life looking after a family on Social Security handouts while my husband did another of his disappearing acts.

Suddenly, it dawns on me exactly what he is planning for the rest of the night. But I hardly know the man and this is not how I had imagined the night would end. I'm not prepared to go to a hotel room with someone who is almost a stranger and I don't really know what he's like.

'No, no, not me. I'm definitely not going upstairs with you,' I blurt out.

Just as the final words have left my lips, I feel an almighty crack across my face and it's as if my jaw is going to explode. I don't know if he's punched or slapped me, but whatever it is has been delivered with a huge amount of force and I'm dazed and in agony.

Just as quickly as he has hit me he is apologising, pulling a handkerchief from his pocket and wiping my mouth and the side of my face.

'I'm sorry,' he says. 'I'm really sorry.' I can see the anger in his face melt away as he speaks.

'Look, I'm well known around here and I can't be made to look a fool. If I book a room for me and someone else, they don't walk out the door and leave me looking stupid.'

I am absolutely terrified and I stammer my excuses: 'I don't do that sort of thing . . . I've got to get back to Dumbarton for eleven o'clock . . .' But I can see that isn't going to wash with him.

'Listen, Mary,' he says in a quiet but determined tone. 'Forget about all that. I know you don't normally do things like this – I wouldn't have fancied you if I thought you did. But I'm telling you now, you're not walking out that door. Even if you go upstairs and spend all night sitting on the side of the bed and don't say a word to me, that's fine. But you're not walking out that door until the morning. I can't afford to have anyone making a fool out of me.'

'I never thought it was going to be like this,' I say.

'Well, I'm sorry you weren't wise enough to realise that when I asked you on a night out I meant the whole night – all night. I don't want to upset you because I like you too much, so we'll go upstairs and I swear to God nothing will happen if you don't want it to. But you're not walking out of this hotel tonight.'

What had begun as a wee bit of excitement for me and no doubt a welcome boost to my ego that someone would ask me – a forty-one-year-old mother of six and a grandmother of three – out on a date had turned into a nightmare.

What I didn't know at the time was that the man I thought was a real gentleman and who had asked me out was one of Scotland's hardest and most feared gangsters. We had first met two years previously, in 1974, while I was visiting my son Gordon after he had been sent to the former St Mary's List D School in Bishopbriggs, near Glasgow. He along with his wife was also visiting St Mary's to see their son. We would be among other parents waiting in the corridor and we'd have the usual conversations about how the children were getting into trouble and how they were coping being in St Mary's.

Both of them were very pleasant and they offered to give me a lift home to Dumbarton, but I already had something arranged. I bumped into him a few times at St Mary's and when his wife wasn't there he would give me a nod of recognition and he had that look on his face that said he wanted to be more than a passing acquaintance.

The next time I saw him was two years later, when Gordon had got into more trouble and was in the former Longriggend Remand Institution in Lanarkshire. One day I was visiting Gordon and I saw this man about to visit his son. He was on his own and at the time we just nodded and he said: 'Still in the same boat?'

'Yes, nothing changes,' I replied.

On the way out from the visit, thinking about the bus and train journey home, I said to myself: 'I bet he's waiting to talk to me.'

And sure enough, there he was. 'Do you want a lift?' he asked.

'I stay a good bit away in Dumbarton,' I said. That's probably taking you out your way.'

'Not a problem – I'll take you home in the car.'

I didn't know who this man was, then. Just that he was very pleasant, exceptionally well dressed and came across as being very impressive. You knew he wasn't the run-of-the-mill father visiting his son on remand. There was just something about him that was attractive to me. He had what I always called a Glasgow face – a hard look but attractive at the same time. The way he behaved and treated me that day, you would never have guessed who and what he really was.

On the way to Dumbarton he said: 'You're a stunning bit of stuff – would you come out with me for a night?'

I was a bit taken aback to say the least and, of course, he was pandering to my ego. My next words were: 'I'm a grandmother of three children, you know.'

'Get away. You don't get grannies looking like you where I come from,' he replied. 'In fact, my mammy never looked as good as you.'

I liked all that patter and his compliments made me feel good. Robert had left me again for one of his jaunts and I was living on my own. So I thought, why not go for a night out with this well-dressed and impressive gentleman?

As he dropped me off in Dumbarton High Street, he asked me again about going out with him and I agreed. He said he would meet me at the Silver Thread Hotel two nights later, and he would pay for a taxi from Dumbarton.

So that's how I ended up sitting in front of a Mr Big of the crime underworld, shivering in fear after he made me an offer I was too terrified to refuse. I had no option but to go upstairs with him.

As soon as I walked into the hotel bedroom I burst into tears as I didn't know what was going to happen to me – was he going to hit me again or was he going to rape me? I had thought he was a gentleman, but after getting such a hard smack in the mouth I knew he wasn't the person I'd thought he was.

He tried to calm me down and began telling me things about himself and his life. 'See round here,' he said, 'I've got a bit of a reputation and there are people who know me. I can't afford to be made a fool of, but don't be scared because I really like you and I wouldn't hurt you.'

He ordered drinks to be brought up to the room and as he stretched out on the bed I sat in a chair in the corner of the room. He must have thought: 'What have I landed myself with here?' His night's ruined and I'm sitting in the corner of the room crying.

Every now and then he would ask if I was all right and apologise for what had happened. 'Please don't let this be the end of this,' he said. 'We can work something out.'

He told me that he ran businesses and I told him about my family and about Gordon always getting into trouble. Obviously he had told me his name, but it never registered with me at the time. But I was soon getting to realise just who this man was.

'I don't like to think that I'm that unattractive,' he explained. 'When I ask a girl out I don't want to be made a fool of. Drinks, a meal, then it's toodaloo, she's off her mark. It doesn't work that way. Mary, I think you're a bit naïve for your age and I'm sorry for thinking that you would know exactly what the score would be.'

We just sat in the room talking and at one point early on I thought about making a run for it through the door, but then a wee voice inside my head told me he wasn't the type to take too kindly to something like that happening to him.

He dozed off a few times and on one of those occasions I got up to go to the en suite bathroom. He must have been sleeping lightly because he heard me getting out of the chair and stirred. 'Don't you be thinking about walking out that door,' he said. 'As soon as the morning comes we'll go out of here together.'

When morning did come, I was more relaxed in his company because he was as good as his word and nothing did happen that night. I actually began to like him again.

When he took me down to breakfast, he said he had to see someone and I was to wait at the hotel for him and he would drive me back to Dumbarton. I had finished breakfast and it was more than an hour later when he still hadn't returned.

I began to think this was him getting me back for last night and he was leaving me stranded.

I had begun thinking about asking people for directions to the train or bus station when he came walking through the door. I noticed he had changed his clothes and I wondered if he had been home to check in with his wife before coming back for me. He apologised again for what had happened the night before and as we walked to his car, he pressed a bundle of notes into my hand. It was £100 and, insisting I take the money, he said: 'Get yourself or the kids something nice with that.'

I was taken completely by surprise when he gave me the money. But I decided I would accept it as a gift because he was absolutely right – I could get something really nice for the children and myself. I had agreed to meet him in the first place because I liked him, not because I knew I was going to get money for sex – or no sex as it turned out.

But perhaps I lost some of my naïvety that night, because I realised what the money was for. It was to make sure I would agree to see him again and the next time there would be no need for a slap in the jaw. I was all right with that because I did like and trust him after he didn't lay a finger on me in the hotel room. No matter how much money he gave me, if I hadn't liked him I wouldn't have gone near him.

I admit it was a great feeling being given the money – it was almost like an adrenalin rush. I knew it was a down-payment for sex in the future, but I never asked for the cash in the first place and I didn't feel any guilt. I thought about all the years I had had nothing and when I had to ask people for the loan of a few shillings to get my children's tea. We had been living on Social Security payments and my children had suffered for that through no fault of their own. By this time I had another child, Mark, who was born on 19 May 1973. Now, becoming pregnant with Mark was another exploit from the 'you'll never believe what's happened to Mary' episodes in my life and I'll come to that in a later chapter. Needless to say, by 1976, life wasn't getting any easier money-wise with an extra mouth to feed, and like any three-year-old, before you knew it, Mark was growing out of his clothes and needing new ones. But I felt it was now the turn of my family and me to benefit from some cash coming my way for a change. I realised I had the body and the face to use in those days and I was going to use them to make a better life for my children.

When you have to constantly tell your children they can't have something they want because you can't afford it, the disappointment and the tears on their faces become too much for you. The thought of being able to say 'Yes' and watching the happiness on their faces was all the justification I needed to keep doing what I was doing without feeling guilty. If I could make my children happy, that was enough incentive for me to do anything to achieve this.

As we drove from Paisley to Dumbarton that morning I agreed to see him again. This time he promised me a weekend in Ayr in two weeks' time. During that fortnight he phoned me several times for lengthy chats and during these I began to get an inkling of exactly who and what he was. Of course, I was curious, but I dared not ask anyone about him, as they would become suspicious as to why I was taking such a close interest in this well-known gangster.

He sent a taxi for me on the Friday of our weekend away. I had arranged babysitters for the weekend, saying I was going to stay with a friend. The taxi picked me up and then drove to Glasgow to pick up my soon-to-be-lover before heading down the A77 to Ayr.

We checked into the Almont Hotel, in Charlotte Street. He had picked the nicest room in the hotel, which was huge and had three single beds and a double bed. The night we arrived he took me to a show at the Gaiety Theatre in Ayr and the following night we stayed at the hotel for dinner, as there was entertainment laid on there.

It was a lovely weekend of being pampered and treated like I was special. By now I was completely relaxed in his company and had become quite attracted to him. This time round there was no naïvety or dubiety that I would sleep with him and the single beds in the hotel room remained undisturbed.

In a taxi on the way home on the Sunday of that weekend, he gave me another gift. This time it was £200 and it was money put to good use – making sure my kids weren't embarrassed by having to wear really cheap jeans when they went out to meet their friends.

It had been a running sore with my three older boys, Robert, John and Gordon, who had to make do with Nordoc jeans – it was all I could afford after buying their school clothes and good Sunday clothes for chapel. They were always asking for a pair of Wrangler jeans, which were the most popular with the young ones and, unfortunately, the most expensive.

I used to listen to the boys talking about the insults they had to endure from other kids about those jeans. I was in the living room one day and the boys were in the kitchen having their tea. There was a small hatch between the living room and the kitchen that was partially open and I could hear what was being said. All you heard from Gordon was: 'F*****g Nordoc jeans! What a showing-up I got today. They were shouting "Nordoc, Nordoc – your mammy got them out of Mackays."'

In those days Mackays was a shop where you could buy cheap clothes, and since I was on the breadline I was a regular customer. I told the boys to cut the label off them and no one would know they were Nordoc, but they said everyone would know that's why there wouldn't be a label on the jeans. It hurt me that my children were being made fun of because I couldn't afford Wrangler jeans.

With the money I got from my new lover after the weekend in Ayr, I bought six pairs of Wrangler jeans – two pairs for each of the boys. You should have seen their faces when they came home from school and I told them I had bought them new jeans.

I could see the despair in their faces at the news and Gordon said: 'Aw, mammy – no' those Nordoc jeans again. You get a red neck wearing those jeans.'

But when I pulled the Wrangler jeans out of the bags I could see their disappointment turn to delight as their eyes widened and they realised that at last they could be like many of the other kids wearing a brand-name pair of jeans.

'Can I put them on now?' asked John.

'Can I go out and tell my pal, Pat?' said Robert.

'I'm going to tell everyone,' added Gordon. 'I'm just going to run around the street with my new jeans on and I'm tucking my T-shirt in so you can see the Wrangler label.'

That was a real joy for me, seeing the look on the boys' faces because, at last, I was able to afford to buy them a pair of jeans that didn't embarrass them. It was the look on their faces and knowing I had been able to do something that meant they could go out to play, proud as punch at getting their new Wranglers, and nobody would be talking about them. In my mind and in my moral code, that's what made it all right for me to become the mistress and accept gifts of money for sleeping with someone. Don't agree? Well, you should have seen the look of happiness on the faces of my boys as they rushed out to play in their new Wrangler jeans.

In many ways I was always a bit of a coward, but when it came to my children I would face up to anything and anyone. A typical example of this was in 1964, when Gordon was only two and had an extremely painful boil in his ear.

The doctor had visited us and given me drops for Gordon. But the pain must have been excruciating, as he never stopped crying all day and all night. The following morning, waiting for the doctor to visit again, I tried to comfort Gordon and help him get some sleep. Suddenly there was a loud banging coming from the end of the house and Gordon started screaming louder than before.

I went to the back door to see where the noise was coming from and there were two workmen hammering at the brickwork. 'Could you stop that hammering?' I asked. 'My son's not well and I'm trying to get him to sleep.'

'Get lost – I've got a job to do,' replied one of the men.

'Could you not go elsewhere and come back here later?' I pleaded with them. 'My wee boy can't stand the noise.'

'Tough,' said the workman.

I went back inside the house to wait for the doctor, but the banging got worse and the man who had given me all the cheek was now on a ladder close to my upstairs window. The tears were running down Gordon's face and he was screaming in pain. I went to the window and said: 'Can you not hear how upset my son is? Can you not stop for a wee while?'

'No can do. Now give me peace to get on with my work.'

He obviously thought he could act all macho with a woman, but I'd had enough of his cheek. In a blind rage, I went downstairs, filled a bucket with cold water and carried it to the bedroom. I opened the window and said to the workman: 'This is for you.' As he heard my words he looked up and I poured the bucket of water over his head.

He fell off the ladder and as he struggled off the ground he shouted up at me: 'You bastard. I'm going for the police.'

When I got back into the living room, the boil in Gordon's ear had burst and there was blood and pus pouring down his face. Fortunately, minutes later the doctor arrived and cleaned away the mess from Gordon's ear and face.

While the doctor was attending to Gordon two policemen arrived at the door and said they had received a complaint about me assaulting a workman. I explained what had happened and the doctor backed me up and said Gordon would have been in terrible pain. The policeman took one look at the state of Gordon's ear, had a word with the other workman, who admitted I had politely asked them to stop hammering, and told the man who had called them: 'You better get out of here before you are the one that gets charged.'

Like any mother, I would have done anything to protect my children.

My relationship with my gangster lover continued for fifteen years and we would meet up as often as we could. Sometimes it would be once a fortnight, then it would be once a month and then there would be times when we'd be together three times in one week. I haven't named him, as when we were going out together we were both married and we agreed to keep our trysts as discreet as possible. I didn't brag about who I was seeing then and I'm not going to break my word to him and start doing it now. Also, his family is still well known and if some of them don't like the idea of me revealing their dad had a long-term affair with someone like me, then I may end up with more than a smack in the mouth.

Normally, we would go to hotels for an overnight stay, but I also met him in a house in Balloch, which is only a few miles from where I stayed in Dumbarton. He had keys to the four-in-a-block council house and we would go there for a Friday and Saturday night. We would arrive on a Friday night and there would be a note left on the table from the person who had the house – 'back on Sunday night' or 'back on Monday morning'.

I always made sure that someone responsible was looking after the children when I went away on my overnight or weekend jaunts. Sometimes after a weekend together he would give me as much as £500 and he was always there to help me pay the bills. One night I was telling him how I had a lot of bills to take care of and he handed me £1,000.

Whenever my husband, Robert, came back to the house I would stop seeing him and that could be for several months at a time. That was a strange principle I had, that if Robert was back in the house I wouldn't go with another man. I felt that if Robert was home doing the decent thing and bringing money into the house to look after the family, I would also do the decent thing and be the faithful wife to him. But as soon as he was off again and not sending any money home I would go back to seeing the lover who was very generous with his money.

I didn't really have to go to any great lengths to hide the fact I was meeting him because most of the time I was picked up in a taxi and taken out of Dumbarton to where we were meeting. The excuse I made was that I was going to stay with one of my friends overnight, and I don't know if people became suspicious. My sister Frances would say she had popped in to see me after Mass on a Saturday night and I wasn't there. 'I'd love to know what you get up to,' she would tell me.

I didn't see the relationship as being with someone who was merely buying sexual favours from me. He said he loved me and I think he did. I loved him, although in a different way from the one man I had truly loved in my life. I loved being with him and I missed him when I wasn't with him. I loved the feeling that I was with someone who commanded respect wherever he went, and the presence he had. Whether he deserved to have that respect is a different matter, considering his lifestyle and how he made his money, but he was never anything but kind and considerate to me.

But at the same time as he was saying that he loved me, he made it clear that he would never leave his wife despite the fact that he admitted he hadn't loved her for years. 'She's always stood by me,' he said. 'When I had nothing she was there with me and she's more than just a wife – she's a great friend to me and I would never do anything to hurt her.'

When we were together I would ask him about his lifestyle and say that I had heard people describe him as a gangster. 'What is a gangster? It's only a name. If being a gangster means that you're nobody's mug and you pull a few strokes and all that, then, aye, that's right. But don't let that interfere with you and me.'

He would make out that when people got themselves some power others get jealous and sometimes 'you've got to put them in their place'. When I told him about things that had happened in my life he would say that he wished he was able to put more backbone into me and that I would stand up for myself.

'If you want something,' he said, 'you have to go after it, no matter how hard it seems, and see if you get where you want to be. And don't let anyone take it off you.'

He added: 'Anyway, half the things you hear about me are lies. Don't let that turn you against me or think bad about me because I would never intentionally hurt anybody.'

When he said that, my mind went back to the night at the Silver Thread Hotel when I got a smack in the mouth for saying I wasn't going to go upstairs to the bedroom with him. But he was good to me and I was having a great time with him and if he apologised once, he apologised a thousand times for what had happened that night.

Every time we met he would give me money and I would spend it on the children, the house or myself. The outward signs of my new-found wealth caused a few eyebrows to be raised and set more than a few tongues wagging. And of course there were a lot of questions – especially from my mother-in-law, Jessie Campbell.

The first time I had fitted carpets in my house was when we stayed in Carman View, in Dumbarton. It was a big thing at the time for people living in council houses when they were able to afford fitted carpets and I was buying them with the money I got from my gangland lover. I didn't tell anyone the carpets were coming after I'd ordered them from a shop in Glasgow because I knew I would be hit by a barrage of questions about how I could afford them and obviously I couldn't tell them the truth.

It wasn't just the living room, but every room in the house was laid with fitted carpets on the Saturday. The first time my mother-in-law came round was on the Monday and you should have seen the look on her face when she walked through the door.

'What in the name of God is this?' she exclaimed. 'What are you doing with fitted carpets?'

'Oh, I just thought I'd get them in since I'd paid off everything else in the house,' I replied.

'You'll have my boy up to his eyeballs in debt,' she said, which was rather ironic since Robert was out of the house at the time and I was paying for everything.

'No, no, it won't cost Robert a penny because I'm paying for everything,' I said.

'I think this is disgraceful. The cheek of you on Social Security and you're sitting here with fitted carpets,' said Jessie.

But there were more surprises to come in the form of a cream-coloured, leather three-piece suite and a phone. In those days, it was unusual for people like us living on Social Security handouts to have a phone in the house – it wasn't like nowadays, when everyone even seems to have a mobile phone.

Jessie got another shock when someone told her that I'd had a phone installed and she just had to see it for herself. She stormed through the front door.

'I hope that's a kid-on phone you've got there,' she said.

'No, it's real and it's working.'

'What do you want a phone for? It's doctors that have phones and you don't need one.'

'It's handy for getting in touch with the school,' was my lame excuse.

'What happened to your legs and the bus that you can't go to the school yourself if you want to see about the children?' she said.

'It gives out a better impression,' I countered.

'You're getting right carried away with yourself,' she said. 'You know the old saying – put a beggar on horseback and it will ride to hell.'

But Jessie wasn't finished with her lecture. 'I got told about this and I couldn't believe it. I just had to come in and see for myself. You know what's going to happen when the first bill comes in. You won't be able to pay it and how are you going to look then? You'll make a right fool of yourself when someone comes and takes the phone away and you end up in the small debt court for all this carry-on.'

This tirade from Jessie made me determined that the phone would never be cut off because I couldn't pay the bills. I swore to myself that she would never see the day they took the phone away and, touch wood, neither it has.

I was still young then and I wanted a wee bit of praise for providing a better standard of living for my family. I was hoping she would say it was good that the kids had a nice place to come home to – but I was getting none of that from Jessie.

Thankfully it was a different story from my brother Jimmy and sister Tilly who were both still living in England. When Jimmy came up on holiday and paid me a visit he said: 'My God, the house is looking good. That's a great thing for a woman bringing up a family.'

Tilly was also very supportive: 'I'm glad to see you're doing well,' she said. 'It gives the children a nice feeling that they're growing up in something worthwhile and more praise to you that you're doing it on your own.'

I'm not sure that Jessie bought my explanation that I was paying up the carpets and new furniture on hire purchase. Once she let rip: 'The money for this is coming from someplace and wherever it's coming from, it's come from no good.'

And another time she went even further when I protested that I was paying everything up and it made me think she knew what was really going on. She stared into my face and said: 'Don't tell me your lies that it's on tick. It will all come out in the wash. There's some folk will lie on their back for anything.'

Looking back, Jessie probably did suspect something was going on. After all, she was an old head, and all of a sudden she was seeing me dolled up with the best of clothes, the boys running around in Wranglers, the house with fitted carpets, leather suites and a phone – and still on Social Security.

My marriage to Robert officially ended in May 1989, when we were divorced. I was still seeing my gangster lover at this time, of course, though our long relationship had nothing to do with the divorce. To be honest, my marriage was over long before then.

When he was younger, my son John bought me a record for Mother's Day – it was 'Son of Hickory Holler's Tramp' sung by O. C. Smith. This is a song about a woman who was left destitute to look after her children when her husband walked out on them. To feed and clothe her family the mother took to selling her body to the local menfolk.

When I was given the record I said to John: 'Do you know what that song is all about?'

'Yes,' he replied.

'Well what do you want to hurt me like that for?'

'I don't want to hurt you – I want to tell you how much I love you.'

I had no idea if John knew the things I did to feed and clothe my children and give them a better life, but the irony of the song wasn't lost on me. After I had spoken to him about the record and he explained his own feelings, I no longer felt hurt. Especially when my birthday came a few days later and he bought another record for me – Scots singer Neil Reid's tear-jerker 'Mother of Mine'.

To be honest, I don't regret one minute of what I did or the money that came with it, which was used to better my family. I always protected my children from what I was doing and I would never have brought my lover back to the house.

My gangster lover is dead now and I was seeing him until a few weeks before he passed away. It was a part of my life – a necessary part of my life – and I'm not ashamed. In the same circumstances I would do it all again. If you fall overboard from a ship and somebody throws you a lifebelt, you take it. I took my lifebelt and I'm not sorry I did.

'Your Boy Never Made It This Time'

I'm lying on my bed curled up in the foetal position and my body shakes uncontrollably. I'm gripped by an awful fear and dread that I can neither understand nor explain. And worse still, it won't go away.

For days now, I've been living with this gnawing feeling of doom that has invaded my very being. My stomach is like lead, my heart is beating faster and my arms and legs shake. My head aches as I desperately search for the reason why I feel this way.

There is nothing outwardly wrong with me. I don't have other symptoms of the cold or flu, or any signs of other illness for that matter. I'm simply engulfed in terror every day and all day, every night and all night. I decide I'd better keep these terrible feelings to myself – otherwise people will think I'm going mad. Anyway, what can I say to my family and friends?

'Listen, there's something wrong with me because I'm frightened.'

'What are you frightened of, Mary?' they would ask.

'Eh . . . I don't really know. I'm just frightened.'

No, I'll have to face this one on my own.

I'm not usually an early-to-bed person, but since this nightmare started, I've been lying under the covers as soon as everyone in the house has gone out for the evening. I don't normally sleep in this foetal position as I find it very uncomfortable, but even if it takes hours to nod off, sleep is my only succour.

But as soon as I awake, I'm haunted by these feelings of

terror and I can't take much more of this. As the days pass by and the horrible sensation stays with me like a dark cloak wrapped round and round my body, I begin to understand a little why this is happening to me.

A terrible premonition enters my head – something dreadful is going to happen to my beloved son, Gordon. This anxiety about something happening to Gordon grows into a realisation that somehow Gordon is going to die. Don't ask me how on earth I came to this conclusion, but it has crept up on me, this insight into something I can't bear to comprehend.

It's almost the end of the second week of my torture and on the Friday I decide I can't take any more as I start to think that I am going mad. I make an appointment to see my doctor at the local health centre. All that day the feeling that Gordon is going to die has grown stronger and stronger. The fear is still there, but now there is a gripping certainty in my mind and in my heart that my son is going to die. No, even worse – a certainty he is going to be murdered.

I don't have an appointment, but in the afternoon I make my way to the health centre and ask to see Dr Anne Mitchelson, my GP. The receptionist, Morag McGinlay, obviously realises there is something wrong with me and she manages to fit me in.

I walk into the surgery, sit down and Dr Mitchelson asks: 'What's wrong, Mary? What can I do for you?'

'Doctor, my Gordon is going to be murdered.'

'What do you mean? Has someone threatened him?'

'No, not that I know of.'

'Well, is it because of his lifestyle that you think he is going to be murdered?'

'No. I just know deep inside me that he's going to die and that he's going to be murdered.'

Dr Mitchelson must think I'm having a breakdown, but I'm coherent and after asking me a few questions she realises that a nervous breakdown isn't the problem. She gives me some herbal tablets to calm me down and promises to visit me on the Monday.

The next day the shaking and the terrible feelings of fear are as strong as ever and at night I decide to have a bath before going to bed. I'm walking from the bathroom up the hall to the bedroom when the phone rings and I pick it up. A girl's voice on the other end says: 'Mrs Campbell, I work at the Burgh Bar and Gordon's been injured – I think he's been stabbed on the arm. Do you want to go out to the Vale of Leven Hospital where Gordon is? Somebody could come out and take you there.'

At that very moment the shaking stops and the fear that has plagued me for two weeks suddenly disappears.

'Gordon's dead,' I tell the girl. And without uttering another word, she puts the phone down.

The high-pitched tone coming through the handset echoes in my ears as I realise that my worst nightmare has become a reality. In those few seconds holding a phone to my ear with no one at the other end of the line, a huge part of me dies along with my son, Gordon. My life changed forever on that night of Saturday, 13 April 1991.

To make matters worse, I'd had a huge fall-out with Gordon six weeks before and had told him not to come near my house. His wife Lorraine had come to see me, complaining that Gordon was staying out at nights and she suspected he was having affairs with other women. I told her I would talk to him about it and the next time Gordon was in the house I had some stern words with him.

'What's all this I'm hearing about you running around with other women?' I asked him. 'You've got a wife and family up the road and you should be spending your time with them.'

'That's a load of nonsense,' Gordon replied. 'Anytime I'm away overnight, I'm doing some business. You know what

Lorraine's like. She wants to be at your side every minute and that can't happen. If I get picked up by the police and she's in the car with me, she's going to get lifted as well. And how is that going to look with two children needing to be looked after? You don't want them being taken into care, do you?'

What Gordon – known by the nickname 'Cippsy' (pronounced Kippsy) – was saying was feasible. I knew he was dealing in cannabis and he would have to be away for nights at a time if he was travelling to London and other parts of the country to pick up a consignment of the drug. Oh, how he had my heart roasted by getting involved in buying and selling cannabis and he just wouldn't heed my warnings about what could happen to him.

I dropped the subject of him carrying on with other women, as he never listened to me anyway, but Lorraine continued to ask me to speak to Gordon as she still suspected he was up to something. One of my regrets is that I always thought the worst of Gordon because of all the scrapes he would get into as a child, and then getting into trouble with the law as a teenager. I adored Gordon, but I never took his word that he hadn't been up to no good in case he thought I was encouraging him. Even his friends used to ask me why I always took other people's word against Gordon's.

One day I had had enough of hearing Gordon was playing around with other women. He came into the house and I had another go at him and the argument got a bit over-heated.

'Until you start going home to your own house every night, don't come back near me,' I told him. 'I don't want you near me when you are hurting your wife like that.'

I ended up screaming my head off at him: 'Get out of here and don't you come back. I don't want anything to do with you until that lassie knows you are not messing around with other women.'

Gordon stormed out, shouting: 'One day you'll realise that I'm not as bad as you think I am and that I don't tell lies all the time.'

For six weeks I refused to let him come into the house and I never spoke to him. That's why I never told him about those weird feelings that something bad was going to happen to him. I probably wouldn't have told him anyway as his reply would probably have been: 'Come off it, Mum – you're being a right drama queen. Nothing's going to happen to me. Are you going off your head, or what?'

The night before Gordon died his older brother John came into the house and said: 'Gordon's outside and he wants to know if it's time up yet, has he done his punishment and can he come back into the house?'

I said he couldn't; I decided I would make the lesson last a bit longer and let it go for another two weeks.

'Sorry, son,' I told John, who said I was being rotten and his brother only wanted to come in for five minutes.

Although nothing could have been further from the truth, I foolishly replied: 'Tell Gordon I don't care if I never see his face again.' The pain still runs deep inside me that I never did – not when he was alive, anyway.

Why didn't I let Gordon into the house to see me when I had such feelings that something dreadful was going to happen to him? I wish I could answer that. Even now I have no idea why certain emotions took control at that moment and I ignored my fears for his life. I have struggled with that question ever since Gordon died and the turmoil inside me never subsides and neither do the tears. I'm crying just talking about it now.

Was it because I have inherited some of the twisted stubbornness of my father? Did I let my anger with Gordon overcome the fear prompted by my premonition of his death? Surely not? But I don't know. Was the fear so strong that I tried to hide it away by saying I didn't want to see

Gordon? Or was I subconsciously thinking that Gordon had survived so many scrapes before that nothing could possibly harm him and these subconscious thoughts came to the fore at that exact moment?

I could also have been afraid of Gordon laughing at me, because that is surely what he would have done if I had told him what my feelings were and that I feared he would soon be dead. That would have led to another row between us.

Whatever the reasons for me telling John not to let his brother into the house, I will never know why I didn't just take Gordon in my arms, hug him tightly, tell him my innermost feelings of despair and beg him not to go anywhere until they had gone. It is the biggest regret of my life not letting Gordon into the house that day. If God would grant me only a few seconds to say something to Gordon it would be that I was sorry for my actions day and that I love him dearly.

The following morning Lorraine came to see me and said that Gordon had gone to Glasgow to buy a couple of suits and a couple of overcoats for himself. His daughter Alana was to make her First Communion the following month and the new clothes were for that occasion. He was also visiting a jeweller in the city to buy a real pearl necklace and earrings for Alana as a present for her big day.

I knew where the money was coming from for all these fancy clothes he was buying and I went off on a rant trying to act like the angry old granny. 'That's evil money he's using, that is.' I said. 'He doesn't need any more suits and coats – he's got plenty clothes. No good will come of all this.'

But Lorraine was happy and in her element as she and Gordon were due to go out together to a party in Dixon Bowling Club in Dumbarton later that Saturday evening. So off she toddled back to her own house to get ready for a night when she would have Gordon all to herself. But at teatime I got a phone call from an exasperated Lorraine. A so-called friend of Gordon's had been phoning constantly, asking him to come to the Burgh Bar for a drink.

'Can you not talk to him, Mary?' said Lorraine. 'Everything is ready for us to go out and I'm just waiting for the babysitter to arrive. Now he's talking about going to the Burgh Bar for half an hour.'

'Stand up for yourself, Lorraine,' I told her. 'Tell Gordon not to be so ridiculous – he's having a night out with his wife.'

'But this guy keeps on phoning,' Lorraine said. 'Cippsy told him he can't go to the Burgh Bar, but he keeps on phoning. Now Cippsy says the only way he's going to get some peace is to go down to the Burgh Bar for half an hour and have a pint with him.'

More than an hour later, Lorraine was back on the phone to me in tears. 'Mary, he's not back yet,' she said. 'I've phoned the Burgh Bar twice and they're saying Cippsy's not there, but I know he is.'

Lorraine didn't believe for a minute that Gordon wasn't in that pub because it was the voice of the person who had been pestering Gordon to go out that she could hear saying he wasn't there. I told Lorraine there wasn't much we could do about it. The last thing Gordon would have wanted was his mother or his wife marching into the Burgh Bar and dragging him home to get ready for a night out. That wouldn't have done anything to enhance his hardman reputation and he would have been raging if that had happened. It wasn't long after that when the phone rang with the barmaid from the Burgh Bar calling me to say Gordon had been stabbed.

Four months later, a twenty-two-year-old man, Patrick McDaid from Duntocher, near Clydebank, appeared in the dock charged with Gordon's murder. He admitted stabbing

Gordon, but walked free from court having been found not guilty after claiming he had acted in self-defence. What was said at the trial at the High Court in Glasgow is not the version of events given to me. I have to be very careful legally what I say here and who I identify because I could end up being charged with contempt of court.

A couple of months before Gordon died, three of his closest friends came to me and said they were worried about Gordon getting involved with a drug user and small-time dealer who had double-crossed a drugs gang from a neighbouring town. This gang had previously asked to go into partnership with Gordon but he had refused, telling them he was making enough money selling cannabis on his own patch and he didn't need them. So right away, there was bad blood between this gang and Gordon.

This individual who had started to curry favour with Gordon apparently double-crossed this gang in a drugs deal and owed them money. They were after him and he was staying in different houses almost every night so they couldn't track him down. This was the same person who called Gordon's house fourteen times begging him to go to the Burgh Bar for a drink the Saturday night Gordon was killed.

I was told by underworld sources that the price this individual paid for clearing his debt with the drugs gang was to set my Gordon up by luring him to the Burgh Bar so he could be attacked. Gordon was never very good at holding his drink and he would rarely get drunk as he wanted to keep his wits about him. But that Saturday night he sat in the Burgh Bar drinking for hours and was in no fit state to take care of himself in a fight.

I was also told that while he was in the pub, Gordon was goaded into going outside to fight and he walked into an ambush. However, according to the law and the decision of a jury, this version of events is not the truth. The court decided that although Patrick McDaid stabbed Gordon, he did not murder him. I have come to my own verdict on what happened that night.

And the truth for this mother is that she no longer has her beloved son because her boy was stabbed and left dying on the pavement in Dumbarton High Street.

The time Gordon's three friends came to warn me about him getting involved with that family of gangsters and the individual they were after for double-crossing them in a drugs deal, I decided to do something about it. I asked Gordon: 'What's this I'm hearing about you getting involved with the boy who's in trouble with that family of gangsters? They'll end up killing you, because I knew their daddy and he was right round the bend – a real lunatic. And I also know they're out looking for the boy you've started hanging around with and has been coming to your house.' And I warned him: 'You'll end up getting murdered.'

But, typical Gordon, he just stood looking out of the window and replied: 'You know the old saying, Mary – *che sarà, sarà.*'

I went off my head. 'You think you're so smart coming away with all this "what will be" stuff. I'm telling you, if you get involved with this lot you'll end up getting killed.'

'Cool the beans,' he said. 'Everything's got to be a big drama with you – you're a real Bette Davis. You've the most vivid imagination of anyone I've ever come across.'

I was raging with him and said: 'My heart's broken with you. Get yourself out of here before I drop down dead worrying about you.'

If only Gordon had listened to me, but maybe even if he had it might have been too late, as the die may already have been cast.

The first person I phoned after the barmaid from the Burgh Bar called was my niece Anne, who was staying in Paisley. It would have been around 10 p.m. and when she answered I blurted out: 'Gordon's been stabbed. He's been taken to the Vale of Leven Hospital.'

About twenty minutes later, Anne walked through my door, gave me a cuddle and asked if there was any news from the hospital. Gordon's dad, Robert – who was by that time living in another part of town – had gone to the hospital, but I had heard nothing from him and that made me fear the worst.

I went back and forward into my bedroom to look at a photograph of Gordon and I keep telling Anne: 'He's gone. Gordon is gone.'

Anne said she would make a phone call to the hospital for me and try to find out how Gordon was. She went out into the hall where the phone was. I could hear her talking on the phone, but I couldn't make out what was being said. When Anne came back into the living room, I got all the confirmation I needed – as if I needed any at that time.

When she first arrived, Anne had been sitting in a chair right next to me. But when she came back in from the hall after phoning, she sat on the couch at the other end of the room. Although the hospital refused to say how Gordon was, Anne knew herself that the news wasn't going to be good. Deep inside, I was hoping against hope that I was wrong about Gordon being dead. But the last flickering vestiges of that hope disappeared when I saw the look on Anne's face.

I felt as if my world had come to an end. I repeated to myself: 'Please God, let this be a mistake. Let it be somebody else. Let it be a mistake and it's not really Gordon who's died – they've got the wrong name at the hospital.'

In the early hours of the morning, Robert Campbell came back to the house from the hospital. He walked into the living room, walked over to the window and said: 'Your boy never made it this time.' Apparently Gordon was still alive when the paramedics arrived at Dumbarton High

Street, but despite their efforts to save him in the ambulance, he died shortly after arriving at the hospital.

That was the final confirmation – if I ever needed confirmation – that Gordon was dead. While I was in a state of shock, Anne must have gone back on the phone to tell the family what had happened. Before I knew it, the house was choc-a-bloc with people, but I didn't want to believe what had happened and when anyone tried to say something to me I would snap at them: 'I don't want to listen to you. Don't talk to me.'

Everything that happened in those hours after I got the dreadful news is a blur, but I have been told that I refused to take an injection from the on-call doctor to help me cope. And that I embarrassed everyone in the room by being outrageously rude to the local priest who came to the house to offer me some comfort.

Apparently the priest, Father McKenzie, sat down beside me and said: 'It's a terrible thing that's happened, Mary.'

And I replied: 'It's you that should be dead – it shouldn't be Gordon. Why would they take my Gordon, and him so beautiful, and leave someone with a fat face like yours on this f*****g earth.' Then I slapped him across the face and told him: 'You've got a cheek coming in here and telling me that my son is dead when you can't even say Mass right.'

The people in the room were utterly shocked by what I was saying to Father McKenzie and someone said: 'But, Mary, you don't even go to Mass, so how can you say that about the Father?'

I was hurling insults at this poor priest, and all he was saying to the others was: 'Leave Mary alone. She's entitled to say what she wants.'

Father McKenzie stayed for quite a long time that night and he was, in fact, quite a good-looking man. He obviously understood the turmoil I was going through and just let me rant and rave at him. He was a really nice man and I now feel terrible about the way I treated him that night when all he wanted to do was help me. My apologies; please forgive me, Father.

Most of my close family and friends were at the house and I told every one of them not to talk to me and I didn't want to hear anything about Gordon being dead. Obviously I was in complete denial and refused to believe it and didn't want anything or anyone trying to persuade me that he wasn't still alive. I didn't even want anyone mentioning his name. 'If you say his name again, you can just get out of this house,' I was telling people.

'Mary, I'm really sorry . . .' they would say.

'Shut up – don't talk to me,' I replied.

My sister Frances recognised what was happening and that I wasn't going to accept the reality of Gordon being dead. The house was so full of people the only place Frances could talk to me alone was in the toilet. She took me in there and said: 'Listen, Mary, you're going to have to stop acting like this. Gordon's dead and you're going to have to accept it, and there's going to be lots of people coming in and out of the house wanting to see you. It's going to be like a circus in here for the next couple of weeks, but I will be by your side all the time. Just think, Gordon's with his granny now.'

Frances was right to try to make me acknowledge what had happened and she was as good as her word, because over the next few weeks she was never far away from me.

But even to this day there is a small part of me that still doesn't believe Gordon is dead and I expect him to come walking through the door again. I was in so much shock that I didn't cry when Gordon died – not that night, nor at his funeral. I was so numb I couldn't let out my emotions. It took me eight years before I shed a tear over Gordon's death, although inside I wept an ocean of tears.

I had been brought up a devout Catholic, but as soon as Gordon died I felt a terrible resentment towards God. From my point of view, Gordon was the most perfect-looking human being that ever came into this world. We all talk about how feet are the most horrible things you can have, but I thought that Gordon's feet – even his toes – were perfect. That's how I felt about Gordon.

God had given me something so perfect in physical form then decided he would take it away from me. What kind of horrible trick is that to play on someone? My years of devotion and belief in God died that night along with Gordon.

I was desperate to see him, but the police wouldn't let me go to the mortuary because there would have to be a post-mortem for the Procurator Fiscal and then another post-mortem for any defence lawyers.

The days passed by with the most empty feeling in the world in my heart. I ached to see my Gordon again, to look at his face, to touch his skin, to speak to him. During this time I would go through a variety of emotions. First I wanted to be dead myself, so I could be with him. Then I wanted him to be kept at the hospital forever so I could visit him, even though he was dead.

I have to pay tribute to Detective Chief Inspector Craw-ford, who was leading the murder enquiry. He would come to see me every day to keep me informed of what was happening with the case and to ask if there was anything he could do for me.

My reply was always the same: 'Can I see Gordon?'

And his reply was also always the same: 'No. I'm sorry, Mary, the Procurator Fiscal won't allow it.'

I would get angry with him and say: 'Well don't keep asking if there is anything you can do for me when you know fine well you can't give me the only thing I want.' Frances would always walk him to the door and one day I think she had a word with him, pushing for me to be allowed to see Gordon in the mortuary.

Whatever she said one of the days he had visited, Mr Crawford came back the next day with the news I was so desperate to hear: 'I have been on the phone to the Crown Office for three hours and you can get in to see Gordon. You can have ten minutes with him,' he said.

'But nobody is to know you are going to the mortuary and there will only be three people allowed in – you, your sister and someone you can trust to drive you there.'

We were told no one was to know where we were going and anyone who asked where we were going was told that I was being taken for a run to get a breath of fresh air and a break from the house.

My niece, Anne – Frances's daughter – agreed to drive us to the hospital mortuary. First, we drove from my house in Cardross Road to the police station in the town, where we were met by an unmarked police car. We followed it to the Vale of Leven Hospital. The only thing going through my mind during the journey was that at last, I was going to see Gordon.

When we got out the car we walked down a small dark passage to the mortuary. Frances and Anne were holding me up as my legs had gone and I was about to collapse. I told myself, 'I'm going to see him and I'll be able to touch my beloved Gordon.'

We got to a window with a curtain that was closed. Someone pulled the strings attached to the curtain and suddenly they opened and on the other side of the glass, there was Gordon's face.

Then it all started. I completely lost control and I screeched: 'Who the f**k do you think you are? That's my son and I don't want to look at him through a window. I want to go round there. Let me get beside him – I want to see my Gordon.'

The place was in chaos and the mortuary attendant was

saying to the police: 'I told you this would happen. We'll need to get her out of here.' But Mr Crawford said: 'No. I think we'll make an exception here and let Mrs Campbell see her son. I'll handle this.'

I calmed down and was taken into the room where Gordon was lying. I was immediately struck by how nice the place was. I was expecting to see big metal tables and drawers with dead people in them getting pulled out. But they had put Gordon into a lovely room with baskets of flowers all around and he was lying on a bed with covers and a pillow under his head. Gordon looked like a patient sleeping in a hospital bed.

As I got closer to Gordon's body, I noticed a small black brush stuck on his head. I moved forward to take it away, but someone pulled my hands back. It was a machine for collecting evidence from hair. I also noticed that Gordon's upper front teeth were over his bottom lip as if he was biting down. 'Frances,' I said. 'Fix his teeth. He's a handsome boy and his teeth were never like that.' She pulled his lips from under his teeth and Gordon looked fine again.

Suddenly, I exploded with grief. I jumped onto the bed, on top of my dead son, and started shouting at him: 'Stop all this carry on. Stop kidding on you're dead.'

The policemen were trying to lift me back off the bed and I was shouting: 'I warned you about all this. I knew this would happen one day. Don't think you're going to get away with this. You are not going to be dead.'

I was completely hysterical and the mortuary attendant was telling the policemen: 'Get her out of here. If I'd thought this commotion was going to happen I would never have let you in here.'

Eventually a combination of Frances, Anne and Mr Crawford persuaded me to come out of the room with the obviously false promise that they would bring me back the next day.

Doll Me Up When I Get Buried

After Gordon had been at the funeral of the father of one of his friends, he said to me that he hated seeing the man lying in a coffin wearing what he described as a 'big white gown'. He said: 'If anything ever happens to me, you doll me up when I get buried.'

I said: 'Don't talk daft. They only do that kind of stuff in America and anyway I'll be long gone when your time comes around – tell your wife and daughters to do those things.'

I shivered when that conversation came back to me as the arrangements were being made for Gordon's funeral. It was typical Gordon, that statement. But I made sure that even although he was lying in a coffin, Gordon was dressed as if he was going out for a special occasion. John Kane, the undertaker, came to see me and I gave him underpants, socks, shirt, tie, shoes and the brand-new suit Gordon had bought the day he died to wear at his daughter's First Communion. And yes, Alana did get the pearl necklace and earrings Gordon had ordered from the jeweller in Glasgow that day. Only he wasn't there to give them to her himself.

Right up until the day Gordon's body was released for his funeral, Lorraine had said his body could come to my house for a couple of days before going to the chapel and then to the cemetery. Lorraine had agreed to this because I stayed only a few hundred yards from their house in Ardoch Crescent and Gordon's two children, Alana and Kelly, had been taken to stay with friends after he died. We didn't want them to see their daddy dead.

But on Friday, 19 April, Lorraine changed her mind and said she wanted Gordon to come back to their own house before the funeral. If this is at all possible, I was even more hurt that I wasn't getting Gordon back to my house. I was also feeling guilty that I hadn't spoken to Gordon for six weeks after we had the fall-out about him not being at home every night. I felt cheated.

My sister Frances was an old head and she'd suspected that Lorraine might change her mind about Gordon and that he wouldn't be coming to my house. She had told me not to put too much store in what people say under extreme emotional circumstances and warned me she might change her mind. Frances knew how much I wanted to see Gordon on my own before he was taken to chapel and then to be buried at the cemetery. So she contacted the police and asked them to organise for the undertaker to take Gordon to a funeral parlour in Dumbarton for an hour before he was taken to his house. With my dear friend Kathleen Carr by my side, we got to sit with my Gordon for an hour before he went to Lorraine's before the funeral. I was grateful for that opportunity, but it was only a tiny grain of comfort in a desert of grief.

Once again, I have to pay tribute to DCI Crawford for those few precious minutes with Gordon. He is a man who understands the love of a mother for her son and the intense felt grief when that son dies.

The local paper reported that Gordon's was the biggest funeral ever seen in Dumbarton. Once again, the Sunday night Gordon went into the chapel and the funeral itself the following morning is just one big blur to me. The only two people I remember seeing in that packed church were Detective Chief Inspector Crawford and his colleague Detective Inspector Boyle, who had been so good to me. As I walked into the chapel I felt a gentle touch on my shoulder and when I turned round it was these two policemen offering their condolences to me. In the chapel I couldn't bear to look at Gordon's coffin, as it was a reminder of who was in there.

The other thing I remember about the funeral was the unusually loud noise, especially at Dumbarton Cemetery where Gordon was laid to rest. Later, I found out that there were police helicopters hovering above the cemetery.

There was a massive turnout to Gordon's funeral, with many, many hundreds of people – possibly even more than a thousand – coming to pay their last respects. There were people outside the chapel kneeling in prayer during the Mass.

And there were some well-known 'faces' from the Glasgow gangland scene there as well. Two of these were Joe 'Bananas' Hanlon and Bobby Glover, who were themselves later murdered, said to be in retaliation to the killing of crimelord Arthur Thompson's son, Arthur Junior.

My niece Mary told me she had been quite frightened at the funeral when she saw big men with long, black coats coming out of flash cars at the cemetery. She'd known Gordon dealt in cannabis, but had had no idea he'd kept the company of the big-time gangsters like that.

After the funeral we went to the Denny Club in Dumbarton for the usual tea, sandwiches and sausage rolls, before coming back to my house. I wasn't long back when I heard a commotion at my front door. I heard a voice saying: 'We must speak to Mrs Campbell.' I went to the door and two men in suits and carrying briefcases were standing on the front step. I thought they might have been from the police and it was something to do with the investigation.

'We've had an anonymous tip-off that you have a lodger staying with you – a Robert Campbell – and you haven't informed Social Security about it,' one of them said.

A friend of the family, John McCourt, was there with me

and he told them that I had just buried my son that day and had just come back from the funeral. I told the DSS officials: 'Yes, Robert Campbell is staying here, but he's my dead son's father and has only been here since my boy died.' At that, the pair of them apologised and went on their way.

How sick can some people be? Everyone in Dumbarton, the Vale of Leven and Clydebank knew when Gordon's funeral was and someone called Social Security to say I had a lodger staying with me when I shouldn't have been claiming benefits. They must have been hoping the DSS officers would come to my house checking up on the day of Gordon's funeral.

Although we were divorced and he had his own home, Robert stayed at my house from time to time – but sleeping in a separate room – for several years after Gordon's death, to give me some comfort. He had stopped drinking and had quietened down considerably – for most of the time, anyway.

But that was just the start of a hate campaign against me. I started getting anonymous phone calls when a voice would say things like: 'How do you feel now that your blue-eyed boy is dead?' and 'How do you not just dig a hole and lie beside him?'

I told the police about the phone calls and they said it could be someone with a grudge against Gordon and since they couldn't get at him any more, they would torment his mother. They began to investigate.

These vile phone calls went on for almost a year until on my next birthday – 31 March – two policemen came into the house and told me they had managed to trace the number of the person making the anonymous phone calls. The police had gone to their house and eventually that person admitted they had been making the nuisance calls. When they told me the name of the person who was making the calls everyone in the room was shocked. It was someone we all knew. For legal reasons I can't say who it was, but they know who they are, my family and friends know who they are, and they should be utterly ashamed of themselves for doing that to a woman who was distraught by the loss of her son.

The police asked if I wanted the person charged. Robert Campbell was all for having them thrown into jail, but my son, Robert, argued that it would only bring more heartache to the family. All I was interested in was getting the calls stopped and the police reckoned they would be able to do that now the culprit had been caught and they would get a warning from the police.

After the funeral I made daily journeys to the cemetery to be at Gordon's graveside. That was the only place I wanted to be so I could feel close to my son. To many people this might seem like an obsession and they may think it would have been better for me just to get on with my life. But I didn't have a life any more – my life was lying in the cemetery. It was a terrible time. I would sit at Gordon's graveside and just hope he would come out of the grave to be with me. Unless you have gone through the heartache of losing a child, I don't expect anyone to understand why I would do and think things like that. Even now, all these years after Gordon's death, I visit his graveside several times a week.

At first I didn't really know what to do or how best to cope with the grief. I spoke to Dr Mitchelson about it and said that sometimes I got really upset because if Gordon had done what I'd told him to do and not got mixed up with that individual involved with the drugs gang, he would still be with me today.

She told me I should speak to Gordon and let him know how I felt. If I was angry with him, I should tell him. If my heart felt broken, I should tell him that. 'Talk to him the way you would if he were here today,' she said. 'Tell him what he has done to you and that you haven't got a life any more because of that.'

I have a huge picture of Gordon on the wall of my living room and, like the doctor advised, I sometimes talk to the picture as if it was Gordon I'm speaking to. What I say depends on the mood I'm in that day. 'I miss you terrible,' I sometimes say. But on other days I'm angry with him and say; 'Look at you now, Mr Big Shot. You're that smart you're dead. Some gangster you turned out to be; getting yourself killed was a really clever thing to do. The rest of them are all still floating about the streets, but you're lying up the cemetery.'

I'll say things like that on days when I feel really hurt and bitter about what happened. But the next day I might go over to the picture and say: 'I'm sorry what I said to you yesterday. I still love you very much.'

I cannot thank Dr Mitchelson enough for all she has done for me over the years. Her warmth, compassion and support have played a huge part in keeping me sane and she has lifted me from the depths of despair many, many times. I would have been lost without her.

Another GP who has given me the strength to carry on is Dr Tom Barlow – a man not given to soft words. His sympathy helped me through one particularly bad day when he said: 'God help you, Mary. I would never want to be in your head.'

I had always wondered why I had those intense feelings of fear and doom the two weeks before Gordon died, and trying to find the reason I visited a well-known psychic, Rita Rogers. She told me there is a very rare phenomenon called the invisible chord. This is a spiritual link between mother and child and she told me she thought there was this invisible chord between Gordon and me. She said that those horrible feelings and the shaking was me going through Gordon's death throes.

I always wished Gordon had never chosen the lifestyle he did, because he would probably be alive today if he hadn't. I used to pray that he would change and be more like his brothers Mark or Robert who, ironically, went on to become a police officer. It hurt me when Gordon got himself involved in the drugs scene, although many people have told me that Gordon kept hard drugs out of Dumbarton for a long time. He made plenty of money selling the soft drug cannabis but he didn't want anything to do with heroin, cocaine or any of the other hard drugs.

I wanted him to have a good life and never to be short of money like I was, but I wanted him to earn all that in a good way. To me he had the looks, the intelligence and the courage to do well without getting involved in the drugs scene. He certainly had a grand lifestyle from selling cannabis, but at the age of twenty-eight he paid the ultimate price for those few years of the high life.

Since Gordon died, I have simply just existed. You go through the motions of living, but life as you know it is over. Any mum who has had to go through the horror knows exactly what I mean. It won't lessen the hurt by giving it the name of nightmare – because nightmares come to an end when you wake up. I'm never going to wake up one morning and find that Gordon is still alive.

The nothingness I feel goes on and on and there's a silent scream going on inside you day after day. It's probably best that the scream stays inside, for if it ever were to be released I can't imagine the horrible sound a tormented heart and mind would make. My world is a grey, grey place now. I am haunted by the thought of a hand being raised with a knife in it. I imagine Gordon coming out of that pub. Did he know he was going to die? What went through his mind as the blade plunged through his heart? Was he afraid and was he in pain? These are the questions that haunt me every day,

and why should my beautiful son be taken from me by one
lunge with a knife?

That knife went though Gordon's body and killed him.
That knife also went through my heart and my life was gone
too. Gone as my Gordon drew his last breath.

The aftershock and emotional turmoil in the weeks and
months after Gordon's death certainly took their toll. So
much so that it split my family apart, with the damage done
still evident today. I was living in a parallel universe for a
long time after Gordon was killed – a world in which the
only inhabitants were Gordon and me. Everything else just
didn't register. There could have been World War Three
going on outside my front door and I couldn't have cared
less and I probably wouldn't have even noticed anyway.
The only thing I thought about all day, every day, was
Gordon not being with me. And the only thing I cared about
was getting up to the cemetery every day to be by Gordon's
graveside.

But life had to go on for other people around me – and it
did, with all the trials and tribulations that everyday living
brings. Almost a month after Gordon died my youngest
son, Mark, had been working for my daughter Alana's
husband's company cutting down trees. This Friday night
Mark came home from work at 8 p.m. covered from head to
toe in oil. The black gooey liquid was running down his
face, and his clothes were covered in it.

Robert was in the house at the time and he went off his
head when he saw the state of Mark. 'Some f*****g job
this,' shouted Robert. 'He's supposed to get £90 a week, but
he's not had a penny and they send him home in a state like
that.'

Mark had to take all his clothes off standing in the garden
path outside our front door before he could go into the
house, as the oil would have stained the carpets. Poor

Mark's clothes were ruined and they had to be taken up to the back of the garden and burnt.

Mark then jumped into a bath and scrubbed the oil off himself and although he was almost eighteen, he looked a poor wee soul, sitting in the living room in his yellow towelling bathrobe, tears running down his cheeks.

Of course Robert was on the warpath about the way Mark had come home after his work and the next day when Alana came into the house as usual, Robert launched into a tirade. 'You should have seen the state that wean came in last night covered in oil,' he shouted. 'We had to burn his clothes because they were ruined. I'll tell you one thing, Mark's not going back to that job,' said Robert.

'Where is Mark?' asked Alana.

'He's in his bed exhausted. It's outrageous the way that boy's been treated.'

Alana went through to Mark's bedroom and seemingly gave him a lecture about the money he would be losing if he didn't go back to the job. But Mark was having none of it and told Alana he wasn't going back to the job.

By this time Robert had got his second wind and he had another go at Alana. 'What about his £90 a week? He's been working there for weeks and hasn't seen a penny.'

'You've got to work for a month before you get any wages,' Alana replied.

'Well, that boy's finished and he's not working another day. Tell your man he can stick his money.'

I was in the living room while all this bawling and shouting was going on and I didn't say a word. I was just wishing they would all go away so I could get up to the cemetery to visit Gordon's grave. The argument ended with Alana telling Robert that she was leaving and she wasn't coming back, and of course Robert's rejoinder was that he 'couldn't give a monkey's' if he never saw her again.

Robert's fury was no doubt fuelled by his simmering

anger that neither Alana nor my other daughter, Annette, had come back to my house after Gordon's funeral a few weeks prior to the row over Mark's job. No one knows why they never came back to the house, but it was noticed by other members of the family – particularly Tilly – who had commented on their absence. Me, I couldn't have told you who was in the house that day or who wasn't. I was in such a state the Queen of Sheba could have been sitting in my living room and I wouldn't have noticed.

The morning after Robert's row with Alana, the phone rang in my house and it was Annette. I said 'hello' as usual, thinking there was nothing untoward and it was just one of her regular phone calls asking how I was bearing up.

'You threw my sister out the house yesterday,' she said. 'And if my sister is not to get back in the house, then I'm not coming back to the house.'

'Alana wasn't thrown out of the house. She walked out and it was her who said she wasn't coming back,' I replied. 'Anyway this has nothing to do with me. It was your daddy she was arguing with. That's what's wrong with this family – someone will say something and someone else will make it sound something different.' It was only a month since I'd buried my son and I couldn't have cared less what happened with the rest of the world.

'Listen, Annette – if you don't want to come back to the house, then don't, and that goes for Alana as well,' I said. To be honest, the only person I wanted to see walking through my front door at that time was Gordon.

Sadly, neither Alana nor Annette has been to see me since that row with Robert took place in 1991. I was appalled that my two daughters could treat me like that, especially as they were never away from my house before that row over Mark's job. Every night Alana would pass my house on her way home from work and she would always call in to see me. And every Saturday from when Alana was married to her first husband, she would come to my house for her dinner and every fortnight I would go to her house for my Sunday dinner.

Almost every day in life, Annette would visit me and sometimes she would stay all day. Neither Alana nor Annette would be in the house without getting a kiss and a cuddle from me – that's how close we were. One of my friends used to say my house was like Grand Central Station, it was that busy, and that you would have thought my girls didn't have husbands to go home to.

I did get a phone call out of the blue from Annette one Saturday night in 2001 to tell me she was getting married again and that she missed me and loved me and was sorry for what had happened. She was about to fly out to Las Vegas for the wedding ceremony, but was planning a reception when she came back to Dumbarton. Annette asked if I would come to the reception and I said I would love to be there. She then said that she and Joseph – her new husband-to-be – would come to visit me the following night. However, Annette never turned up and I haven't heard from her since.

A couple of years after that, I was in Helensburgh with my nieces, Margaret and Mary. We walked into a clothes shop and who would be inside but Alana and her second husband, Tony. I'm sure Alana saw me because suddenly her bag fell to the floor and everything spilled out of it onto the ground. They quickly busied themselves picking stuff up and putting it back in the handbag. Alana didn't make any attempt to recognise I was in the shop and I didn't want to cause any embarrassment. So I walked to the other end of the shop and looked at the display of nightdresses until the pair of them left.

It's a sad, sad way for a mother-and-daughter relation-ship to be, but it wasn't of my making. It wasn't me Alana had the fall-out with over Mark's job before she stormed out of the house declaring she would never return. Then Annette had decided to believe that I had barred her sister from my house and showed a misguided solidarity by refusing to visit me. I definitely feel the aggrieved party in all this. After all I had just been through with Gordon, the last thing I needed four weeks after burying my son was my two daughters to disappear from my life.

Nowadays, I might see Alana and Annette at the odd wedding or funeral, but we never speak to each other. I still feel hurt that the two daughters who were such a huge part of my life, and I in theirs, should have treated me the way they did over an argument that had nothing to do with me and at a time when everyone was on edge and their emotions were raw. I don't think I should beg for Alana and Annette to speak to me again nor apologise to them for something I didn't do. What they did to me broke my heart and I was stunned that it had happened. They know how to get in touch with me. After all, none of us is getting any younger and we're a long time dead.

If losing my beloved son Gordon and then my two daughters deciding they weren't talking to me wasn't enough, even more heartache was to follow – this time at the hands of Gordon's widow, Lorraine.

After Gordon was killed, his daughters Alana and Kelly would come to my house to stay every weekend. This went on for about a year until one Friday the girls never turned up. I phoned Lorraine and one of the girls answered and said: 'It's my gran.' Then I heard Lorraine saying: 'Put the phone down.' I called back several times, but the phone was never answered. I thought maybe Lorraine was going through a bad time after Gordon's death, so I just left it.

I never heard anything from Lorraine or the girls the whole of the following week and when they didn't appear the next Friday either I began to wonder what was going on. My fears were confirmed when a letter arrived from

Lorraine's lawyer telling me that I wasn't to see my grand-daughters any more and falsely accusing me of upsetting the children by making remarks about a man Lorraine was seeing. I was astounded. I had never mentioned anything to the girls about anyone Lorraine may or may not have been seeing.

Then another bombshell – a second lawyer's letter arrived accusing me of showing Alana and Kerry – who were then seven and five years old – videos that were 'unsuitable for children'. This was an absolute lie. When I told Robert – who was still coming back and forward to the house to see me – and Frances and Tilly about this they insisted that I should go to a lawyer and reply to these outrageous and false accusations. Especially as the night I was supposed to have shown the girls these 'unsuitable' videos, I wasn't even in the house looking after them. I was at a ladies' night and my other, older granddaughter, Kelly-Anne McGovern, was babysitting the girls along with Robert and a long-time family friend and Granny Boyle's grandson, Andy Dobbin.

I had my lawyer write back denying these allegations in no uncertain terms. The letter Lorraine's lawyer then sent offered me visits with the girls, but supervised by my daughter, Alana. This was becoming a sick joke, I thought. I had looked after these girls ever since they were born and now I was to be supervised by someone who wasn't even talking to me. My lawyer advised me not to give in, so I replied saying that this was unacceptable.

I got another letter from Lorraine's lawyer offering that I could see Alana and Kelly between 2 p.m. and 4 p.m. every Tuesday and Friday. Again, I said that I didn't accept these conditions and my lawyer wrote back to that effect. The reply to this letter was that I could see the girls any time I wanted.

However, very serious allegations had been made against me and now that it was accepted they weren't true, my lawyer said I should get an apology. My solicitor wrote back asking for a full retraction and apology, but Lorraine's lawyer said that he could no longer make contact with her to take instruction on this demand.

I was rightly disgusted at what had been said about me and I wanted publicly to clear my name, as I didn't know who else she had said these terrible things about me to. Lorraine's lawyer was contacted by my solicitor and he said he had no objection to the following public notice that appeared in my local newspaper, the *Lennox Herald*. The public notice read: 'I, Mrs Mary Campbell, would like to thank the loyal members of my family and many friends for their support through my recent unpleasant ordeal. Now that my name is completely cleared, once again my sincere thanks to all who made this possible.'

The last time I heard from Lorraine was when she told one of the girls to put the phone down when I called to ask why they hadn't come to stay with me that Friday night. I have no idea why she would make these stories up about me and want to stop Alana and Kelly seeing me. Maybe now that she had started going out with men again she thought I would turn away from her. But if that is what she believed, nothing could have been further from the truth. Even then, only a year after Gordon's death, I realised that she was a young woman and had her whole life ahead of her and that included having another partner or a husband.

After all my heartbreak at losing Gordon, I thought nothing else could ever happen to me that would bring me as much pain – but I was wrong.

Another Son Gone

There are only two of us in the house when I pull open a drawer, take out ten tea towels, walk into the kitchenette and place them on the worktop beside the sink.

'What are you doing that for?' asks my son John.

'I know Mark's dead. The police will soon be here to tell us and before you know it the house is going to be full of people making cups of tea and there'll be loads of dishes to get done,' I reply.

John looks at me, but says nothing more. We've all been here before, almost three years before, when Gordon was murdered. This time my youngest boy, Mark, has been missing since Monday and now it's Wednesday. Three days since I last saw him head off into town as I started to make his favourite dinner of stewed sausage, onions, turnip and potatoes. Not a phone call, no message sent with a pal to let me know where he was and no success with the searches going on all over Dumbarton.

As I say, I'd been there before with Gordon and I just knew Mark was dead. How did I know? I had that same feeling of dread that I had when Gordon was murdered. I knew Mark was a good, dependable and loyal boy who loved his mother and wouldn't do anything to upset me – especially since he knew more than most how I still hadn't got over the trauma of losing Gordon in such a violent way.

Mark was gone and I knew he wasn't coming back. I also knew what the aftermath would be like, when eventually there would be a couple of police officers standing in the middle of my living room looking awkward and not wanting to break the inevitable news to a mother.

And, sure enough, there was that dreaded but expected knock on the door. I was in the kitchenette with my tea towels when it happened and hadn't heard anything. But John answered the door, came into the kitchenette and said: 'Mammy, there's a policeman and a policewoman in the living room.'

The policewoman's face was chalk-white. After all, she was just a young lassie and maybe not so used to dealing with death at such close quarters. The two of them look at me and the policeman says: 'Would you like to sit down?'

'No, it's all right,' I reply.

'We've got Dr Doig coming.'

'Mark's dead, isn't he?'

'Has someone already been here?' he asks with a perplexed look on his face.

'No – but you're not saying that he isn't dead.'

The conversation was interrupted as Dr Anne Doig, another doctor from the practice I went to, walked into the living room, put her arms round me and said: 'Oh, Mary, I can't believe I've had to come to the same mother twice in three years for something like this.'

She made me sit down and the policeman continued with his unpleasant duties. 'Your son Mark was found dead in a house in Bellsmyre,' he told me.

'Have you got who murdered him?' I asked.

'No, Mark took his own life – he hanged himself.'

That's when the calmness went. I knew Mark was dead, but I certainly wasn't expecting to hear he had taken his own life. When the policeman's words sank in, numbness went through my whole body. I thought my head was going to burst. It was too horrible to believe that Mark had taken a rope, put it round his neck and hanged himself. Just like when I had been told Gordon had been murdered, I couldn't cry. I didn't cry for eight years after that. The doctor had told me that the shock and the grief had been so intense that it took me that long actually to shed a tear for either of the two boys who had so cruelly been taken from me.

I thought there was definitely not a God. It had happened to me once; I had lost a son and now He'd done it to me again – I'd lost another son. I was immersed in a world of my own as the house began to fill with people who had heard about the tragedy. No doubt they were saying all the things that should be said at a time like that, but I was going through the motions and it all washed over me, as I was oblivious. I was talking to myself in my head, thinking it wasn't just two of my boys God had taken from me. There was Frances's son Davie, who was killed in a car crash in 1976. I was extremely close to Davie and treated him like a son of my own, as he had lived in our house for some time in the mid Sixties.

'That's three boys God has taken from me,' I said to myself over and over. 'What have I ever done to God to deserve this?'

Then a different emotion overwhelmed me and my anger turned to Mark. 'What if they are telling the truth and Mark has killed himself?' I thought. 'Why did he do this to me after his brother had been murdered and he knew how much that had devastated my life?'

What tiny semblance of a life I had left after Gordon's murder was shattered on that Wednesday night of 23 February 1994. The last person in our family to see Mark was John, as they were both in a café in Dumbarton on a freezing cold day with the snow falling heavily. Mark had been saying to John how he was looking forward to having his dinner as it was his favourite, and the pair of them were about to step out of the door and head for home when Mark's former girlfriend, Frances Connolly, asked to have a word with him.

Mark told John to carry on and head home himself. 'But tell my mammy to put my dinner out – I'll be right at your back after I've spoken to Frances,' Mark said. When John got home he told me Mark was on his way and I'd to plate his dinner. But half an hour went by and he didn't appear. Mark was still not back after an hour and then two hours, three hours, four hours . . .

Ever since Gordon died I had drummed it into Mark that wherever he was, and if he was going to be late home, he should phone and let me know he was safe – even if he had no money and had to reverse the charges.

I telephoned the police later on Monday night and you can understand how at first they would have thought I was just an over-anxious, paranoid mother.

'He didn't come home for his tea. What age is he?' the policeman at the other end of the phone asked.

'He's twenty,' I replied.

'Don't be so ridiculous.'

'You might think that, but you never had a son murdered three years ago.'

'Oh, sorry – is that you, Mrs Campbell? Where do you think Mark might be?'

'I've no idea.'

'Listen, we'll keep an eye out for him and maybe have a look round the pubs to see if he's there.'

Give them their due, the police phoned back later, but only to say they hadn't found Mark.

I was phoning everyone I could think of and even got a hold of Mark's diary and called every name he had a telephone number beside. Of course, I phoned the hospital to see if anyone called Mark Campbell had been admitted, but I was no further forward. The following day, Tuesday and then Wednesday was more of the same, calling everyone I could think of, but nobody had seen Mark since he was in the café late on Monday afternoon. Of course, all my desperate phone calls trying to find out where Mark was stopped when the two police officers came to tell me the tragic news.

My grandson Philip McGovern and his pal Thomas Cavan found Mark in a house in Bellsmyre after spending the previous two days looking for him. It was a flat that Robert had previously stayed in after we divorced, but no one had been living there for a while. Why Mark should be in that flat I will never know. Apparently, they found Mark with the rope from a boxing punch bag round his neck, which was tied to a beam in the loft.

But did Mark take his own life? There was no suicide note left and although many, many people take their own lives without there being any indication that they were feeling that way, it came as a total shock to everyone. It's the one thing about Mark's death that haunts me to this day – not knowing why he took his own life and if he didn't, was it an accident in a prank that went wrong, or did somebody kill him? There was something that could point to suicide, but then again, there are inconsistencies that make me wonder.

Mark had been suffering with back pains and he was due to have an operation to remove a tumour from his spine. That much I knew, but what I didn't know until after his death was that doctors had told him the operation could leave him paralysed. Mark kept this to himself, not wanting to burden me with even more bad news after Gordon's murder.

Mark was born with a big, dark blue birthmark at the base of his spine. The doctors were at first concerned and told me he might have spina bifida and they wanted to do more tests. He was kept in hospital for several weeks before the doctors came back and told me that the birthmark was superficial and that everything would be fine. As Mark grew up everything was fine and we believed it really was just a simple birthmark. But when he was fourteen Mark started to get sore stomachs and despite numerous trips to the doctors we could never find out what was causing the pain. Everything from stress to something he had eaten was suggested until Dr Barlow, a GP from the medical centre who we didn't normally see, noticed the birthmark when he was examining Mark. 'I know this might sound ridiculous,' he said. 'But I think the stomach pain might be coming from the boy's back. I don't like the look of the centre of the birthmark.'

But just as quickly as they came, the stomach pains disappeared and when Dr Barlow asked him if he wanted something done about the birthmark, Mark said he wasn't bothered as long as he didn't have a sore stomach any more. But about three years later, in 1990, I noticed blood coming from the centre of the birthmark and when I questioned Mark, he admitted he had been suffering from a sore back. Although he played it down and said it was just 'every now and then', I was having none of it and insisted he went back to see Dr Barlow, who referred Mark to the former Canniesburn Hospital, in Glasgow. Doctors there examined Mark and said they wanted a neurologist to examine him, as a straightforward birthmark shouldn't be painful.

For the next three years Mark was in and out of hospitals as a day patient, getting all sorts of treatment to try to get rid of the birthmark and the pain in his back. Of course, by this time Gordon had been murdered and I was living in my own black world, thinking about nothing else other than my murdered son.

I know now that Mark must have suffered terrible agony from his back, as the painkillers he was prescribed were extremely strong. But he was such a thoughtful and caring son he didn't want me to know just how bad the pain was, nor how serious it was. Now and again I would see Mark lying on his stomach across his bed and when I asked him why he was doing that he said it was the only way to get some relief from his sore back. But when I questioned him further it would always be the same answer: 'You've got enough to worry about. My back's not sore all the time.'

I went with Mark on his first few visits to hospital, but after that he said he wanted to go by himself as he was a grown man and not a child any more. He didn't want people to think he was a child and needed his mammy to come with him to hospital. Our close family friends, Terry and Marion Cunningham, would drive Mark to his appointments, but every time Mark came back from hospital and I asked how he got on, he would just say: 'Fine. They're going to give me another appointment.'

This went on for more than two years until December 1993, when Terry Cunningham told me that Mark had been told three months previously that doctors had discovered he had a tumour on the base of his spine. However, Mark had sworn Terry to secrecy and didn't want him telling me. Even though it was nearly three years since Gordon had been murdered, I was still distraught with grief and everything else was still passing me by. But this was another blow and it shocked me to the core.

I felt a terrible guilt. I had been so wrapped up in my grief over Gordon, I hadn't been able to see the pain and anguish my youngest son was going through. I was numb and couldn't believe something so terrible was happening to me again.

I waited until Mark was in the kitchenette by himself before I went in and asked: 'Why didn't you tell me about the doctors saying you had a tumour on your spine?'

'Mammy, you've had nothing on your mind but Gordon since he went. I'm not so bad – at least I'm still here. I don't blame you and I know your life is finished because of what happened to Gordon,' Mark replied.

I hugged him tightly. 'I'm really sorry, and I do love you. It's just that I don't know how to show love any more,' I told him. I thought I would have had all the time in the world to look after my youngest boy once I had got over Gordon, but as it turned out, nothing could have been further from the truth and that still hurts me to this day.

Even after that emotional conversation with him, Mark still protected me from his real suffering. The doctors had told him that he was to have the operation to remove the tumour in March the following year. But the prognosis was that there was a 50 per cent chance he might not walk again as he could be paralysed from the waist down after the surgeons had removed the tumour. Mark never told me this. It was only after Mark died that his former girlfriend Frances mentioned it. She too had been warned by Mark not to mention anything about this to me. 'My mammy's got enough on her plate with Gordon's murder, so don't say anything,' Mark had told her.

Sure, Mark had told me he was going to have an operation, but all he had said was that it might take a long time for him to recover. I'm sure that was him preparing me for the worst in case I was wondering why he couldn't walk when he came out of hospital.

Maybe it was the thought of spending the rest of his life in a wheelchair if he came out of the operation paralysed that drove Mark to suicide. This is me taking over Mark's thoughts now, but maybe he thought that if Gordon had still been alive to help me and I wasn't the state I was in, I would have been able to cope looking after him in a wheelchair. But he could have just looked at me and said to himself: 'She can hardly talk to anyone, let alone look after someone who is paralysed. Gordon's gone and she doesn't even want her own life, let alone to take on the life of someone who is in a wheelchair; that would be an even bigger burden for her to carry.'

Mark was the type of person who wouldn't want me to go through any more grief and he would think having to look after him would be too much for me. He was such a caring and thoughtful person. He had such high principles that he would rather take his own life than put an extra burden on me. But I would have been glad still to have Mark, whether he was in a wheelchair or not. If he could somehow hear me now I would say to Mark: 'I would rather have you in a wheelchair for the rest of your life, so long as you would still have been here on this earth with me.'

But a lot of the time I think about the inconsistencies in the suicide theory that will always make me wonder if that really was the case.

First, Mark never left a note and that is something that I would have expected him to do if he had committed suicide. He would have written a letter because he wrote about everything, whether it was letters, notes or even poems. He was always writing things down. I can't imagine Mark not leaving a note, as he was fanatical about making sure everything was tidy and in its place. If a person like that does want to commit suicide I would expect them to leave a note expressing their feelings in words, explaining why they were doing it, and not leaving any loose ends. It would have been second nature for Mark to pick up a pen and write me a letter saying: 'Mammy, I'm sorry, but this operation's not going to happen because you've got enough to deal with in your life and I don't want to be an extra burden on you.'

Then there was the £250 I had given him to pay the gas and phone bill. Well, the bills were still in his pocket when he was found dead and they weren't stamped as having been paid, but the money was gone. The only money I got back as having been in Mark's possession was 38p – they said that was all the money found on Mark's body and I've still got those coins in an envelope tucked away in a drawer. So where did the £250 go? Did someone steal it while he was alive and was he killed for that money? I know people have been murdered for less. Or did someone rob him after he was dead?

I don't think he gave the money to his ex-girlfriend Frances either, because if he wanted money for anything like that, Mark would know he only had to ask me and I would have given him whatever he needed. I would have trusted Mark with my life and if he said he was going to pay those bills for me, then something terrible would have to have happened for him not to do that.

I have twice asked Frances what happened that Monday when she met Mark in the café – once a few weeks after Mark died and the second time on the first anniversary of his death. But she would only say that she last saw Mark at the Spar shop in Bellsmyre. So, Frances wasn't able to shed any light on what happened to the money, what was said or what happened between Mark leaving the café with her and walking to Bellsmyre.

Another mystery to me is how Mark got up into the loft to tie the rope around the beam. At the Fatal Accident Inquiry into Mark's death it was stated that a small red stool was found directly below the hatch to the loft. But we had been told that the police had borrowed the stool from a neighbour to get into the loft, and when Robert visited the flat the day after Mark was found, all the kitchen chairs were placed neatly under the table and a pair of step ladders Robert knew was in the house were still in the cupboard.

At the inquest it was said that the stool gave Mark a bit of height and Mark climbed up the wall 'like Spider-man' and pulled himself up into the loft. That's how they described it – he climbed up 'like Spider-man'. I might just be a mother in denial, but that sounds strange to me, especially when there was no stool in the house at that time.

There were also other clues to Mark's state of mind and they certainly didn't point to his being suicidal. He had got a place in college to study accountancy the following September and he was going to classes in Dumbarton Academy to brush up on his computer skills. Mark was also due to take his driving test and he had already been to see a car he was going to buy if he passed.

Mark was also making plans for his twenty-first birthday party in May and writing a list of people he would invite and the places where he could hold the party. And he was in the middle of making his own wreath to take to Gordon's graveside on what would have been his big brother's birthday the following week. The wreath was half-finished and lying in Mark's room.

But my biggest doubt came when a policeman who was investigating Mark's death came to visit me and said: 'I've been in the police for twenty-odd years and I've come across cases like this before. I always get a gut feeling about things as soon as I see them and my gut feeling is that your boy never did this to himself. If it's any consolation to you, my opinion is that I don't think your boy was there on his own.'

You can imagine how I tear myself apart at times with all those conflicting thoughts going through my head. Even if Mark did commit suicide, I don't believe it is the coward's way out. I am a coward and I have thought many times about wanting to die, but I couldn't bring myself to commit suicide.

For someone to have had the tragedies in their life I've had – the deaths of my nephew Davie, my sons Gordon and Mark and even more heartache in 1999 when my granddaughter Kelly-Anne McGovern died of silent pneumonia at only twenty-one – you would probably expect them to want to escape by killing themselves. But I'm a coward and I don't have the guts to kill myself and be gone from the dark, dark place that I find myself in sometimes.

The emotions and feelings I have can change from day to day. At the start, shortly after Mark died I experienced a terrible feeling that he had deserted me and let me down. I have large photographs of both Gordon and Mark on my living-room wall and I would sometimes look at Mark and say: 'How could you do this to me? I always thought you would be my rock and now you've gone away and left me.' And I also felt resentment because I thought maybe Mark loved Gordon more than me and he hanged himself because he wanted to be with him instead of me.

Thankfully, those feelings went away eventually, but I would sometimes then turn my anger to Gordon, look at his picture and say: 'This is all your fault. If you hadn't got yourself murdered, Mark would still be here because he would know you would be around to look after him, even if he was paralysed and in a wheelchair.' If Gordon had still been alive, I know that he would have done everything he could to help Mark because he truly loved his wee brother.

People say time is a great healer – well it's done nothing to make me feel better. The other one people come away with is that you have to pick yourself up and get on with your life. I'm afraid that after losing my two sons I sometimes feel as if I don't have a life and it's just an existence. Some days, I can be in the depths of despair until someone says something amusing or makes a joke and that can see me through another day. By the time I have laughed, it has broken the spell of sorrow that has been cast over me.

A good example of this relief is when I phoned the author who is helping me write this book one day, and when he asked how I was, I told him: 'I'm having one of those days. I'm really down and I feel like killing myself.'

'Today's not a good day for suicide, Mary,' he said. 'Why don't you leave it until your book's published?'

Black humour indeed, but I had a laugh and it broke me free of my despair – for a time, anyway.

Obviously people are extremely sympathetic and do their best to make me feel a little better, but no one – unless they too have had both their sons taken from them – can fully understand, imagine or appreciate just what it feels like.

I can only describe it as like being in a dungeon. Now, I've never been in a dungeon, but I can imagine what it's like – although my dungeon doesn't have any doors or windows. All I can see is four walls, and those walls go on forever and ever upwards and there is nothing but darkness. I bounce from one wall to the other looking for a door, but there is no door, there is no escape from this horrible darkness.

I want to scream. I know there is a huge, gigantic scream deep inside me in the pit of my stomach and if I could only get that scream out I might feel better. I feel the scream passing up through my stomach and into my throat – but the scream never gets any further and doesn't come out. It stays silent and it stays inside me. A monster – that's my silent scream and that's how I feel about my grief. I can't get rid of the monster inside me.

My GP, Dr Mitchelson, and I were talking one day about why I couldn't cry, not even a small tear. She said it was because I was carrying too much grief and advised that I should see a bereavement councillor, who suggested I take someone I trusted to a quiet place and scream my head off. I don't know why, but I can't bring myself to do that. I don't know if it's the embarrassment or the fear of acting ridiculous.

For a long time after Mark's death I didn't want to go out in public, but when I did venture out for the first few times, it would be to visit my GP at the health centre in Dumbarton. The receptionist there, Morag McGinlay, was – and still is – a tower of strength. She would let me stand at the side of the reception area out of sight of the rest of the patients in the waiting room. She spared me the ordeal of being stared at and being asked questions by other people who obviously knew what had happened. Human nature being what it is, people are curious about tragedies, but I could not face speaking about Mark's death. God bless this young woman who realised what I was going through and spared me even more pain.

I know this may sound callous, but I used to watch television and see mothers who have lost children sitting there crying their eyes out and I would think how lucky they were. I loved Gordon and Mark just as much as they loved their children, but they could cry and get rid of their monster. I couldn't cry, I couldn't get relief – the monster was still there deep, deep inside me and it wasn't going away.

My Husband's A Killer

The newspaper headline says it all – 'My husband is a killer'. The Mary Kelly jinx has struck again and I'm reading about myself and how my husband had stabbed his live-in lover to death after we had separated.

I was sixty-six years old when I married Frank McLaren, who is seven years younger than me, and you'd think at my age I would have learned my lesson, but it appears not. To say my relationship with Frank was farcical is a bit of an understatement. We lived together for six years, got married in March 2001, and four months later, in July of that same year, I locked him out of the house and told him not to come back because of his heavy drinking. Over the years I have certainly given the gossips something to talk about, but this time they were going into overdrive.

Oh, what a tangled web we weave. The long and tortuous road that led me to being the wife of a man who kills his lover and gets three and a half years in jail after pleading guilty to culpable homicide began nearly thirty years previously.

Rewind to 1972: Robert has disappeared on one of his jaunts again and I'm left on my own. One Saturday night I go to the Denny Social Club in Dumbarton with my brother Willie, his wife Sadie and one of my pals, Agnes Beattie. Willie tells us that there is a great singer and piano player going to do a turn at the club that night and he's called Frank McLaren. 'If this boy would just keep off the drink, he could really go places,' says Willie.

Sure enough, this Frank McLaren went down a storm and was a smashing singer. After his spot he came over to our table to say hello to Willie. 'This is my sister, Mary,' Willie says, introducing me to Frank.

'I know you,' Frank says, looking at me.

'No, I don't think we've ever met,' I reply.

'I used to be your milk boy when you stayed in Cumbrae Crescent. I fair fancied you then and I used to leave you extra pints of milk.'

This is a right patter merchant, I think, but I enjoy the attention he's giving me and we get up on the floor to dance.

'Where's your man Boxer tonight?' asks Frank.

'He's away.'

'I heard that he never turned out to be much of a good guy. I'm not married myself.'

Now, that might have been theoretically a true statement, but he had missed out a few other rather salient facts, as I was later to find out. I believed him when he told me he was single and, after a few dances, Frank asks: 'Can I see you home?'

I thought, 'He's not married, Robert is off on his wanderings, so why not?' I didn't say anything to Willie or Sadie about Frank seeing me home and when they were heading off, I just said I would wait to hear Frank do another spot singing later on that night. We went back to Agnes's house that night and that was the start of my relationship with Frank McLaren.

Over the next few weeks I would go to pubs and clubs to hear Frank singing. I'll admit he was a good-looking young man with long, jet-black, curly hair that a woman would die for. I did find out years later from one of his irate wives that Frank got his hairstyle by putting in women's curlers before he would go out at night. So there you are, looks, as well as what he was telling me about being single, can be deceiving.

About three months after I started going with Frank, who

should turn up on the scene again but Robert? He knew I had been going out with Frank McLaren, but Robert said he was going to get a job and house in Huddersfield and asked if I would come with him and make another go of our marriage. I thought a fresh start might help things and as I got on really well with his brother Ian and his wife, Ellen, who also stayed in Huddersfield, I agreed to pack up my belongings and head south with the children.

I told Frank I was leaving Dumbarton and getting back with Robert and as far as our relationship was concerned, that was that. But six weeks after I had moved to Huddersfield with Robert, who turned up at our door? None other than Frank McLaren.

Frank and Robert knew each other from Dumbarton and when Robert asked him what he was doing in Huddersfield, Frank gave him a tale about two guys from Manchester hearing him sing and suggesting they could get him work in the clubs in the north-west of England. 'I knew you were in Huddersfield now,' Frank said to Robert. 'And I've got a booking to sing Friday and Saturday nights at a working men's club at the end of your road. Do you know of anywhere I could get digs?'

Now, Robert might have been a lot of things in those days, but he wasn't daft and he knew I had been seeing Frank back in Dumbarton. So Robert arranged for Frank to stay in digs at his brother's house, where there was a spare room. No doubt to make sure he could keep tabs on him.

Within a few days of Frank appearing in Huddersfield, I got a surprise letter from Willie saying he and Sadie were coming down to visit us the following weekend. Willie and Sadie duly arrived for their weekend in sunny Huddersfield and he acted surprised when I told him Frank McLaren was also here. I've no doubt Willie knew fine well that Frank had appeared out of nowhere and that was the reason for his trip south.

'Let's all go to Blackpool,' said Willie. 'And why don't we ask Frank to come as well?'

Both Ian and Willie had the car so it was organised that Ellen, Robert, me and two of the kids would go in Ian's car and Willie would take Sadie, Frank and our other two children in his car.

While we were in Blackpool, Willie made sure he got me on his own and asked: 'What do you know about Frank McLaren?'

'He's just a single guy that's got the chance of some work singing in the clubs down here,' I replied.

'Single, is he?' said Willie. 'What about the young woman up in Bellsmyre who has five kids by him?'

I knew nothing about this, as Frank had told me he stayed with his mother in Castlehill. Although I maybe should have thought a bit more about why a good-looking young man like Frank, barely thirty, wouldn't have a regular girlfriend and still stayed with his mother. And before I could challenge Frank, he announced that he was going back to Dumbarton the next day. Everything happened so suddenly that I've no doubt Willie's trip to Huddersfield was to warn Frank to leave me alone and turn his attentions elsewhere.

Unfortunately, Willie was a bit late with his intervention as a doctor soon confirmed what I had suspected and feared immediately before I left Dumbarton for Huddersfield – I was pregnant, and Frank was the baby's father. Once again, I had conceived during an affair while Robert was off gallivanting. Just my luck.

I told Robert I was expecting and we all just acted as if the baby was his. Robert had got us a council house in Huddersfield and one of our neighbours was a Scot who had married an English girl. After a few months he came into our house to see me and said he suspected Robert was carrying on with his wife.

Why was I not surprised? And it was further justification

in my mind that if Robert was being unfaithful to me, I was going to be unfaithful to him to get back for the hurt he'd caused me over the years. I still say I would have been a good wee wife if I hadn't found out about all the shenanigans he was getting up to.

But it looked as though I could be facing another problem, since the irate husband was going to tell Robert to stay away from his wife; I knew Robert's usual reaction to this kind of situation was to do a runner and I didn't want to be left in Huddersfield by myself. I decided that I'd had enough, and I wanted to go back to Dumbarton. I'd been feeling like this for a while – wanting to go back home – and this latest incident set the seal on it.

I told Robert I was going back to Dumbarton and he said I should stay with his mother for a few weeks until I got a council house, then he and the rest of the family would follow me back to Scotland. I had told Frank about being pregnant, but said I was back with Robert and we were going to get a house in Dumbarton. Mark was born on 19 May 1973 and I settled back into the old routine with Robert. Although Robert's mother, Jessie, always said that she didn't think her son was Mark's father, it wasn't until many years later, during an argument, that I admitted that Frank was Mark's dad, but by that time our marriage was a bit of a sham and it never made any difference to our relationship.

For a few years after Mark was born I would get the odd phone call from Frank – who was now staying in Liverpool – asking how I was. And any time he was back in Dumbarton, he would try to visit me, but I always refused to see Frank, telling one of my boys to say I wasn't in when he came to the door. After that happened a few times he got the message and completely disappeared out of my life.

That was until the night Mark's body was found. At one point, with everyone coming and going in my house, I turned round and Frank was standing in the middle of my living room with his brother.

'Tell me it's not my son,' he said.

'It is, Frank. It's Mark who's dead.'

After that, every day without fail Frank would turn up at my house with a bunch of flowers, a jar of coffee or a packet of biscuits or cakes in a wee bag for me. I began to see what I thought was a 'new' Frank McLaren – someone who was kind and compassionate with not a word out of place. He told me he had been married, but was divorced and was back living with his mother in Dumbarton. I believed him.

In hindsight I know now that Frank saw me as being vulnerable, breaking my heart for my boy, and here was a chance if he played his cards right to maybe rekindle a flame there. I even got a call from his mother who asked if Frank was pestering me and did he have a drink in him when he was visiting me.

It never clicked that there might have been an ulterior motive and he was acting the complete gentleman to get on my good side and worm his way back into my affections. I never noticed Frank being the worse for wear with the drink, although I do recall he would come into the house for an evening and bring a couple of cans of lager with him. What I didn't know – because I was never a drinker myself – was that it was extra-strong lager and just enough to keep his alcohol level topped up. No, there was never anything untoward about Frank's behaviour in the months after Mark died. Not a word out of place, none of the Casanova patter you would normally get from him. Frank was a fly man right enough. He knew that if he was to have any chance of getting in my good books, one bad move and he would have been rumbled.

Mark thought Robert was his dad until he was sixteen, when Gordon played a rotten trick on him and revealed that

Frank was his real father. Gordon and his pals had sneaked Mark into The Keep public house in Dumbarton even though he was under age. Who would be singing that night, but Frank McLaren?

Mark was sitting there enjoying himself drinking a pint with the 'men', as he would have seen it. That was until he turned to Gordon and his pals and said: 'That guy's a great singer. He even sounds like Tom Jones.'

'Aye, so he is,' said Gordon with a smirk on his face. 'And he's your dad.'

'You're a dirty liar,' said Mark.

'I am not. Remember when you were younger and you sang at cousin Anne's wedding and you brought the house down? Where did you think that came from? Your mammy can't sing. You take it off your dad – that guy over there who's a great singer.'

Well, Mark burst into the house in floods of tears and said: 'Do you know what Gordon has done to me? Him and all his pals are laughing at me up in The Keep just now.'

'What is it? I've told you not to bother about Gordon when he's winding you up.'

'He says that man singing up The Keep is my dad. He says his name's Frank McLaren and he's my dad.'

I was raging with Gordon for doing that and I can just imagine that Gordon and his pals were wanting rid of Mark from the pub and Gordon would be signing behind Mark's back to the rest of the crowd how he would do that. No doubt he thought it was great laugh. Mark certainly wasn't laughing and neither was I that night. I had to sit Mark down and tell him all about Frank McLaren being his dad.

Like many big brother–wee brother relationships, the older one would take a rise out of his younger sibling, but as quick as a row erupted they would make up again. That's exactly what happened on this occasion. The next day Gordon's car was parked outside our gate and Mark went out to see what was happening.

'Did you report me to your mammy for what I said last night?' Gordon asked.

'I certainly did and my mammy says you've not to get in the house for doing that.'

'Don't you worry, wee man. Give it a fortnight, a couple of bunches of flowers and everything will be all right.'

Gordon then handed Mark £100 and said: 'There you are. You know I didn't really mean to hurt you – we were only having a laugh.'

As far as Mark was concerned, that was Gordon back on his pedestal and all was forgiven.

But back to Mr McLaren. He was really playing it cute, keeping everything platonic, no doubt realising that Robert had stopped staying at my house a couple of months after Mark's death. For the next ten months he would always be there, keeping me company with a sympathetic word or a kind deed – until the New Year of 1995.

I was still under the impression that Frank wasn't married and he had promised my son John that we would see in the New Year together. I had met Frank's sister, Rita, who was in Dumbarton visiting her mother over the festive period and we agreed to meet for dinner at the Dumbuck Hotel on Hogmanay. We were sitting at the table and she said: 'What do you think of Frank going back down to Liverpool to see his wife? On Hogmanay, of all days.'

I almost choked on what I was eating. I was really angry, hurt and felt let-down. Especially for John, who was looking forward to spending Hogmanay with life-and-soul-of-the-party Frank.

On 2 January the phone rang and it was Frank. 'Mary,' he said. 'I can't stick this down here. I'll tell you the truth now – I'm married.'

'I know fine well you are – Rita told me.'

'When I came down here I started thinking of you and I want to come back to Dumbarton and be with you.'

'Well you can come to Dumbarton all you like, but don't come near my door. You're a rotten swine pretending all the time you were Mr Nice Guy and letting John down like that.' I slammed the phone down – message delivered.

I should have listened to my sister Frances who – along with a steady stream of family and friends – never liked Frank and had continually warned me not to have anything to do with him. They said I was daft to give him the time of day.

The next thing I knew was that Frank's mother died at the end of January and he came to my house to let me know about the funeral arrangements. Despite the way he had behaved I felt sorry for his loss and I had to give him the same respect and sympathy that he had given me when Mark died.

After the funeral, Frank told me he had applied for a quickie divorce and asked if we could start seeing each other. I wasn't getting caught out a second time with his lies, so I told him not to come back until he could prove he was officially divorced. Within a few weeks he was back with the news that he was now divorced.

'What about you and me getting married?' he asked.

'I couldn't marry you because I've promised our Frances that I wouldn't and I'm not going to break that promise to her while she's alive,' I replied. And I had promised, because to say Frances didn't approve of my relationship with Frank was an understatement.

'She could live for another twenty-odd years,' he replied.

'I don't care. I've promised Frances that I wouldn't marry you and that's the way it's going to be.'

He protested a bit more, but he soon realised that I wouldn't budge and eventually it was: 'We could live together then.' I agreed because I thought that I loved him, but in reality it was probably just loneliness and someone to fill a void. I had the idea that with Frank in my life, I would be able to keep a little bit of Mark there as well. So Frank McLaren moved in with me in May 1995.

There hadn't been much in my life to make me laugh in the four years prior to getting together with Frank. What with Gordon's murder and then Mark's death I was certainly in need of cheering up, and that's exactly what Frank did. Even though he drank far too much, I put up with it because he was a funny drunk. Some people take on a horrible persona and just want to fight everyone when they have had too much to drink, but Frank was exactly the opposite. All he wanted to do when he was drunk was play the piano, sing songs, tell jokes and be the centre of attention. He was a drunk you could laugh with and people used to come round to our house on a Saturday and Sunday night because they knew Frank would have a good drink in him and he would entertain them by playing lots of different tunes on his keyboard and giving them all a song.

It was also a relief from my grief to have all those people around me having a good time with Frank singing and telling funny stories. There's a hell of a lot you can criticise Frank McLaren for, but one of the gifts he did have was to make me and other people laugh.

Four years after Frank moved in with me, my sister Frances died, on 3 December 1999, and that was a huge loss to me. Even as adults, Frances always saw herself as being the big sister who needed to look after her sometimes foolhardy younger sibling and keep her on the right road. She was probably right on that score. Frances was very strict in what she saw as right and wrong and wouldn't be slow to give me a good talking-to. But when the chips were down and I needed help, Frances was always there. If she heard from one of her girls that they had bumped into me and I wasn't feeling too good, she would be on the phone straight away or would come round for a chat.

It was just over a year after Frances died that Frank once again asked me to marry him. We were in the house with my niece Maggie and her boyfriend Paul at the time, having a good laugh amongst ourselves, when Frank suggested we tie the knot. After many, many refusals, this time I said: 'Yes – why not? It'll probably be a good laugh right enough. I'll be sixty-six in a few weeks' time so I might as well have a last go at it before that.'

Maggie asked: 'Are you sure you want to do this?'

'Even if we get one good day out of it, a nice meal and a day out, it will be a rare laugh and something to look back on,' I replied.

So, that was me, going to be Mrs McLaren and getting married at the age of sixty-five for a laugh. That's the God's honest truth – I agreed to get married for a laugh. What on earth possessed me to think that way, I'll never know. Even Maggie and Paul trying to get me to think it through couldn't stop me.

'Listen, with everything that's happened to me and my two boys, Gordon and Mark, I don't really care what I do or what happens to me,' I told them.

I knew what the reaction of my family and friends would be, so we decided to keep the wedding a secret. We got a special licence to get married at the Vale of Leven Register Office – instead of the one in Dumbarton – with only Maggie and Paul present as witnesses, on 29 March 2001 – two days before my sixty-sixth birthday.

As I had thought, it was a laugh getting married in secret, but when we were back at Maggie's place after the ceremony some reality kicked in.

'Oh my God, how am I going to tell everybody that I've gone and got married again?' I asked. Paul came up with a plan that since it was my birthday in two days' time I would have a wee birthday party in my house and invite family and friends along. When they were there, I would drop the bombshell that I had got married in secret.

Sure enough they all came, handed over birthday presents, wished me Happy Birthday and I blew all the candles out on the cake. It was a normal birthday celebration until Paul asked for everyone's attention and started to make an announcement.

'I've something to tell you all. Just so you know, Mary, Frank, Maggie and I had a lovely day out on Thursday and, as a matter of fact, Mary is now officially Mrs McLaren. Mary and Frank got married.'

A round of congratulations, handshakes, hugs and kisses? No, the announcement was met by a deafening silence in the room. My brother George looked at me and said: 'I knew you weren't right in the head.'

'Thanks, George,' I replied.

Someone else said: 'No offence, Mary – but I'm out of here.'

Another of my friends added: 'You married that? God forgive you, Mary. There's something up with your head. I'm away as well.'

More and more people started to head out of the door saying: 'I told you she was going round the bend. Is that not terrible? She's completely lost it, marrying that Frank McLaren.'

As for Frank, who was well on his way to his usual state of inebriation – well, his reaction to all this commotion was to ask: 'Would any of youse like a wee tune on the piano?'

When he came out with that immortal line, I couldn't stop laughing. Well, that was my wedding reception when I got married for the second time. And needless to say the wedding presents were as scarce as a full bottle of vodka when Frank McLaren was around.

In hindsight, my 'wedding guests' that day were absolutely right – I must have been off my head to marry Frank McLaren. Very quickly after the wedding Frank's behaviour and drinking got steadily worse. The laughs got fewer and fewer as he drank more and more. I came to my senses and realised what a mistake I had made. The mirth he brought me had now turned to misery and I decided that my only option was to end the marriage and put him out of the house.

In the summer of 2002 we had decided to go on holiday to Blackpool along with my son John and one of his pals, Davie Watson. I told Frank that I was going to sleep with John while we were in the hotel and he would be sharing with Davie Watson.

It turned out to be a holiday from hell, with Frank drunk all the time, and at the end he was told by the hotel owners never to come back again. There was an expensive piano in the hotel lounge which belonged to the owner's grandson. Of course, as soon as Frank set eyes on the piano he was telling everyone how no one in the world could play the piano like he could and he would prove it.

He was out of his head with the drink and started playing this piano without asking anyone's permission. When the hotel owner remonstrated with Frank, he started causing an argument, swearing and firing insults at anyone within hearing distance. If the marriage wasn't finished before that Blackpool holiday, then it was well and truly dead and buried after that trip.

We got the bus back to Scotland and I knew Frank would be desperate for a drink by the time we got home to Dumbarton. When we got back inside the house and before any unpacking was done, I gave Frank £10 and told him to go and treat himself to a bottle of vodka just to round off the holiday. He probably thought he'd died and gone to heaven after a week on the drink in Blackpool and then me giving him money for even more. 'You're the best, Mary – never had a wife like you,' he said.

'Well I've never had a husband like you and I'm not putting up with any more of your drinking,' I thought to myself.

So, off he went to the local Co-op store to buy himself his bottle of vodka. But while he was away, I dumped his suitcase on the doorstep and locked the door. I knew he didn't have a key with him.

Five minutes later the letterbox opened and there was Frank. 'Mary, the door's locked. Come and let me in.'

I just sat in the living room with John and his pal Davie.

Frank must have cottoned on to what was happening when he saw his suitcase on the doorstep. That's when his patter started.

'Mary, for f***'s sake, come and open the door. I know I probably overdone it with the drink and I didn't give you and the boys a very good time when we were on holiday.'

And then the dramatics. 'Mary, I'll even smash this bottle of vodka and not touch another drop.'

Nobody was taking him on in the house and when he realised the charm offensive wasn't working, he changed tactics. 'You're a right cow, Mary,' he shouted. 'I never thought you would pull a stunt like this. You'll never do this to me again. If you don't open this door I'll not be back and you'll regret this.'

Sweet music to my ears, that threat, and I was glad to see the back of him. But after a few days he was constantly on the phone, sending me cards and bunches of flowers, asking for me to take him back, but I had come to my senses and always refused.

Frank got himself a house in Burnside Street, Dumbarton and then the soft side of me came to the fore again and I sent John round with dishes, an electric blanket, duvet and groceries. He was regularly trying to get me to take him back, but I had been bitten once and that was one too many times. Eventually, I heard Frank had taken up with another woman who had moved in with him and I thought I was rid of him for good. That was until two years later, in July 2004.

It started with a phone call from a staff nurse in the Christie Ward of the Vale of Leven Hospital where John had been taken after another of his breakdowns. The nurse said a man claiming to be John's stepfather had come to the ward to see him and he was drunk. She asked me to tell my husband to stay away from the ward if he was going to be in that state.

I hadn't spoken to Frank for more than a year, so I sent him a note on a blank card saying: 'Would you please refrain from visiting the Christie Ward, as I was told today you and a female companion visited my son and you were under the influence of alcohol. Please do not embarrass John by going back. Yours sincerely, Mary McLaren.'

But little did I know when I mailed that card that I would be blamed in court for causing the row that led to Frank stabbing to death his forty-year-old live-in lover, Angela Clifford.

Having written and posted the note I thought nothing of it until a few days later there was a knock on my door and two policemen were standing in front of me. I invited them into the house – by this time I had moved to a high-rise flat in Dumbarton – and one of them said: 'We've got something to tell you about your husband.'

'Is he dead?' I asked. And for good reason, as three different doctors had warned Frank that if he didn't stop drinking he would soon be dead.

The policeman replied: 'No, Mrs McLaren, it's worse than that. I'm afraid he stabbed a woman to death in his flat.'

At first I found it hard to believe that Frank would kill someone, as I didn't think he had enough badness in him to take someone's life. In fact, he appeared in court originally charged with murder and was eventually given bail. I didn't hear from him until a week before his trial in January 2005. He called me and pleaded to see me one more time in case he was given a long jail sentence, although he claimed to me that Angela Clifford getting stabbed was an accident.

Once again, my soft side took over and against my better judgement I agreed to meet him in the Argyll Bar, in Helensburgh. Frank thought he was going to see me on my own, but there was no way I was taking that kind of chance and I took a friend, May Martin, with me. He was raging when I appeared with May for what would be a tragic, terrifying, but at the same time funny and surreal meeting.

His opening gambit was that he thought I was coming alone and that he wasn't going to buy May a drink.

'I don't care who you buy drink for, Frank,' I said. 'You begged and pleaded with me to come here and see you. I've done that, now what is it you want to say?'

'What I've done, sweetheart,' he said. 'I've booked a double room at the Commodore Hotel and you and I are going to spend the night there and have our last night there because we've got our future to talk about.'

'There's is no way that's happening because we don't have a future. Say what you've got to say with my pal sitting here.'

'No, Mary, this has got to be done in private.'

I might have done some daft things in my time, but to go to a hotel on my own with someone who is due up in court for killing a woman is not one of them.

Frank's next line of attack was to tell me that he was going to go up on stage in the bar and sing what he described as 'our favourite song', 'Always On My Mind'. I was sitting there thinking he'd really gone stone mad. There was a woman lying up in the cemetery, Frank was due in court charged with killing her, and all he was thinking about was getting up on stage to sing 'Always On My Mind'.

May Martin was looking at me and I mouthed to her: 'Please help me get out of here.' I never thought I would be so scared of Frank McLaren as I was that night. And when he would touch my hand I shivered and couldn't think about anything else but that those hands had killed someone. I was desperate to get out of that pub and as far away from Frank McLaren as possible.

There was a girl already up on stage singing and being accompanied by the keyboard player and Frank was shouting: 'Wait till you hear a real singer when I get up there.'

Then his turn came and Frank made his way onto the stage. He had his back to us as he was telling the keyboard player what song he was going to sing and what key it was in. That was my chance to escape and both May and I bolted out of that bar as if our lives depended on it. We jumped into May's car and even before she got the motor started and into gear, Frank was out of the pub cursing at us at the top of his voice. 'You lousy bastards – get out of that car.' We could still hear him shouting as May put the foot down on the accelerator and we sped off.

The next time I heard from Frank was the night before his trial at the High Court in Glasgow. It was a Sunday and he appeared to be talking sensibly. He promised that he wouldn't come near me and he wasn't asking me to visit him if he got sent to jail. The next day the phone rang and a voice on the other end of the line said: 'Your husband wants a word with you – it'll have to be quick.'

Then I heard Frank's voice: 'Mary, that's me got a jail sentence. It wasn't that bad – just three and a half years. Love you, sweetheart. I'll be in touch.'

'Take as long as you like to get in touch,' I was thinking, surprised at how light his jail sentence was. I was expecting him to get fifteen years for killing that woman, but at an earlier hearing Frank had pleaded guilty to a lesser charge of culpable homicide and that was why the sentence was so light.

'At least I'll get some peace and quiet for a year or two,' I said to myself. But that peace and quiet only lasted a couple of days until I saw the report of Frank's case in Dumbarton's local newspaper, the *Lennox Herald*.

It was reported that the court was told that Frank had stabbed Angela Clifford in the chest in an argument over the card I had sent him. It was as if I had been trying to rekindle our relationship with the card, and nothing could have been further from the truth. I called the newspaper and the following week they ran a story giving my side of events and pointing out the card was only asking Frank to stay away from the hospital where John was.

Before Frank killed that woman, I knew I had no feelings for him and it was gratitude for being nice to me after Mark died that I had mistaken for love. He had certainly played a good game in winning my affections. After we were living together for a while, he admitted that he had waited thirty years to get me and a few months of cutting back on the drink and acting the gentleman was a small sacrifice to pay after so long. I know now that I never loved Frank McLaren – it was his kindness and the state of my mind at the time after Mark's death that made me think I did. Hurting as bad as I was then, if anyone did or said something nice about the two boys I had lost I clung onto it, because it was a part of them. I appreciated the things people said about Gordon and Mark because it was as if they were still there when people were talking about them.

But by the end of my relationship with Frank, I was disgusted with myself. How had I got myself into the situation of believing in and ending up living with someone like Frank, with all his drinking and the problems that brought? If I'd had half a brain I wouldn't have let Frank McLaren anywhere near me and I'm ashamed of how stupid I was. But he was good at exploiting the sadness, loneliness and vulnerability I felt at the time.

Yes, Frank McLaren certainly knew how to play me, just like he played his piano.

My Secret Grandson

It is a moment of bliss and sadness all rolled into one. The young man has tears running down his face as he steps over to the chair where I'm sitting and puts his arms round me. I, too, am crying, for I have just been told that this handsome young lad is my grandson – a grandson I never knew existed. And a son that my boy Gordon didn't know he had. It had started as a normal day for me, but by the late afternoon my world would have changed in the best possible way.

It's just after 2 p.m. and the intercom buzzer in my high-rise flat goes. I pick up the receiver and ask: 'Who is it?'

A female voice with an English accent replies: 'I'm looking for a Mrs McLaren.'

'This is Mrs McLaren – what can I do for you?'

I hear another voice in the background, this time it's a man's voice and he is saying something to the woman. I'm a bit suspicious and wonder if they are trying to sell me something. Although there is something about the voice that is vaguely familiar.

'Can I get into the flats to speak to you, please?' the woman asks.

'What for? Are you selling something?'

'No. It's personal and I don't think it's right to discuss it like this.'

Out of curiosity, I press the button to open the main door of the block of flats. I also open my front door and step out onto the landing to meet the two strangers coming out of the lift on the second floor where my home is. If they are selling something, then I'll find out before I let them into my home.

I hear the elevator coming and when the door opens the young man is standing facing the woman and he has his back to me. It takes a second or two for the woman to realise I'm on the landing waiting for them. As soon as the boy turns round to step out of the lift I'm ever so slightly taken aback. 'He looks like one of us,' I think to myself, meaning he looks like one of our family. And the more I look at his face I even think he looks like my Gordon.

The woman steps forward and says: 'I don't know how to put this, but it might come as a shock. I hope what I've got to tell you is a pleasant surprise, though.'

By this time I'm rattled and really worried about what these two strangers could tell me that would come as a shock. My legs start to shake as they always do when I become nervous. Then she blurts out: 'This is Gordon's son. His name's Scott.'

I was stunned. I'd no idea Gordon had a son and within the next few minutes I was to discover that Gordon didn't know either. But I soon realised that in my heart I must have known from the first second I set eyes on the boy. I looked at Scott's face and saw how closely he resembled Gordon.

I asked them into the house and they both sat on the couch. I was still shaking when the woman explained that her name was Erin Farridy and she was Scott's mum. I managed to gain my composure enough to offer to make them both a coffee and as soon as I got into the kitchen, I took a Valium tablet to calm me down. Normally, I would take the Valium at night, but I thought in the circumstances a little bit of medicinal calmness shouldn't wait until then – I needed it now.

When I took the coffees into the living room and sat down, Erin said: 'I know Gordon is no longer with us, but Scott wanted to meet his grandmother.'

When I heard those words my heart began to pound. There was never a moment that I doubted what she was saying because the more I looked at Scott, the more I saw of Gordon in his face. Even the way he spoke with a slight burr was just like my Gordon.

Suddenly, I burst into tears and so did Erin. Scott lifted himself off the couch, came over to my chair and gave me a hug. How proud my Gordon would have been with not only a handsome boy for a son, but that he was caring enough to comfort me like that.

The next few hours were an emotional roller coaster for me – one minute brimming over with joy and the next experiencing deep, deep sadness with tears flowing freely.

Erin began to tell me the story of how she and Gordon met and started going out together. Gordon was eighteen when he decided he'd like to try his luck in London and get a job. A girl from Dumbarton, Kate Hamill, had been living in London for some time and she found a place for Gordon. Kate knew Erin and when Gordon first went down to London she introduced them to each other. When Gordon would phone home I would ask him if he had found a steady girlfriend, but he would always just answer that he was seeing this girl or that girl off and on. I had no idea he was seeing Erin on a regular basis.

Erin told me she had taken Gordon home to meet her widowed mum, Sarah, and they had got on really well. After a few months Gordon had told Erin that he missed Scotland where all his family and friends were and he was thinking of coming back to Dumbarton. Then Erin fell pregnant and although she was tempted to tell Gordon she was having his baby, she decided not to after talking to her mother about it.

'I talked it over with my mum and we decided that it would be wrong to trap Gordon into a marriage he might not have been happy in at such a young age. My mum said we would manage on our own and maybe we could tell Gordon when he was older and a bit more mature,' said Erin. 'Although I've no doubt he would have "done the right thing" as people say, and married me if I had wanted him to. But we knew he was missing his family in Scotland and wanted to go back, so we decided to keep my pregnancy secret.'

What a lovely girl, I thought, doing that and putting Gordon's feelings before her own at what must have been a very traumatic time in her life, finding out she was pregnant.

Erin said that she and her mother had always intended to tell Gordon about the baby, but the next thing she knew was when Kate Hamill had told her that Gordon had got engaged. Erin didn't want to turn up in Dumbarton with Gordon about to be married and drop the bombshell that he had a baby son.

After Scott was born the months flew by and turned into years. When Scott was three Erin married Jack, whom she had been going out with for some time. He had been friendly with Gordon when he was working in London and knew Scott was Gordon's baby. Just the same, he adopted Scott and brought him up as one of his own.

The reason Scott had come to see me when he was now twenty-three was that he was getting married the following year and was planning to emigrate to Canada soon after his wedding. Erin and Scott knew Gordon had been killed, but they wanted to know the full details. This was very painful for all of us and many tears were shed as I recounted how Gordon had been stabbed to death and the subsequent court case.

Then Scott looked at the big photograph of Gordon I have on my wall. 'That's my dad there, isn't it?' he said. Then I made what I thought at the time was a huge blunder. 'Yes, that's your dad. That's him on his wedding day.' As soon as the words had left my mouth I wished I hadn't said that in case the boy was thinking that maybe it should have been his mother who was marrying Gordon. But my fears were unfounded, as Scott never blinked an eyelid.

The three of us talked for nearly three hours and they told me they were staying at the Dumbuck Hotel and that Jack was with them, although he had stayed back at the hotel until Erin and Scott had seen me first.

They asked if they could come back and visit me later that night, and would it be all right to bring Jack with them. I said of course it would and why didn't they all just stay at my house instead of the hotel. So they went back to the hotel to check out, collect their luggage and all three of them came back to see me that evening.

While they were away, I thought how sad it was that Gordon – who had always said he wanted a son – never knew he really did have a boy of his own. Gordon was dead and he never knew the pride and joy of things like watching his boy kick a football for the first time or taking him for his first haircut. A wave of sadness washed over me. People say it gets better as time goes by, but that's not true if it's one of your children who has been taken from you. Maybe time does heal if it's your mammy or daddy, or your aunt or uncle, but not if it's one of your children.

But I was on that emotional roller coaster and there was also the jubilation of discovering I had a grandson, and such a handsome one at that. Ironically, the fact that Gordon did, after all, have a son made me, perhaps not happy, but gave me a sense of satisfaction, despite feeling sad that he never lived to see his boy.

When Erin, Scott and Jack came back to my flat that evening we talked and talked about Gordon. And when Erin and Jack went to their bed, Scott and I talked even more. I was floating on a cloud of happiness that night as I told him everything about his dad and what he was like growing up – the good and the bad things – and of course, we went over the tragic end that befell him.

It was like having a bit of Gordon back again, spending the hours until dawn with Scott. I just couldn't get enough of him. For a lot of the time he sat on the edge of the chair with his arm around me. After a while I didn't even notice; it felt so natural for him to do that. After all, I was his gran. He reminded me so much of Gordon that if you painted a son for Gordon, he would be like Scott. Like getting two for the price of one.

We laughed when he gave me a peck on the cheek and asked: 'Have you no intention of giving me a kiss tonight?'

'I usually leave that to the men,' I replied.

The light of a new day was starting to stream through my windows when we decided I had better go to bed and get some sleep. Scott was to sleep on the couch and as I left the room he said: 'Gran, I love you. I would have regretted it for the rest of my life if I hadn't met you.'

As we hugged for the final time that night I looked over Scott's shoulder at Gordon's photograph on my wall and thought: 'You were here with me tonight, Gordon. And it's thanks to this lovely young man – your son.'

I lay in my bed recounting what a strange day this had been and I had to convince myself everything had really happened. I had a good feeling because I knew my 'new' grandson was in the next room watching a home video of his dad and his two young step-sisters which was filmed one Christmas.

When I got up a few hours later, Scott had watched the video and told me: 'I've seen photos of my dad that my mum showed me and I've seen the pictures you showed me last night. But to see him on video moving around and hearing him speak is really the icing on the cake. I know now why people say he had a big personality and that's how he came across in the video and you can't get that from a photograph. He was everything my mum told me he was.'

My heart swelled with pride just to hear Scott talk about his dad like that.

Most of that day was spent at Dumbarton Cemetery,

where Gordon is buried. It was October and it was a cold, cold day with a biting wind. First we went to a florist in Dumbarton and bought flowers for the grave. It broke my heart to see Scott laying the flowers at his dad's grave and talking to him.

'I'm going abroad to start a new life for myself and I think you will be proud of me. I'm sorry we'll have to wait a while before we see each other.'

Erin had to walk away from the graveside as the emotion was too much for her and she started crying. Jack followed to comfort her. Scott turned to me and said: 'I'll always have a picture in my mind of where my dad's resting place is. I'd been told what happened to my dad and I always wanted to come here to do this. I can't get any nearer to him than I am today, but I know he will always be with me.'

Scott kissed his fingers and laid them on the top of Gordon's gravestone. Then he stepped over to Mark's grave and spoke to him. 'You were just a kid,' he said. 'God bless you too, Uncle Mark. I'll see you as well one day.'

Then he turned to go back to Gordon's grave and asked me if he could have a wee word. I knew what he meant – he wanted some time alone with his dad. I walked across the path to a bench and sat there watching Scott at his daddy's graveside. I sat thinking about Gordon and had my own conversation with him: 'There you are, son. Your boy has come to see you.'

Erin, Scott and Jack stayed for another couple of days before they went back to London and that time was filled with a marathon of stories. Before they left they made sure I agreed to come to Scott's wedding in a few weeks' time. And best of all, Scott promised that he and his Debra would come back to Dumbarton to visit me before they left for Canada the following year.

This may sound selfish, but after they left I wished that he wasn't going to Canada, because I wanted Scott to be closer to me and be able to visit me regularly. I felt like this wonderful feeling I had, knowing about Gordon's son, was a will-o'-the-wisp type of thing. But then I thought I should be grateful for what had happened and that I had actually got to know about the grandson I didn't know I had. The promise Scott made to bring his bride back to Scotland to see me gave me a wee thing to hold onto.

Although I was overjoyed, I only told one person about Scott. That was a very close friend of many years and a constant companion at the time, Matt Thornton. I was afraid that even after all those years, the people behind Gordon's death might still bear a grudge and come after Scott. Paranoid? Maybe, but I wasn't taking the chance.

Matt met Scott, his mum and step-dad during their three-day visit to Dumbarton and he reckoned he was 'his father's double'. As you can imagine, that pleased me no end. And it was Matt who accompanied me to Scott's wedding in London a few weeks later. We stayed with Erin and Jack and that's when we met another lovely lady in Erin's mum, Sarah. She couldn't have been more gracious in her welcome to us and she talked freely of Gordon. Of course, there were tears when I told her how Gordon met his death. But, God bless her, she said: 'God only takes the best early. Gordon was a lovely boy, so full of fun, and he left me with so many lovely memories.' And not for the first time on that trip I was moved to tears when she pointed to Scott and said: 'More importantly, look what else he left me.'

Sarah told me that his trip to Scotland to meet his new gran was all Scott had talked about when he returned home. And he admitted to her that he now felt a 'whole person now' as he had felt there was a part of him that wasn't complete.

On the day of the wedding I was the proverbial bag of nerves, but Matt calmed me down by asking: 'Did you ever think you would see Gordon's son standing waiting for his bride at the altar? You are always praying for miracles – well, here's one unfolding before your very eyes, so enjoy it while you can.'

What Matt said was true, but like all miracles I could hardly believe it was happening. When we got to the church Scott was standing at the front with his best man, dressed in a dark suit, pink shirt, burgundy tie and cummerbund, black shoes and a pale burgundy carnation in his lapel. He looked really handsome and my mind went back twenty years to when Gordon got married, and I remembered how handsome he looked on his wedding day.

The music started and I turned my head to see Debra coming into the church on her father's arm. She was radiant in an off-the-shoulder gown with a small tiara set in the middle of her hair. Her bouquet was made from pink and white roses intertwined with greenery and three brides-maids and two little pageboys followed her down the aisle. My emotions began to get the better of me and I felt faint, but Sarah must have noticed and she moved to stand beside me. She knew as a mother and a gran how this was affecting me.

Later, at the reception, I felt honoured that I was seated at the top table and as the champagne flowed, I had my usual glass of Coke. When it came to the first dance, the band played 'True Love' – from the classic movie, *High Society* – as Scott and Debra walked onto the floor. Guests applauded and cameras clicked all over the hall. They made a picture of happiness.

Scott then led his mum onto the floor for the second dance and when that was over, he walked over to where I was sitting and asked: 'Would you like to dance with me, Gran?'

It was a dream come true for me to step onto the dance floor in the arms of my handsome grandson. As we danced to the song 'Somewhere My Love' from the *Dr Zhivago* movie, I was taken back in time to my Gordon's wedding reception, because that was the song the band played when the two of us danced that night. Later, I found out that Scott has specifically asked for the band to play that song because he knew how much it meant to me. He also made sure the band played the Tina Turner hit, 'Simply the Best', which he knew was my song for his dad.

There are some experiences in life that you just can't do justice to in words. Scott's wedding day was one of them. I treasure a photograph of Scott and Debra having the first dance of the reception and it's the picture of them I look at most because it brings back the memory of that wonderful day.

While I was in London for the wedding, Scott and Debra told me of their plans to settle in Canada the following year and they promised to visit me in Scotland before they emigrated. In March 2005, Scott and Debra did come to see me and we spent three days and three nights in the Glenmorag Hotel, Dunoon, on the Clyde coast. Matt Thornton came with us to make up a foursome and we had a wonderful time. I spent most of the day sitting talking to Scott about his daddy, telling him about Gordon growing up and the scrapes he got into. Matt did me a real favour by making sure Debra was entertained so I could have Scott to myself.

One of the times we were sitting together in the grounds of the hotel, I turned to Scott to say: 'You are all I dreamed a grandchild would be.'

'Gran, I'm so sorry for all you have suffered in your life – the loss of my father, Uncle Mark and all the other ones you have loved and lost. I'm glad I came to meet you and now I feel as if I've known you all my life.'

I looked at him and there was such an ache in my heart, as he had such a close resemblance to his dad. I put my hand up to his face and the tears started again.

Scott and Debra are now living in Canada and they have spoken about starting a family once they are truly settled and financially secure. We are in regular contact, but my one small regret is that my fear of flying stops me going over to Canada to visit them. It's wonderful to hear Scott's voice on the phone and he always ends the call by saying: 'You are a person worth loving, Gran.'

Once when we were speaking on the phone about the possibility of a family, Debra said: 'No prizes for guessing the baby's name if it's a boy.'

I was so grateful to hear her say this that I was silent for a few seconds. Then she said: 'Are you still there, Gran?'

'Yes, sweetheart, I'm still here.'

'Do you disapprove?'

'I'm just so happy to hear you say that. That would be lovely.'

Scott will never know just how much joy he has brought to me. We may be thousands of miles apart, but we're closer than some not a mile away. Distance is nothing where love is concerned. When we are talking on the phone, he will often ask: 'Have you been to see my dad this week and did you tell him I love him?'

'Yes, Scott, I did tell him,' I will reply. 'And I'm sure he heard me.'

I don't have any contact with Robert – my former husband and Scott's granddad – so I haven't told him about our secret grandson. I did tell Scott all about my life with Robert and left it to him to make the decision whether to contact him, but as far as I know he hasn't tried to contact his granddad.

Who would have guessed that when the buzzer went on my intercom the person on the other end of the line would bring me such happiness? It has been a huge bonus in my life to have Scott and I would never have believed in a million years that this could have happened to me. Sometimes when

I'm feeling really down – no Gordon, no Mark and there's another of my friends no longer with us – I think of Scott and I get some relief from the thought that Gordon did have a son after all, and I get 'Gran' birthday cards and 'Gran' Christmas cards.

In some ways Scott has made me feel that Gordon is somehow still living and that a part of Gordon is in a faraway land where no one can hurt him any more.

What Mary Did Next

My hand shakes as I untie the thick string around the top of the red velvet bag and pull the opening wide enough to carefully lift out the container inside the bag. I hold what can only be described as something like a glass sweetie jar in both hands and walk over to the graveside. Only it's not sweets in the jar, but the ashes of one of my best friends, Matt Thornton, who died after a long battle against cancer.

I unscrew the top of the jar and pour the ashes around the grave of Matt's mother, Catherine. Earlier that day I had gone to Cardross Crematorium and told the staff I was Matt's next of kin and was there to collect his ashes. As far as I was concerned, I was only carrying out Matt's wishes. But others thought different and I ended up being charged by the police for my actions.

It all began a week or so earlier, on 20 June 2006, when Matt died in the Vale of Leven Hospital of the cancer that had taken over his body. I had known Matt for many, many years as a friend, when Robert and I would go out with Matt and his wife in a foursome. Since then, Matt had been divorced and I – well, you know about everything that had happened to me, including being divorced as well.

In the previous few years Matt had been my constant companion and he couldn't have done enough for me in that time. We were such close friends that Matt had told hospital staff that although he did have grown-up children, I was to be named next of kin on hospital records. When Matt knew he was dying of the cancer, he told me that he wanted to be buried in Dumbarton Cemetery next to his mother, and I promised I would make sure that happened.

I was desperately sad the day Matt died, but that sadness turned to despair and anger when one of his daughters phoned me to say that the family had decided he was to be cremated. I told her that her dad's last wish was to be buried beside his mother, but that made no difference and she insisted her dad was going to be cremated and his ashes spread at Ardmore Point, near Cardross on the River Clyde.

I knew Matt wouldn't have wanted that, but there was nothing I could do as his family were taking control of the funeral arrangements. What was even worse was that Matt's body was not even going to be taken to the chapel overnight before his funeral. One of Matt's best friends, Billy Hughes, heard about this and contacted me. 'Matt was a good Catholic and the least he deserves is his night lying in chapel,' he said. 'I'm going to see the priest about this.'

That's what Billy did and eventually the family agreed that Matt would go into St Patrick's Chapel in Dumbarton overnight, and the following day a Funeral Mass would take place in his name. I went to the Funeral Mass but I didn't want to go to the crematorium because I was so upset about Matt not being buried next to his mother as he had wished.

Not being able to grant Matt's wish to be buried next to his mother preyed on my mind. A few days after Matt was cremated I was in Asda shopping and I bumped into one of Matt's daughters, Pauline. 'Hello, Mary,' she said. 'We're going to scatter Dad's ashes at Ardmore Point.'

I didn't say anything, but Pauline mentioning that made me angry and I thought to myself: 'Aye, that will be right. That's not what your dad wanted and that's not going to happen. He wanted to be next to his mother and I'm going to make sure that's what happens.'

The next morning I got a taxi to Cardross Crematorium

and walked into the office. 'I'm Matthew Thornton's next of kin,' I announced. 'And I'm hear to collect his ashes.'

'Have you any proof you're next of kin?' the young man asked.

'Phone Ward Three of the Vale of Leven Hospital and Mr Thornton's GP, Dr Haggerty, and they'll confirm it,' I replied.

He called both the hospital and Dr Haggerty and both times he was told I was down as Matt's next of kin. Having been given confirmation, he handed the ashes over to me. I had kept the taxi waiting and as soon as I got into the back of the car, I said to the driver: 'Dumbarton Cemetery, please, and as quick as you like.'

I had no idea where Matt's mother was buried in Dumbarton Cemetery, and when I got there, I had to ask one of the workers to look up their records for the grave of Catherine Thornton. The boy was very obliging and looked up a huge book and then drove me to her grave at the other end of the cemetery.

I took the jar full of ashes out of the red velvet bag and started scattering them on the ground around Matt's mother's grave. I then poured some Holy Water on the ground, laid flowers I had brought with me and said a silent prayer for my dear departed friend.

I left the cemetery and went back home satisfied that I had carried out Matt's wishes about being laid to rest beside his mother. But soon I was to get the shock of my life.

Two days after my mission to the crematorium and the cemetery, the entry buzzer went in my flat and I immediately answered. 'It's the police here. Can we come up to your flat?' the voice said. I pressed the button to open the outside door for them and as I waited for them to arrive, I thought to myself: 'Oh my God, I wonder who's dead now?'

I could hear the lift door open and I saw two black shadows outside my door. I let the policemen into the house and as they walked up the hall I asked them: 'What's happened now – who's dead?'

'Nobody's dead,' one of the policemen said. 'But in another sense you're kind of right there.' The policemen sat on the couch and asked me if I was at Cardross Crematorium the other day.

'Yes I was,' I answer.

'Did you take Matthew Thornton's ashes?'

'I did.'

'What have you done with them?'

'I took them up the cemetery and scattered them at his mother's grave.'

'I don't think you had any right to do that. Do you know his family are going mad about what you did?'

'But I've every right to do that. I'm Matt's next of kin and before he died Matt told me he wanted to be buried beside his mother.'

'Ah, well, we didn't know that you were his next of kin. We'll have to check that out and we'll have to inform the dead man's family about what you are saying about being his next of kin.'

'You do that,' I replied. 'All you need to do is phone the hospital or Matt's doctor and they will tell you Matt had me down as his next of kin.'

Two weeks later, the same two policemen came to my door and one of them said: 'We're awful sorry about this, but you are to be officially charged over what you did, taking the ashes from the crematorium. It's the first time I have ever heard of someone being charged after taking someone's ashes from the crematorium. I don't think they were sure what to charge you with, but I've been told to charge you with committing a breach of the peace. This is a weird one, right enough.'

The policemen told me I would receive a letter in a few weeks' time from the Procurator Fiscal telling me what the next stage in the case would be. The policeman cautioned and charged me in July 2006 and I still haven't heard anything from the Procurator Fiscal to this day.

It could only happen to me – someone making a complaint to the police claiming I had stolen Matt's ashes to spread them on his mother's grave, and then being officially charged with breach of the peace. My lawyer says that it is now so long since I was originally charged, and I still haven't been summoned to court, nothing more will come of it. Till I draw my last breath, I will be adamant I was doing the right thing by making sure Matt had his wish granted to be lying next to his mother in Dumbarton Cemetery – even if I could only manage to get his ashes there.

It was a real shock to me when the two policemen came to my door and charged me with breach of the peace – I was seventy-one years old, for goodness' sake. I can laugh about it now and I'm sure that, somewhere up in heaven, Matt is having a good chuckle to himself as well.

I've heard people talk about me and say: 'You'll never believe what's happened to Mary.' And sometimes I find it hard to believe as well. As I've already told you, one of my earliest memories as a child is my father shouting that I was nothing but a jinx. I would hate to think I had ever brought bad luck on him, my family or friends, despite what he said that night. I do, however, believe it has been me who has been jinxed, after all that has happened and I have suffered in my life.

How I survived, I will never really know. But survive I most certainly have, although sometimes it has felt like throughout my life I was walking on a path of thorns. But walk that path I did and I still do – with my head held high.

Postscript

The first time I saw Mary Kelly she was standing in the school playground on our first day at school. We were told by our teacher, Miss Slorach, to take a partner by the hand and then we were to queue in an orderly manner. Although I didn't know who she was, I took Mary's hand and she smiled at me. How then were we to know that that hand-clasp would bond a friendship lasting nearly seventy years, and a better friend would be hard for me to find.

On our way through life we would lose touch at times, but would always come together again. Some might tut-tut at the more, let's say, 'extrovert' elements of Mary's life over the years, but as the Native American Indian prayer says: 'Grant me the wisdom that I may judge no man until I have walked two moons in his moccasins.'

Mary was treated badly as a child and a teenager. So when she saw a way of escape, she took it. I love my friend and admire the courage she has shown through a lifetime of heartache and tragedies. Although Mary would say she has no courage, she has found the inner strength to survive ordeals that would have destroyed a lesser person. So where did Mary get her courage from? Ironically, it was the hardships and tragedy that gave Mary her courage. For the sake of her children and herself, Mary needed to survive what life threw at her, and survive she has. There can't be many people in this life who have suffered the blows that Mary has. But Mary Kelly is a survivor and despite all that has befallen her, she and I can still share a laugh between the tears.

My friend Mary is a great example of survival against the odds and I am glad our paths crossed all those years ago with a simple handclasp.

Kathleen Carr,
Mary Kelly's lifelong friend